W9-ADP-825

Choosing Not Choosing

CHOOSING NOT CHOOSING

Dickinson's Fascicles

SHARON CAMERON

THE UNIVERSITY OF CHICAGO PRESS
Chicago & London

SHARON CAMERON, Kenan Professor of English at The Johns Hopkins University, is the author of *Lyric Time: Dickinson and the Limits of Genre* (1979), *The Corporeal Self: Allegories of the Body in Melville and Hawthorne* (1981), *Writing Nature: Henry Thoreau's Journal* (1985), and *Thinking in Henry James* (1989).

The University of Chicago Press, Chicago 60637
The University of Chicago Press, Ltd., London
© 1992 by The University of Chicago
All rights reserved. Published 1992
Printed in the United States of America
01 00 99 98 97 96 95 94 93 92   5 4 3 2 1

ISBN (cloth): 0-226-09232-1
ISBN (paper): 0-226-09234-8

Library of Congress Cataloging-in-Publication Data

Cameron, Sharon.
Choosing not choosing : Dickinson's fascicles / Sharon Cameron.
p. cm.
Includes bibliographical references and index.
1. Dickinson, Emily, 1830–1886—Criticism, Textual. 2. Dickinson, Emily, 1830–1886—Manuscripts. 3. Manuscripts, American—Editing. 4. Poetry—Editing. I. Title.
PS1541.Z5C287   1992
811'.4—dc20

92-15544
CIP

♾ The paper used in this publication meets the minimum requirements of the American National Standard for Information Sciences—Permanence of Paper for Printed Library Materials, ANSI Z39.48-1984.

CONTENTS

ACKNOWLEDGMENTS

PORTIONS OF CHAPTER ONE were given as a lecture and collo-
quium at the University of Utah. A summary of the book's argument
appeared in the Houghton Library's exhibition catalogue, *The Marks in
the Fields: Essays on the Uses of Manuscripts,* edited by Rodney G. Dennis
with Elizabeth Falsey (Cambridge, Mass.: The Houghton Library,
1992).

My largest debt is to R. W. Franklin's *The Manuscript Books of Emily
Dickinson.* Although I argue with Franklin's interpretation of Dickinson's
packets or fascicles, no work on Dickinson's fascicles could have been
done without Franklin's textual reconstruction of them, and readers of
poetry in general, as well as Dickinson's readers, have reason to be grateful for his edition. I am also indebted to Roxanne Rhodes, whose unpub-
lished paper on Dickinson's variants first suggested to me the possibility
of reading variants as non-exclusive alternatives. Not least I wish to
thank Rodney G. Dennis, former Curator of Manuscripts at the Houghton Library, and Elizabeth A. Falsey, Acting Curator of Manuscripts at
the Houghton Library. Rodney Dennis granted me permission to look at
the Dickinson fascicles and also to photograph illustrative samples so
that the reader could see representative facsimiles of the manuscripts discussed. Elizabeth Falsey was a model of tact in deliberating the complex
issues involved in questions of rephotographing fragile manuscripts.

Finally, I am grateful for the contributions of the readers of my own
manuscript: for Garrett Stewart, Walter Michaels and Allen Grossman,
in particular; their suggestions and criticisms changed the shape and the
content of many of these pages. At numerous stages of the book's production Barry Weller's judgments as a critic and editor substantively and
beneficially affected its outcome. I am also grateful to Steven Tatum,
Jonathan Crewe, Larzer Ziff, Peter Sacks and Jonathan Goldberg. My
book would have more deficiencies without the suggestions of these col-
leagues, who in large and small ways sharpened the discussion. The book
was written in an office made available through the graciousness of Roger

Brown, in particular, and of the Psychology Department of Harvard University, in general. Conversations with Roger Brown about anomalous orders enabled me to conceptualize terms in which to understand the Dickinson fascicles.

Cambridge, Massachusetts, 1992

TEXTUAL NOTE

ALTHOUGH *Choosing Not Choosing* considers Emily Dickinson's packets or fascicles, throughout my book I represent the manuscript poems in the transcript of the three-volume Johnson variorum edition, which lists variant words at the ends of poems. When in my discussion I consider a single line that includes variants, I enclose the variants in brackets, with slash marks separating the alternative words. When I discuss variants without quoting a whole line, brackets are omitted, and a slash mark alone indicates the presence of alternatives. However, it is important to my argument that the reader see the association of the poems in Dickinson's fascicles, as well as that she visualize Dickinson's variants on the manuscript page. I therefore refer the reader to the appendixes and figures within, and—for those manuscripts of which no facsimile is here presented—to Ralph Franklin's *The Manuscript Books of Emily Dickinson.*

Appendix A arranges the texts of the poems in the order in which they appear in the fascicles which I discuss in detail: Fascicles 15, 16, and 20, and two of the poems in Fascicle 13. Each fascicle is prefaced by a list of the first lines of the poems it contains, in which list I follow the practice of Franklin's edition in using a space to indicate the beginning of a new bifolium or singleton, as well as its practice of providing the number assigned to the poems in the Johnson edition. For information about the physical characteristics of the manuscripts the reader should consult Franklin's description, preceding each fascicle, as well as the introduction and appendixes to his edition.

Appendix B is a facsimile of Fascicle 20, minus the first two poems. Appendix A supplies a transcript for the poems which Franklin speculates were copied on the missing leaf. (See his persuasive discussion of the identity of the missing poems, I:434.) In presenting a facsimile of Fascicle 20 rather than Fascicle 16—the other whole fascicle discussed comprehensively in this book—I wish the reader to see the way in which words are made variant to each other. Fascicle 16 better illustrates the way in which poems are made variant. As it is the former kind of variant that requires visualization, I have chosen to reproduce Fascicle 20, despite the missing first leaf, for, as I have noted, the poems on that leaf are not really in dispute. But even this preliminary distinction—fascicles which illustrate variant words versus fascicles which illustrate variant poems—simplifies my understanding of the complex relations in Dickinson's fascicle texts. As I shall explain, both variant words and variant poems are in effect interlineated or intercalated in the manuscript books.

The *x*'s, numbers, and words at the top of some of the manuscript pages are not Emily Dickinson's, but rather the markings of her early editors.

In general, in Emily Dickinson's fascicles each sheet is folded once to constitute a bifolium. The list of figures (pp. viii–ix above) indicates the poems' first lines, the numbers assigned to them in Johnson's edition, the fascicle numbers, and the first or second rectos or versos of each bifolium in which they occur. The captions provide only the fascicle, bifolium, and recto and verso number. I use the abbreviation "bf" for "bifolium."

I

Unread Dickinson

I. THE SUBJECT OF CONTEXT

ℰℨ𝔁ℵ𝔥𝔇

To LOOK AT THE HISTORY of Dickinson criticism is to see that what is memorialized are her ellipses, her canceled connections, the "revoked . . . referentiality" of the poetry. The phrase is from Geoffrey Hartman's *Criticism in the Wilderness,* but one thinks also of Jay Leyda's description of Dickinson as writing "riddle[s]," poems of the "omitted center . . ."; of Robert Weisbuch's characterization of this poetry as "sceneless," producing "analogical language which exists in parallel to a world of experience, as its definition"; of David Porter's assessment that "here is the verbal equivalent of *sfumato,* the technique in expressionistic painting whereby information . . . on a canvas is given only piecemeal and thereby necessarily stimulates the imaginative projection of the viewer, who, out of his own experience, supplies the missing . . . context"; of an earlier claim of my own that the poems "excavate the territory that lies past the range of all phenomenal sense." Or, to allow Hartman to make the point one more time: Dickinson, the "dangerous" purifier, italicizes "leanness," more than leanness even—the "zero" meaning of the hyphen that punctuates the poetry. In Hartman's discussion, the hyphen becomes emblematic. "Perhaps because it both joins and divides, [it is like] a hymen. . . . That hyphen-hymen persephonates Emily."[1]

But does it?[2] What if this way of reading her poetry belies the way it was written, or, once written, put together (both internally structured and also made contiguous)? What if these poems are less alien than we

1. See Geoffrey Hartman, *Criticism in the Wilderness: The Study of Literature* (New Haven: Yale University Press, 1980), pp. 129, 130–31, 126, and, inclusively, 122–32; Jay Leyda, *The Years and Hours of Emily Dickinson* (New Haven: Yale University Press, 1960), I:xxi; Robert Weisbuch, *Emily Dickinson's Poetry* (Chicago: University of Chicago Press, 1975), p. 19; David Porter, *The Art of Emily Dickinson's Early Poetry* (Cambridge, Mass.: Harvard University Press, 1966), p. 99; Sharon Cameron, *Lyric Time: Dickinson and the Limits of Genre* (Baltimore: Johns Hopkins University Press, 1979), p. 9.

2. Certainly the history of Dickinson criticism from the 1890s to the present, as these quotations indicate, has preserved a consistent account of the poet. It has stressed the separations in the poems (among grammatical and syntactical units), as well as the separation of any given utterance from a decipherable situation that it could be said to represent; and it has stressed vexed connections among them. Spe-

had supposed? Or not alien in the way we had supposed? What if they are not quite as sceneless or cryptic (even apparently subjectless) as the characterizations insist? Or what if the scenes and subjects can be said to unfold between and among the poems as well as within them?

In positing such questions I may seem to be creating a predictable opposition, and to be preparing the ground for an argument that I do not intend to make. I want therefore to offer preliminary clarification. To understand the lyric as a contained structure would seem to imply something that is bounded, albeit—in Dickinson's case—something that is also piecemeal. Conversely, to understand Dickinson's piecemeal lyrics as governed by a fascicle structure would seem to imply a unity produced by a reading of connections between and among poems. But in the following pages I shall be arguing, to the contrary, that unity is not produced by reading Dickinson's lyrics in the fascicle context. Unity is not produced since what is revealed in the fascicles is not only connections *among* poems about the same thing, not only intertextuality in the sense that different poems might be *about* the same thing, or present problems about the same or similar topic/s, or even reiterate aspects of each other. What is more radically revealed is a question about what constitutes the identity of the poem. Thus, although it will become apparent that some of Dickinson's poems raise the problem of identity by thematizing it, Dickinson's fascicles can rather be seen to *embody* the problem of identity. I shall be concerned with elaborating the distinction between thematizing identity and embodying it, an *embodying* of identity manifest when aspects of a poem thought to be extrinsic to it—variants to the poem, variant poems—must be understood as being half-incorporated by that poem.

---

cifically, as the chronology of the poems is not seen to signal development, critics are deprived of one conventional way of discussing the poetry, and this deprivation is often countered by certain primitive groupings of the poems, according to thematic similarities, formal properties, evaluative assessments which discriminate poems that are successful from those that are not—with the constant implication that there is no inherent way of understanding relations among the poems. The taxonomies advanced for Dickinson's poems are different from those advanced for other poets, because when the poems are sorted it is precisely to emphasize idiosyncrasies and repetitions (of traits, themes, syntactic features), as if what Dickinson had to teach us were that there is no way to comprehend the alien except by the most critically reductive strategies of categorizing and comparison.

The anomaly of the situation I have begun to describe is immediately apparent. For assumptions about boundedness are so fundamental to our suppositions about lyrics as in effect to become definitional of the genre. This is revealed in the originary definitions most brilliantly laid out in the enabling propositions of Allen Grossman's *Summa Lyrica*.[3] With respect to the boundedness of the lyric, Grossman writes: "The frame of the poem (its prosody or closure) is coterminous with the whole poem, and must be conceived as bounding the poem both circumferentially (the outer juncture with *all* being) and internally (the inner juncture, produced syllable by syllable, with its *own* being). The minimal function of closure is to fence the poem from all other statements, and most strenuously from alternative statements of the same kind." Even Grossman's qualification, "The closural frame may be more or less permeable. In Wordsworth it is more permeable . . . ; in Ben Jonson it is less," does not affect Grossman's reiterated conclusion: "The quality of singularity manifested in each instant of utterance is in each case of manifestation, syllable by syllable, the frame of the poem (that is, its closure)" (4.5). It will be one of the tasks of the following pages to explain the way that Dickinson's fascicles trouble the idea of limit or frame on which, as Grossman reminds us, our suppositions of lyric fundamentally depend.

To consider poems as individual lyrics is to suppose boundedness. To consider poems as related—as, say, a sequence would relate them—is differently to suppose boundedness, in that poems which are seen to be connected must first be seen to be discrete. To consider poems as not discrete but also as not related is to complicate the negotiations between interior and exterior. This Dickinson does by raising questions about the identity of the text. With respect to Dickinson's fascicles—to anticipate my argument—the variant is a way of getting at what the text "is." That is, in Dickinson's poems, variant words (and poems which we come to see as variants of each other) raise the question of what counts as the identity of the text in question. The question raised is: If this word—or this second poem—conventionally understood to be *outside* the poem is rather *integral* to the poem, how is the poem delimited? What *is* the poem? I shall argue that words that are variants are part of the poem outside of which they ostensibly lie, as poems in the same fascicle may

---

3. In *The Sighted Singer* (Baltimore: Johns Hopkins University Press, 1992), pp. 205–374. Subsequent citations to this work refer, in parentheses, to individual sections of *Summa Lyrica*.

sometimes be seen as variants of each other. In Dickinson's fascicles—
where "variants" are more than the editorial term for discrete delimited
choices—variants indicate both the desire for limit and the difficulty in
enforcing it. The difficulty in enforcing a limit to the poems turns into a
kind of limitlessness, for, as I shall demonstrate in numerous instances,
it is impossible to say where the text ends because the variants extend the
text's identity in ways that make it seem potentially limitless. (This
holds true even though not all Dickinson's poems have variants and even
though I shall sometimes discuss poems without focusing on the variants. For although the variants are crucial to my examination, I treat
them like any other significant part of the poem, to be taken up or not,
depending on their pertinence to a particular discussion.)

In pointing to such an extension of the text's identity, I am not, to
reiterate, talking only or even primarily about intertextuality. I am not
suggesting that the relation among Dickinson's poems is significantly
intertextual. For the intertextual question, What are the relations among
these poems? assumes that "these" are different poems. In this chapter,
although I initially ask such questions—ask how poems are related, contextualized, or understood in a sequence—I ultimately ask under what
circumstances a relation becomes an identity. In chapter 2 I shall argue
that in writing poems that are variants of each other, Dickinson assumes
not that these poems are *about* the same thing, but rather that they *are*
the same thing. While I claim that poems in the same fascicle must often
be understood as variants of each other, I also claim that when the ostensibly "same" poem is placed in two different fascicles (or in another context, such as a letter), this is rather a case where we must understand the
two poems as *similar* but not as the *same*. The category of the fascicle is
required to produce identity. What looks like the same poem in two
different fascicles may be recognized as the same words without being
recognized as the same poem. Thus the material placement of the poem
is essential to discerning its identity.

Initially, however, my aim is to ask how the situation for understanding Dickinson's poems changes when we consider that they are at once
isolated lyrics, as Thomas H. Johnson presented them in *The Complete
Poems* (and in the variorum text), and poems that have the appearance of
a sequence, as R. W. Franklin presented them when he published *The
Manuscript Books of Emily Dickinson*—a volume crucial for our reassessment of this poetry, about which I shall therefore say a few words before

proceeding.[4] First, the assertion that Franklin presents Dickinson's poems in sequences is one he would not accept. Dickinson organized most of her nearly eighteen hundred poems into her own form of book-making: selected poems copied in ink onto "sheets of letter paper already folded by the manufacturer to produce two leaves" (Franklin, I:xi). Then she stabbed them and bound them with string. Franklin has argued that no aesthetic principle governs their binding. It was, nevertheless, Franklin's goal to reproduce in facsimile the manuscripts which Dickinson bound with string into forty fascicles from about 1858 to 1864 and the fifteen "sets"—poems which, primarily after 1864, she copied but never bound.[5]

Second, Franklin claims the binding was a means of keeping order among her poems. But an alternative speculation is that the fascicles were a form of private publication.[6] Franklin's assumption that they were a means of keeping order among her poems begs the question of what such an order would be. The alternative, that the fascicles were a form of

4. See *The Complete Poems of Emily Dickinson,* ed. Thomas H. Johnson (Boston: Little, Brown, 1960); *The Poems of Emily Dickinson,* ed. Johnson, 3 vols. (Cambridge, Mass.; Harvard University Press, Belknap Press, 1955); and *The Manuscript Books of Emily Dickinson,* ed. R. W. Franklin, 2 vols. (Cambridge, Mass.: Harvard University Press, 1981). As indicated in the Textual Note, when I cite poems I reproduce them in the transcript of Johnson's three-volume variorum edition. When a poem is initially cited, a P and the number assigned by Johnson follow in parentheses. Franklin's edition of *The Manuscript Books* is hereafter cited by volume and page number.

5. The sets have many of the characteristics of the fascicles except that they were not stab-bound and tied. According to Franklin, Dickinson stopped *binding* fascicle sheets around 1864, though there are a few unbound sheets as early as 1862 (set 1 is dated 1862 by Franklin; sets 2–4, 1864). In the late 1860s Dickinson stopped *copying* fascicle sheets. In the 1870s she began copying fascicle sheets again (sets 5–7 are dated between 1864 and 1866, though, as noted, the majority of the poems in the remaining sets [8–15] are from the 1870s), but she never again bound them (Franklin, I:xii–xiii). For a concise discussion of the differences among the bound fascicles, the unbound fascicle sheets, the worksheets, and the miscellaneous fair copies, as well as for Franklin's speculations about the ways Dickinson variously used the bound fascicles, and for a detailed description of how Franklin reassembled them, see the introduction to *The Manuscript Books of Emily Dickinson.*

6. It is important to reiterate that this and the following assertions about Dickinson's intentions with respect to the fascicles are speculative. While the following pages produce an empirical argument about how the fascicles work, and about what the fascicles are, the basis of that argument is, and could only be, speculative.

private publication—halfheartedly endorsed by Franklin in the introduction to the facsimile, and (as I shall explain) contested by him elsewhere—has its plausibility heightened by reference to an essay of Emerson's printed in *The Dial* in 1840, in which he advised authors, in distinction to the dominant strain of poetic tradition, to collect album poetry, for, Emerson writes, a "revolution in literature is now giving importance to the portfolio over the book."[7] In making her lyrics into manuscript books—in effect constituting manuscripts as if they were books—Dickinson may have been responding to a revolution like the one predicated by Emerson. Indeed, once Dickinson had copied poems into fascicles she usually destroyed her worksheets. Such a practice invites us to regard the poems copied in the fascicles in the same way that her manner of collecting them suggests she might herself have regarded them: as definitive, if privately published, texts. The copying and binding, and the destruction of the worksheets, insist that this is the fascicles' status, despite the fact that Dickinson subsequently adopted variants from the fascicle sheets in the "text" she sent to friends, and despite the fact that it is one of the characteristics of the fascicle texts, especially after 1861, that variants to words also exist in fair copy, indeed exist as *part* of the text of the last thirty fascicles. I shall return to this point.[8]

7. "New Poetry," in *Ralph Waldo Emerson: Essays and Lectures,* ed. Joel Porte (New York: The Library of America, 1983), p. 1169. In further references this edition is cited *RWE,* with page references supplied parenthetically in the text.

8. The earliest fascicles have no variants; the first occurrence of a variant is in Fascicle 5, and there are only five other variants for poems through Fascicle 10. These variants, often multiple, and not uniformly positioned at the end of the poem, as in the Johnson edition, are sometimes signaled in the facsimile text by the little " + " signs that Dickinson used near a word to indicate variants to that word (for example, fig. 4). In the facsimile text the variants appear in the following diverse positions: at the end of the poem, to the side of the poem, and underneath or above a particular stanza, word or line. Sometimes the variants to words are virtually inseparable from the text, as in the second stanza of "I think the Hemlock" (fig. 13). Frequently a variant appears above the word: "The [maddest/nearest] dream— recedes—unrealized—" (P 319; fig. 3). Or to the side of the line: "The Cordiality of Death—/ Who [drills/nails] his Welcome in—" (P 286). Or to the side of and at right angles with the poem, as in "There is a pain—so utter—" (P 599) and "Like Some Old fashioned Miracle—" (P 302; fig. 23). Or underneath the word: "An Island in dishonored Grass—/ Whom none but [Daisies,/Beetles—] know" (P 290; fig. 8). In the same poem another variant ("manners") is also noted below the word ("attitudes") that is on the line. But a third variant appears at the end of the poem, "An/Some—Island," making it seem that different ways of noting variants indicate different ways of understanding alternatives in relation to each other. Only in the

There came a Day - at
Summer's full -
Entirely - for me -
I thought that such - were
for the Saints -
When Resurrections - be.
           Revelations

the Sun - as Common - went -
abroad -
the Flowers - accustomed - blew -
        + As if no soul the
+ While on two Souls
Solstice passed -
+ +that
  Which maketh all things new.

the time was scarce profaned -
by speech -   figure + S, n 60 /
the + falling of a - word
was needless - as at - Sacrament -
the Wardrobe - of Our Lord.

FIG. 1.   Fascicle 13, bf5, 1st recto

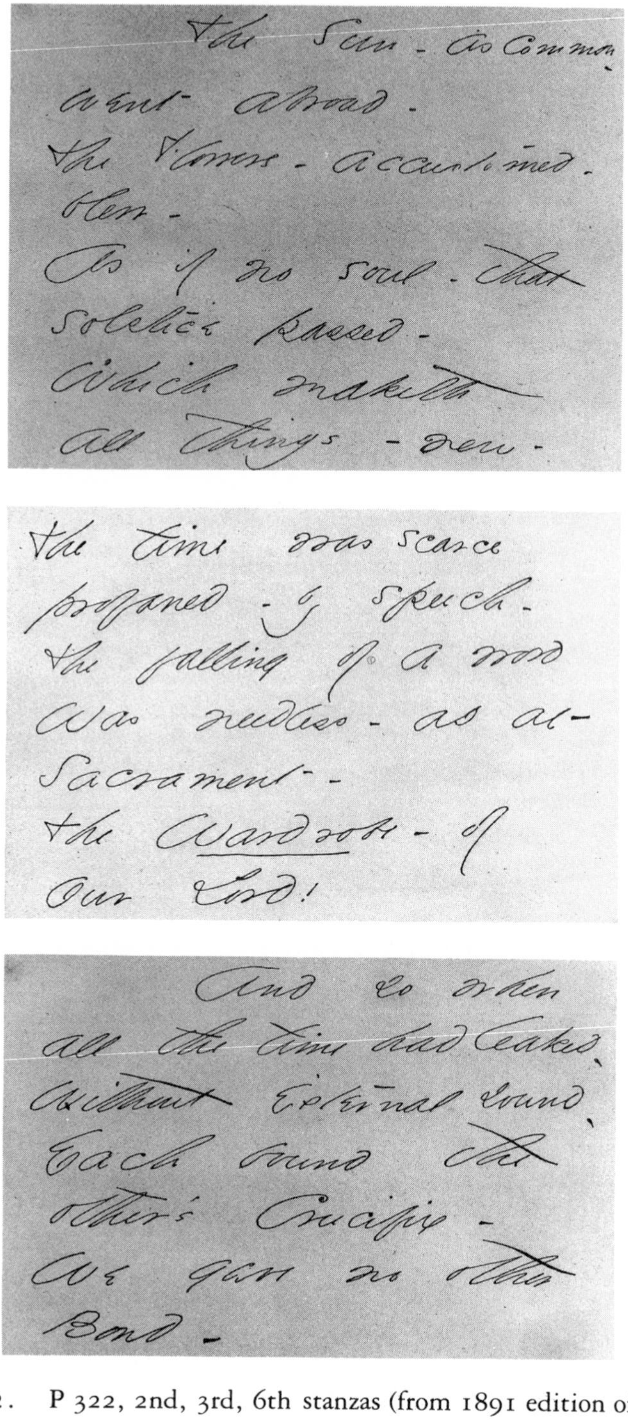

The Sun – as Common
Went abroad –
The Flowers – accustomed –
blew –
As if no soul – ~~that~~
solstice passed –
Which ~~maketh~~
All things – new –

The time was scarce
profaned – by speech –
The falling of a word
Was needless – as at
Sacrament –
The <u>Wardrobe</u> – of
Our Lord!

And so when
all the time had leaked,
~~Without~~ External sound,
Each bound ~~the~~
other's Crucifix –
We gave no ~~other~~
Bond –

FIG. 2. P 322, 2nd, 3rd, 6th stanzas (from 1891 edition of *Poems*)

When Franklin writes that the fascicles were a means of keeping order among Dickinson's poems, he means that they literally helped her to
tidy up: "The disorder that fascicle sheets forestalled may be seen in the
'scraps' of the later years. When she did not copy such sheets and destroy
the previous versions, her poems are found on hundreds of odds and
ends—brown paper bags, magazine clippings, discarded envelopes and
letters, the backs of recipes."[9] Thus Franklin imagines Dickinson's keeping order as her means of making the poems consistent with respect to
their physical appearance, rather than as her means of organizing them.
According to his explanation, the poems are not "artistic gatherings" at
all, but rather "private documents with practical uses, gatherings of con-
venience for poems finished or unfinished" (*SIB*, p. 17).

Yet, as I have noted, Franklin's speculations about what occasioned
these gatherings, his understanding of how Dickinson herself made use
of them, and finally what the material evidence might suggest these
gatherings are, shift in the course of his assertions about them. For example, in the introduction to the facsimile text, Franklin writes that the
fascicles "may have served privately as publication, a personal enactment

later years of the copying are the variants positioned characteristically at the poem's
end, Dickinson having apparently standardized her placement of them.

Infrequently Dickinson drew a line through words to signal their replacement
by alternatives. See, for example, P 241, "I like a look of Agony," in which in the
first line of the second stanza, "Death comes" is decisively crossed out, and replaced
by "The Eyes glaze once—and that is Death—," and P 322, "There came a Day—
at Summer's full—," where substantive decisions against word choices are marked
by lines through those words, with the preferred alternatives unambiguously chosen
(fig. 1, first page of fascicle text of "There came a Day—at Summer's full—"). I say
"unambiguously chosen," but even here the choice unambiguously made may subsequently have been *un*made. A second fair copy, for which no manuscript is extant,
presumably written after the fascicle copying, is reproduced in facsimile on four
pages preceding the title page of *Poems by Emily Dickinson,* Second Series, ed. T. W.
Higginson and Mabel Loomis Todd (Boston: Roberts Brothers, 1891). That fair
copy adopts some of the canceled fascicle readings which had appeared (erroneously)
to have been definitively deleted. In the details from the four-page facsimile of
"There came a day—at Summer's full—," Dickinson restores words in the second,
third, and penultimate stanzas (fig. 2).

However exceptional, these excisions insist, by distinction, that Dickinson's
typical way of *noting* variants is not random, but indicates her way of *understanding*
variants. I elaborate in the body of the text.

9. "The Emily Dickinson Fascicles" in *Studies in Bibliography,* vol. 36, ed. Fred-
son Bowers (Charlottesville: The Bibliographic Society of the University of Virginia,
1983), p. 16. Hereafter this article is cited as *SIB.*

of the public act that, for reasons unexplained, she denied herself" (I:ix). Here Franklin's explanation suggests that what is being "privately published" is not simply the poems but the order of the poems, or—less indisputably—the association of the poems, an association made material because of their discrete gatherings, with the internal structure of those gatherings painstakingly reconstructed by Franklin. The editorial endeavor would imply this, even assuming Franklin's own explanation failed to, since, Franklin continues: although the poems became "an extended letter to the world, . . . no edition of the Dickinson poetry" prior to the facsimile edition "has followed the fascicle order" (I:ix). To follow the fascicle order is, in Franklin's account of his task as described in the introduction to the facsimile, to present the poems "much as [Dickinson] left them for Lavinia and the world" (I:ix). In an article in *Studies in Bibliography,* however, published two years after the facsimile text, Franklin differently claims that the fascicles were a form of "surrogate publication . . . constructed for herself" (*SIB,* p. 16). Were the poems constructed for the world or for herself? Was the publication private or rather surrogate?

Such inconsistencies punctuate Franklin's statements about Dickinson's poems. For instance, Franklin would preserve the idea of the sequence. In fact he is responsible for reestablishing it. But, so doing, he would contest any sense of its significance. Thus order, as Franklin understands it, involves Dickinson's keeping the poems in one place. It involves imagining that the fascicles were the place—like a closet or bureau drawer—where Dickinson elected to put them. But an alternative speculation is that the fascicles were not some convenient place Dickinson devised in which to keep her poems, with this idea at once literalized and made arbitrary, but rather that the fascicles were essential to her placing of them, with the idea of placing as identification and the idea of placing as materially establishing *what* they are in relation to *where* they are, externalized and made inseparable—in effect, privately published. For in the fascicles placing as "setting down," placing as "arranging," and placing as "identifying" by connection with an associated context are indistinguishable.

Claims made about the sets are similarly inconsistent. For example, Franklin asserts of the sets that "the physical evidence is insufficient to arrange them in a specific order" and that the "lack of binding would suggest that none was intended" (*SIB,* p. 10). Such a distinction correctly implies the importance of a different understanding of those poems intended to be bound than of those for which no binding appears to have been intended. Yet this different understanding is betrayed or contradicted when the attributed motive for binding (so Dickinson could "browse" among her poems) and the attributed motive for deciding *not* to bind (the sets indicate, once the poems reached a certain mass, Dickinson may have found it easier to locate poems in unbound fascicle sheets) replicate each other (*SIB,* p. 16). For "browsing," as it is described, *is* the means of locating poems in the fascicles. In Franklin's explanation, the very activity that binding was supposed to facilitate is the very activity that not binding facilitates, and the idea of number of poems as determining whether the binding facilitates or frustrates browsing and finding seems unconvincing to me, since Dickinson continued binding the fascicle sheets until well over eight hundred poems had been copied and bound. Here it would seem important to differentiate fascicles from sets in function as well as in appearance (for Franklin imagines the fascicles as serving a function). It would have to be argued that something was differently intended for the fascicles than for the sets. Franklin's inference about the lack of binding (that no order was intended) understands this difference, but his explanation of the same "function" for the fascicles and sets subverts the understanding, because the needs of "browsing" and "locating" are equally met by bound and unbound fascicle sheets.

In addition, Franklin's speculations about how the variants occur and what can be inferred from the manner of the copying—while not contradictory, like his notions about private/surrogate publication, or insufficiently differentiated, like the speculations which describe the tasks filled by bound and unbound sheets—must be questioned. About the variants: Franklin sees Dickinson as using the fascicles as a private workshop since "when Dickinson went 'public' with a copy to friends, she would produce a fair copy," that is, a copy with no variants (*SIB,* p. 16). Yet in fact, as Franklin points out, the earliest fascicles themselves have no variants. Variants seem to develop in the fair copy of the fascicles about 1861, either because, as Franklin speculates, Dickinson is making different copies for friends (I:x)—differences of which she is keeping a record and which (in the framework of Franklin's explanation) are perceptible to us as the variants; or because, as I shall argue, the variants can instead be understood not as copies or records of differences, but rather as constructions of identity. The variants can be understood by the supposition that what is being developed by Dickinson in her maturity is a poetry that depends on variants which extend a single utterance, conceived as a unitary text, outward into the margins and downward through the fascicle sheet. Sometimes Dickinson returned years later to a fair copy to emend it in pencil, "whereas the initial writing had been in ink" (I:x). To Franklin this would suggest that Dickinson was treating the fascicles as "a continuing workshop where . . . she would enter the specific poetic process again" (I:x). But the return would somewhat differently suggest that the idea of completion was another limit extended temporally as well as spatially by the proliferation of the variants.

Finally when Franklin speculates that the fascicles are meant to order (tidy up) rather than to arrange (make significant), as evidence of this he cites the fact that Dickinson may have had a backlog of poems written before they were copied and bound. This was probably the case in 1862 when, Franklin writes, "Emily Dickinson could have had a significant number of poems in her pool and, in that year, perhaps spurred on by the correspondence with Higginson, set in vigorously to organizing them, now letting poems enter the fascicles trailing many alternates" (SIB, p. 15). An opposite assumption is that Dickinson was saving these poems up to see *how* they would go together, allowing single lyrics, or several lyrics copied onto one bifolium, to remain temporarily separate or piecemeal so that she could ultimately stitch them into the different comprehensive entity that the fascicle gathering made of them. And if it is more probable to suppose (as Franklin also does, SIB, p. 13) that the poems in twenty of Dickinson's forty fascicles were *copied* rather than all (necessarily) written in 1862, then whether Dickinson saved her poems with the idea of eventually organizing them or whether in 1862 she came to group and identify poems previously seen as discrete—identifications marked by the copying and the fascicle binding—is in a sense less significant than that we consider what the gatherings made of these poems. It is important that we consider, as the copying most dramatically in that year instructs us to do, whether structures are being created out of ostensibly discrete entities. Sometimes sheets were copied in different years and only subsequently bound. Of these Franklin writes: "Binding followed copying, sometimes years later mixing sheets from different years. That such sheets were copied in different years suggests that no fascicle-level order governed their preparation" (SIB, p. 17). Yet sheets copied in different years and only subsequently bound rather suggest to me sheets over which a high degree of order has been exercised, suggest that, in the delay between the copying and the binding, what is precisely being governed, made visible, and materially determined, is the preparation of an entity.

Whatever his suppositions about Dickinson's texts, Ralph Franklin's reestablishment of the order in which the sheets in each fascicle were bound is of inestimable value to all readers of Dickinson, and in fact to all readers of poetry. Indeed Franklin's restoration of the internal sequence of the fascicles—no internal order could be established for the sets since they were never bound—in *The Manuscript Books of Emily Dickinson* has immediate practical consequences for Dickinson's reader, for reading Franklin's text of the poems is different from reading Johnson's text of the poems. This is the case even when Franklin and Johnson ascribe identical dates to the poems so that there is the same consecutive relation among several poems in both editions. In the Johnson edition the unit of sense is the individual poem; beyond that, it is whatever arbitrary place the reader decides to close the book. In fact, although Johnson arranges the poems chronologically, that arrangement of poems gives the reader the impression of no arrangement at all, because in a year like 1862 there are over three hundred poems. In the facsimile, these poems do not follow on the page as they do in the Johnson variorum. Rather, as I hope to show, in Franklin they exist in groups with internal sequences.[10] Thus in the Franklin edition the unit of sense is not the individual poem but rather the fascicle book, and one wonders about the relation among the fascicles as well as about the relation between the

10. In the fascicles Dickinson often, though not always, drew a line after the variants that concluded a poem, thereby indicating an end to the unit of sense. But because the poems are ordered and bound and because there are sometimes several poems to the bifolium, the collocation oppositely implies a potential relation among poems. (In Fascicle 14, where poems from 1861, 1858, 1862 are bound in that sequence, the implications of "order" are differently unmistakable.)

Moreover, within the bifolium, the method of copying is varied. It is varied because, as indicated, a line is frequently but not always drawn after a poem, and because, although the bifolia are customarily filled, there are instances of blank half-rectos and -versos. This is particularly the case in Fascicle 11, where whole sheets and half sheets are left blank. But there is also a three-quarters blank first verso in Fascicle 15; nine blank lines and a blank verso conclude Fascicle 18, while in Fascicle 13 the first bifolium contains a three-quarters blank second recto. Such variations indicate that Dickinson may be regulating *which*, as well as *how many*, poems belong in a particular bifolium. The method of copying is also varied because, while the fascicles are ordinarily composed of single, folded sheets—with a disjunct leaf or slip added rarely, where necessary, to continue a poem—Fascicle 11 contains as

fascicles and the sets—or at least the question of such relations is raised by the contiguity of these units. [11]

Despite questions like these, raised inevitably and provocatively by the enormous contribution of Franklin's edition, in the ten years since the publication of *The Manuscript Books of Emily Dickinson* there has been no useful commentary, virtually no commentary at all, on how the gathering of poems into fascicles influences our understanding of how to read Dickinson's verse. Moreover, one of the reasons that the few existing theories about the fascicles have been so unsatisfying is that they variously attempt to account for the fascicles as if they had a single discernible principle of order—for example, a love story. [12]

---

many as four disjunct leaves (see Franklin's tables for Dickinson's manner of accommodating overflow of poems and for the locations of disjunct leaves within particular fascicles, on II:1413 and II:1414, respectively).

Further, while Dickinson characteristically tries to complete a poem on a single page, and if it runs over, it characteristically does so by as many as four lines, in Fascicle 11 there are only two lines on the verso of the fourth sheet. Finally, although Franklin is right to say that the sheet or bifolium is the unit of *manuscript* integrity (an assumption borne out by Dickinson's manner of accommodating overflow from the sheet), the sheet or bifolium is not the unit of *thematic* integrity.

11. The relation "among" the fascicles is itself problematic because, in Franklin's words, Dickinson "did not number or otherwise label" or index them (I:x). Thus, though in the facsimile they are now arranged according to a presumed chronology, it is only arbitrarily that Fascicle 13 precedes Fascicle 14. This is the case because, while one can determine that certain fascicles were copied in the same year, it is now impossible to determine the particular order in which they were copied within that year. Fascicle 13 would seem to precede Fascicle 14 in that the former dates from 1861 while the latter has poems which Franklin dates from 1862, as well as from 1858 and 1861. But Fascicle 11, too, has poems from 1861, and Fascicle 12 poems from 1861 as well as 1860. Moreover, by virtue of these different dates, it would appear that in binding the sheets, Dickinson worked from a pool of manuscripts, and therefore the exact relation of Fascicle 13 to Fascicle 14, if Dickinson intended one, cannot be surmised. Fascicles 11 through 14 are the most problematic of the fascicles, since in them the binding practices are inconsistent. Specifically, Dickinson there deviates from her practice of binding poems presumably copied in the same year.

12. Ruth Miller writes: "So similar are the fascicles that it seems possible to chart one and obtain a blueprint for all. . . . Each is a narrative structure designed to recreate the experience of a woman as she strives for acceptance or knowledge, is rebuffed or fails . . . forces herself to be patient in order to survive, fixes her hope on

But what if there are multiple ways of construing order, or what if there are multiple orders?[13] That Dickinson ordered her poems through the fascicles rather than simply collecting them there could be argued from the method of copying in the fascicles. For instance, although the sheets are customarily filled, there are, as indicated in note 10, diverse instances of blank half-rectos and -versos in the fascicles, such variations suggesting that Dickinson may be regulating *which* poems as well as *how many* poems belong in which bifolium. That Dickinson ordered her poems is argued by other evidence of the manuscripts: by the fact that, for example, on the first leaf of Fascicle 9 (dated by Franklin and Johnson as copied in 1860) Dickinson added "Bound—a trouble—"(P 269, dated as added about 1861), although there would have been room to add this poem elsewhere in that same fascicle (on the second side of the next leaf), and by the fact that in Fascicles 12 and 14 poems from different years—from 1860 and 1861, in the case of 12, and from 1861, 1858, and 1862, in the case of 14—are bound together, although in each of these years Dickinson wrote numerous poems and in other fascicles she characteristically bound poems from the same year together. It

---

another world where Jesus and God await her, and remains content meanwhile" (*The Poetry of Emily Dickinson* [Middletown, Conn.: Wesleyan University Press, 1968], pp. 248–49). William H. Shurr agrees with the idea of a single theme, although he formulates it in the terms indicated by his book's title: *The Marriage of Emily Dickinson: A Study of the Fascicles* (Lexington: The University of Kentucky Press, 1983). And while M. L. Rosenthal and Sally M. Gall argue that the poems cannot "be reduced to a monotonous formula" (*The Modern Poetic Sequence: The Genius of Modern Poetry* [New York: Oxford University Press, 1983], p. 48), their discussion resembles other analyses of the fascicles in producing a narrative within or between the fascicles that shows a progression from one to the other. (See their analysis of Fascicles 15 and 16.) These theories about the poems ultimately unify, whether unification is understood thematically (as by Shurr and Miller) or narratively (as by Rosenthal and Gall).

Finally, many of these discussions supply a putative master narrative about the death of a lover. As will become apparent from my subsequent analysis, I think such a theme informs some of the poems without informing all. But even where present it does not necessarily produce an order, or ways of understanding what orders are in Dickinson's poems, any more than isolating the figure of "the dark lady" produces understandings of order in Shakespeare's sonnets.

13. Such ways of understanding orders as multiple have been variously demonstrated with respect to relations among Shakespeare's sonnets in Stephen Booth's commentary to his edition of the sonnets and, specifically with respect to comple-

is further argued by the example of Fascicle 8, in which a poem is copied twice in different places in the fascicle with variant first lines ("Portraits are to daily faces" [P 170] becomes in the second instance of copying "Pictures are to daily faces"), as if each were a separate poem. Since the repeated poems are separated by several leaves and by nine intervening poems, and since there is space earlier in the fascicle to have copied "Pictures are to daily faces," Dickinson may have been structuring the fascicle by her disparate placements of the so-called same poem. This arrangement of poems—perceptible in Dickinson's copying practices; in her adding to a "completed" fascicle; in her repeating a poem within a fascicle; in her copying on matching leaves poems she then placed in separate fascicles; in her composing a fascicle with poems from different years—suggests a conceptual scheme, although Fascicle 9, the same fascicle that suggests that scheme by virtue of the added poem, also leaves the reader uncertain how the scheme is to be understood, because it is not clear to what the poem is "added" (the immediate sequence of poems? the specific poem preceding it? the whole fascicle?).

Here one could equivocate about questions of order by saying that whether Dickinson produced the order or whether the reader produces the order of the fascicles by registering the poems' juxtaposition there is immaterial, since the question of the author's intention is always undecidable. But the question of intention, at least at one level, is not undecidable—because we know that Dickinson intended something. After all, she copied the poems into the fascicles. The question then is, in doing so, what did she intend? Looking at the fascicles it might even appear that Dickinson's intention was to be indeterminate with respect to the relation among these poems, since lyric structures whose boundaries are conventionally left intact are in the fascicles characteristically punctured by the "outside" (which I shall argue is not an "outside") composed of variants and other poems. Or, to explain the situation in positive terms: it seems that given such violations of boundaries it might differently appear that Dickinson intended to redetermine our very understanding of how the identity of a poetic structure is to be construed.

---

mentary and antithetical relations among meanings in and among single sonnets, in Joel Fineman's "Shakespeare's Perjur'd Eye," *Representations* 7 (Summer 1984): 59–86.

With respect to the binding, we do know, however minimal this knowledge may initially be deemed to be, that Dickinson intended to associate these poems with each other. Thus the question is not whether intentions are relevant. The question is rather how to understand the extraordinarily complex, perhaps even conflicted, set of intentions, beliefs, desires that are registered when Dickinson's poems are read in the fascicles in which she copied them. For to read the poems in the fascicles is to see that the contextual sense of Dickinson is not the canonical sense of Dickinson.

The point, then, is to examine what kinds of connections among poems are apparent when they are read in the fascicles, and perhaps even on what principle the "apparent" will be produced. Connections, while not possible to illustrate in all of the poems in a given fascicle, are demonstrable in a sufficient number of the poems to give the fascicle as a whole the appearance of a structure. This apparent structure consequently affects our understanding of the subjects of the poems. Specifically, as I shall explain, it affects our understanding of what subjects are. By "subjects" I do not here mean the first-person speaker, but I also do not mean the conventionally defined headings that Johnson produces in his "Subject Index," which designate rhetorical and wholly unproblematic topics or themes. In fact, while the poem I shall consider at the beginning of section II of this chapter confirms the standard notion that a lyric of Dickinson's is devoid of a subject, when one returns that lyric to the fascicle context the question of the subject comes back in a different way as a question about the nature of poetic subjects.

· To sum up, then, I mean to ask how reading a lyric in a sequence is different from reading the lyric as independent, for to do the latter is to suppress the context and the relations that govern the lyric in context—a suppression generating that understanding of Dickinson's poems as enigmatic, isolated, culturally incomprehensible phenomena which has dominated most Dickinson criticism, including my own.[14] At issue in the following examination is the question of what happens when context—when the sequence—is not suppressed.

14. Of course, a Dickinson contextualized is not necessarily a Dickinson made culturally intelligible; a literary context does not necessarily produce a cultural explanation. Here we are only in a speculative realm, but to gesture toward some topics which could be explored: There is the question of Emerson's poetry of the "portfolio," on the one hand, and of women's writing, on the other. Both seem cultural contexts in which Dickinson's poetry situates itself. On the subject of con-

To look at what happens when the sequence is not suppressed is to look past normalizing critical accounts of Dickinson. But it is equally to look past more complex, theoretically ambitious accounts, for instance, Hartman's. The criticism that domesticates and normalizes often finds little to talk about beyond the narrative of the love story; the poems make no sense or the sense that they make is completely unproblematic. Such criticism either finds Dickinson alien or makes her comprehensible in unconflicted terms. The criticism that radicalizes Dickinson finds nothing to talk about in completely different terms. Since what this body of criticism discovers in Dickinson is a poetry stripped of referentiality, and paradox purified of content—Hartman's hyphen, which enables the point about the hymen, although Hartman knows it is in fact a dash—such criticism is completely uninterested in problems posed by the textual history or the text. It has transcended the text at the moment of epitomizing it, as the normalizing criticism differently transcends the text by smoothing out its problems or claiming that they are incomprehensible. In both cases, albeit in different directions, the text is left behind.

Likewise, to look at what happens when the sequence is not sup-

---

text, it should also be noted that in the Houghton Library's collection of books owned by the Dickinson family (books that have the autograph signatures of Edward, Susan Gilbert, or Emily Dickinson, or other characteristic indications of family ownership), many of the poetic collections have lines separating the poems. See, for example, *The Poems of Elizabeth Barrett Browning* (New York: C. S. Francis and Co., 1852), where, in volume I, a series of sonnets is separated by lines, as well as Charles Anderson Dana's 1860 volume of *The Household Book of Poetry* (New York: Appleton and Company) and Rufus Griswold's 1844 *Gems from American Poets* (Philadelphia: Harmon Hooker). In these books, as in the journals of the time, it was conventional to divide poems by lines. The lines may indicate division (as in the case of the Dana anthology), but in Browning's case they also appear to indicate association, since no other poems in the volume are segregated by these graphic means. Although the Browning volume has the autograph signature of Susan Gilbert Dickinson, we can assume Emily Dickinson read it. In vol. II, p. 178, of *Poems* the following lines from "A Vision of Poets" are marked in pencil: "There were poets true/ Who died for Beauty, as martyrs do/ For truth—the ends being scarcely two." Although it is unclear whether Dickinson marked these lines, it is clear to me, from the verbal echo of "scarce," in one of her own poems, with Browning's "scarcely," that she had read them: "I died for Beauty—but was scarce/ Adjusted in the Tomb/ When One who died for Truth, was lain . . ." (P 449).

pressed is also to look past the two ways of reproducing the text. For there is a similar textual evasion apparent when one looks at Johnson's and Franklin's editions. The two ways of producing the text correspond to the two kinds of incomprehension illustrated by the normalizing and the theoretically sophisticated criticism. In the case of Johnson, Dickinson's poems are said not to be wholly unproblematic (see the introduction to the variorum text), but they are treated as unproblematic, in that the poems are reproduced as textually resolvable—that is, as possible to delimit. Specifically, they are still separated from the fascicles in which Dickinson bound them in fair copy. They are in addition treated as discrete utterances whose eccentric features can be accommodated by print, and the variants are dropped to the bottom of the page, while in the reader's edition variants are dropped entirely. In the case of Franklin, the problems of Dickinson's text are not ignored. In fact they are produced in the facsimile, even while the significance of what is being revealed by what has been produced is completely denied. I want to ask what happens when Dickinson's fascicles are read. Nothing in the two kinds of criticism or in the two ways of producing the text illustrates what makes the fascicles so interesting. Nor what makes the fascicles central to an understanding of Dickinson's poetic enterprise.

Finally, although my examination of the problems posed by the poems in Dickinson's fascicles—specifically the problems posed by the variants—can be seen as circumscribed in topic, that examination inevitably opens onto other aspects of Dickinson's poetry and onto aspects of other bodies of poetry, as indicated below.

I shall argue that, with respect to the variants, Dickinson sets up a situation that seems exclusionary, and that she then refuses choices which she presents as inevitable. Thus in Dickinson's poetry the apparent need to choose is countered by the refusal to choose. "Not choosing" in this respect is, of course, not itself particular to Dickinson's poetry, for the problem of "or" is common in poetic tradition. Logically there is a "minus or" that is exclusionary and a "plus or" that is inclusionary, as exemplified, for instance, by the poetry of Yeats, Whitman, and Stevens. That is, there are situations where "or" implies a choice *between* this and that, and different situations where "or" implies *both* this and that. If Dickinson's poetry exemplifies the latter situation (in which this *includes* that) while appearing to exemplify the former (this *excludes* that), other poets exemplify more simply the ways in which "or" means "and" or "also." Consider Yeats, whose "nor" in effect means "or":

Labour is blossoming or dancing where
The body is not bruised to pleasure soul,
Nor beauty born out of its own despair,
Nor blear-eyed wisdom out of midnight oil.
O chestnut tree, great rooted blossomer
Are you the leaf, the blossom or the bole?
O body swayed to music, O brightening glance,
How can we know the dancer from the dance?

    ("Among School Children")

and Whitman:

A child said *What is the grass?* . . .
I guess it must be the flag of my disposition, out of hopeful green
    stuff woven.

Or I guess it is the handkerchief of the Lord,

    . . .

Or I guess the grass is itself a child, the produced babe of the
    vegetation.

Or I guess it is a uniform hieroglyphic,
And it means, Sprouting alike . . .
And now it seems to me the beautiful uncut hair of graves.

    (Song of Myself)

Diverge, fine spokes of light, from the shape of my head, or any
    one's head. . . .

    . . .

Play the old role, the role that is great or small according as one
    makes it!

    . . .

The same old role, the role that is what we make it, as great as
    we like,
Or as small as we like, or both great and small.

    . . .

Great or small, you furnish your parts toward the soul.

    ("Crossing Brooklyn Ferry")

And Stevens:

> We live in an old chaos of the sun,
> Or old dependency of day and night,
> Or island solitude, unsponsored free. . . .

>> ("Sunday Morning")

In these instances "or" not only does not require but positively precludes choice. Thus, for Yeats, the identity of the thing cannot be understood outside of its serial manifestations; for Stevens, our origins, if ascertainable, are multiply specified. And for Whitman most of all, not choosing is itself a philosophical choice or position. Thus the grass is a uniform hieroglyph, and the child who asks about the grass is not to be distinguished from the grass which is a child. In fact in the series of examples from "Crossing Brooklyn Ferry" "great *or* small" becomes "great *and* small"—after which "and" again becomes "or" (though "or" is demonstrably shown to *mean* explicitly "and": "great as we like,/ Or as small as we like, or both great and small")—in a rare explication of the relation of alternatives that, the conjunction notwithstanding, are not predicated as alternatives. It will have been observed that in all of these examples, and in poetic discourse generally, not choosing is internal to the text. It exists within the boundaries framed by the poem. Moreover, not only is not choosing contained within the lines of the poem, but also, for a poet like Whitman, ontology is grounded upon it, as Whitman never tires of reiterating. In addition, in a plenitude of examples where alternatives are additive, the identity of persons (of speakers, of addressed readers) and the poetic identity of the text are compounded, as it were, and made to intersect. Thus canceled discriminations among objects in the text are made to coincide with canceled discriminations between the poet and the reader, between the poet and all his readers, so that "what I assume you shall assume,/ For every atom belonging to me as good belongs to you."

By light of the previous examples, what I shall call Dickinson's "not choosing" is exceptional. It is exceptional, however, not because it is not choosing, but rather because the presumption that choosing is necessary is contested by the representation of not choosing, for in the poems the choice of particular words implied by the lyric frame to be imperative is rather shown to be impossible. Thus if there is an inclusive "or" and an exclusive "or," Dickinson's poems seem to exemplify the latter situation (this but not that) while in fact representing the former situation (this as well as that). Thus not choosing in Dickinson's poems is different from not choosing in Whitman's. First, it is different because it is assumed that choice is required, even as the requirement is repeatedly, if subversively, transgressed. Second, not choosing is exceptional in Dickinson's poems because the words occasioning it appear exported to the margins or interlinear spaces. Choice appears to engage words which lie outside the text, at least to lie "outside" as that text has conventionally been defined. This points to a third difference between not choosing in other poetic situations and Dickinson's not choosing. In most poetry the incorporation of "or" situations results in what is in effect a monoglossic situation. Notwithstanding its magnitude, Whitman's "I" is a unitary self. By distinction, in Dickinson's poems not choosing results in a heteroglossic situation. That is, most poems presume one speaking voice, as the lines from Yeats, Whitman, and Stevens indicate. Dickinson's poems appear to follow that convention in which utterance issues from a single voice while in effect transgressing it. For, as the discussion below elaborates, two voices often punctuate the poetry as do double stories—with one of the voices, and often one of the stories, situated outside the ostensible boundaries of the poem. This unacknowledged exteriority, this outside voice, which must be drawn into relation with the poem, in lieu, as it were, of actual assimilation to it, might explain the rhythmic constraint and the dictional consistency characteristic of Dickinson's poems, for perhaps both are necessary to create boundaries around the voice in the poem, to contain it and to distinguish it from the voice situated "outside."

As I shall explain, it is in the variants that the two voices can be seen to emerge. For if in the variants we have the same metrical contour for alternative words, then it cannot be said that the variants indicate Dickinson's attempt to find the "right" word. Moreover, if in the poem (as distinct from in the margin) Dickinson is moving from terms used less frequently ("Beetles," to take one example) to those used more frequently ("Daisies," to take an example from the same pair of variants), then Dickinson "in" the poem is moving into her own terminological world. She is looking for language that can be identified as "hers" and she is finding it at the center. If, on the other hand, the word used most frequently is set in the margins, then conversely Dickinson is looking for her own language and finding it in the margins. So one question to be asked about the variants is, Are the words in the line of greater or lesser frequency than the ones in the margins? Is Dickinson always gravitating toward

"Daisies" and away from "Beetles," or vice versa? For if in the margins Dickinson is gravitating away from high-frequency words, then one could say she is moving toward her own voice in the poem as conventionally defined. The question raised by this issue is something like, Which voice is *her* voice, and is the voice designated as "other" expelled or incorporated? If, conversely, there is no consistency to these placements, if the concordance reveals no pattern to the location of the high-frequency words—high-frequency words are neither always in the center nor always in the margin—then we are left with a situation in which the voice that is owned and the voice that is other are in effect indistinguishable with respect to the question of placement. Thus one might want to ask if the excluded terms are metrically identical with the included terms. If they are the same (or if they are different), what are the implications? One might also ask: Is the word in the copy-text of greater or lesser frequency? If Dickinson is characteristically choosing against the standard, what are the implications of that choice for heteroglossia?[15]

I have noted that my examination of the fascicles opens onto aspects of not choosing in other bodies of poetry. But it also opens onto aspects of not choosing specific to Dickinson's poetry—aspects touched on above with respect to the two voices. I enumerate, albeit briefly, other aspects of doubleness—of choosing not to choose—in Dickinson's poetry that the following explanation of the textual situation helps to enlarge.

1. First, it is a commonplace that at the level of syntax Dickinson is

15. In the ten sets of variants which I have examined, it is not in fact possible to claim that the characteristic word, the one Dickinson uses with most frequency, is "marginalized" or "centralized," for, according to the frequency of these words as specified by the concordance, not only is there no consistent practice, but, further, in many of the poems which contain more than one variant there is also no consistent practice within a given poem (see *A Concordance to the Poems of Emily Dickinson,* ed. S. P. Rosenbaum [Ithaca: Cornell University Press, 1964]). Thus, for example, in "If I may have it, when it's dead" (P 577) in which ten lines contain variants, only five of the variants clearly centralize the word/s used with more frequency. Complicating this situation, in line 27, where there are two alternatives ("touch/greet") to the word on the line ("stroke"), although one of the marginalized words ("touch") is used more frequently than the word on the line, the other ("greet") is used less frequently. Nor in fact, as my discussion below indicates, can these words quite be described as either marginalized or centralized (see the last stanza of "If I may have it, when it's dead," fig. 7). And this interweaving of the marginal and the central, with respect to frequently used words, suggests that Dickinson is not in fact defining her "own" or characteristic language either at the center or in the margin. She is rather speaking "characteristically" from both places at once.

characteristically choosing not to choose. It is not, for instance, clear whether "Slow Gold—but Everlasting—" in "Some—Work for Immortality—/ The Chiefer part, for Time—" (P 406) refers to the compensations of "Time" or those of "Immortality." By association with the previous line the tenor of the metaphor would be "Immortality," not "Time," but in light of the following line it would be "Time" rather than "Immortality." Nothing will produce a resolution to the question about reference, since the syntax is unresolved, and definitively so, for according to the indeterminacy conveyed by the dashes the line cannot but be read in opposite directions and this simultaneously. Such doubleness, both syntactical and semantic, is less complicated in "At least—to pray—is left—is left—" (P 502). But it is quite complicated in the last stanza of "Rehearsal to Ourselves" (P 379): "We will not drop the Dirk—/ Because We love the Wound/ The Dirk Commemorate—Itself/ Remind Us that we died." In these lines there is a choice between reading "Itself" as allied with "Dirk," with the reflexivity applied to the instrument, and reading "Itself" as applied to the wound inflicted by the dirk. In the second interpretation of the syntax the recollection is still fatal, but it is not, as in the first, futile. Since the fatality is caused by the loss—rather than by the recollection of the loss—it is compensated by being also caused by the "Bliss" associated with the loss, and inevitably recollected at the same time. And this choice is unresolvable since no amount of parsing will convert the syntax into conventionally punctuated lines that indicate which noun is underscored as object of the self-reflexive action. The dashes permit, even insist on, these overlapping, disparate meanings, suggesting both the futility of recollection and its compensations.

2. But if Dickinson characteristically does not choose syntactically, she also characteristically does not choose between the story ostensibly being told and the story actually being told. In "I cannot live with You—" (P 640), for instance, choosing not to be with a lover rather means choosing the grounds on which to meet him: it means equating him with the God for whom he has ostensibly been given up. Often apparent in the difficulty of this poetry, as I elaborate below, is the fact that two conflicting stories are told simultaneously. While the disruption caused by the doubleness punctuates the experience of reading the poems, it is also a characteristic of these poems not to acknowledge the existence of double stories, hence not to establish alliances with one or the other of the stories, and thus to predicate a seamlessness belied by

what is being voiced.[16] So voice is at odds with itself in these poems, so much so that the proper term for the disagreement is in fact heteroglossia in another form.

3. Dickinson is also choosing not to choose between the suggestion that certain experiences can be mapped—can be made comprehensible in terms of geographies and exteriors—and the suggestion made by the same poems that such experiences cannot be. Thus, for example, in a poem like "Bereaved of all, I went abroad—" (P 784) a speaker attempts to reside elsewhere than where the loss is, literally to place herself at a geographic distance from loss, although the speaker is more explicit about the futility of such efforts than elsewhere. Such poems, in search of correlatives for interior experience, often resort to the language of measurement in order to insist on the impossibility of it (as in "A nearness to Tremendousness—" [P 963]). Or they raise questions about what it means to define experience in terms of categories without content ("I stepped from Plank to Plank" [P 875]). These poems might be described as sceneless, but in fact they avail themselves of quite elaborate maps, geographies, scenes, and coordinates ("Behind Me—dips Eternity—/ Before Me—Immortality—/ Myself—the Term between—" [P 721]), even if the claim made by the elaborate representations is countered by the categorical emptiness of the same representations, by the fact that what is being mapped is only technically or terminologically coherent. In the poems Dickinson is choosing not to choose whether certain experiences *can* be mapped—whether something that is only categorically comprehensible is comprehensible or not. She is choosing not to choose what the coordinates of an experience are, choosing not to choose whether internal scenes can have external coordinates. And she is choosing not to choose whether certain exteriorizations ("a Funeral, in my Brain" [P 280]) fulfill the task assigned to them—here to make a conceit of repression—or whether, in not forestalling the repression, the exteriorization fails to fulfill the task assigned to it. In fact, this exteriorization is itself equivocal: it gives literal, external form to an inner event but immediately relocates it within ("in my Brain").

---

16. See the discussion of double stories that disrupt each other in "'A Loaded Gun': The Dialectic of Rage" in Cameron, *Lyric Time: Dickinson and the Limits of Genre*, pp. 56–90; but see also the discussion of the apparent seamlessness of these stories in "The Interior Revision," chapter 4 of this book. *Lyric Time* is hereafter cited as *LT,* and page references are supplied parenthetically in the text.

4. Dickinson is also not choosing how particular words are to be read. Consider "None may teach it—Any—" in "There's a certain Slant of light" (P 258) where what is implied is "None may teach it—[not] Any [one else]—"; "None may teach it—Any[thing]—" (it is not subject to alteration); and "None may teach it—[to] Any[one else]—." In "I felt a Funeral, in my Brain" consider the poem's last line: "And Finished knowing—then—," where it is ambiguous whether knowing is finished or whether the experience which prevents knowing is finished. And consider the last line of "After great pain, a formal feeling comes—" (P 341): "First—Chill—then Stupor—then the letting go—" with its ambiguity about whether what "letting go" implies is the ability to feel which would reverse the "Chill" and "Stupor" that have preceded it or whether what is oppositely implied by the whole series of nouns are the final stages of the inability to feel that terminate in death.

5. The refusal to choose—choosing not to choose—how syntax is to be read, how double voices and sometimes contradictory stories are related to each other, how lines which *can* be read in antithetical ways *should* in fact be read, is reiterated in the question mark with which so many of Dickinson's poems conclude: "Which Anguish was the utterest—then—/ To perish, or to live?" (P 414), "Could it be Madness—this?" (P 410), "And could I, further, 'No'?" (P 446), "Say, Jesus Christ of Nazareth—/ Hast thou no Arm for Me?" (P 502), "'My Husband'—women say—/ Stroking the Melody—/ Is *this*—the way?" (P 1072), etc.

6. Finally, Dickinson's choosing not to choose is dramatically reiterated in the questions raised by the discrepancy between the boundedness implied by the quatrain form and the apparent boundlessness implied by the variant. To elaborate these questions: How does one interpret the fact that Dickinson chooses to write in quatrains and in hymn meter—in a structure that goes as far as possible toward bounding and containment—rather than to write in a looser form, as, say, Whitman does? Why is Dickinson writing in a form that bounds, contains, borders and excludes? Why does she write in an exclusionary form when she also through the structure of the variant makes the form all-inclusive? What is the residual challenge that the form poses to her endeavor?

One way to answer these questions is to say that Dickinson is choosing a form so as to subvert it. But a more intelligible intuition might be that Dickinson is rather exploiting a form so as to point to the "identity" or convergence of boundedness and *un*boundedness. Thus what is discernible in the form of the poem as related to the form of the variant is not only displacement, but also condensation. It is almost as if in choosing the most condensed form, Dickinson resolves to produce an equivalent to Freud's analysis of the antithetical sense of primal words—a phenomenon also visible only in condensation.[17] Dickinson condenses to a point where she ends up with formal antitheses which have, as we shall see, thematic equivalents. Both thematic and formal oppositions advance a psychological or philosophical proposition: that in condensation, what is revealed at the core of identity is not just difference but more fundamentally antithesis. In light of such an understanding, the formal boundedness of the quatrain and the subversion of boundedness in the heteroglossia of the variants are not matters of Dickinson's form *subverting* Dickinson's project. They are rather matters of form *revealing* the audacity of the project as founded on identity that can only be understood as deriving its element from opposition.

Before turning to the fascicles, then, my point has been to connect the "not choosing" in Dickinson's poetry with the "not choosing" in other poetic corpuses even while suggesting that not choosing in these other corpuses seems typically to result in monoglossia. Not choosing in Dickinson's poetry rather results in a heteroglossia whose manifestations inform every aspect of the poetry. But we also see the attempts to deny heteroglossia or doubleness, and see as well and nevertheless that exclusive speech—speech which attempts to suppress other voices and meanings—does not in fact achieve exclusion. It is to the most radical manifestations of such double speech—its "illocality" half-positioned, as it were, outside the poem understood as conventional poem—that I ultimately turn in considering issues of identity in Dickinson's poetic text.

---

17. See Freud's 1910 review, "The Antithetical Sense of Primal Words," reprinted in *On Creativity and the Unconscious: Papers on the Psychology of Art, Literature, Love, Religion,* ed. Benjamin Nelson (New York: Harper and Row, 1958), pp. 55–62. Specifically, Freud is here expanding on his earlier observation about dreams: that in dreams opposites are reduced to a unity so that these antitheses may be represented as one thing. Crediting his reading of Karl Abel—a philologist who wrote in 1884—for the amplified understanding of his own earlier observation about dreams, Freud quotes Abel: "'Since every conception is . . . the twin of its opposite, how could it be thought of first, how could it be communicated to others who tried to think it, except by being measured against its opposite?'" (p. 58). Thus in language, as in dreams, identity itself is understood as fundamentally constituted by the contradictory and the antithetical.

II. Excess

IN AN ATYPICAL but logically first example of what we might expect from consideration of a poem in its fascicle placement, recourse to the fascicle context can prove simply clarifying. In "It's like the Light—" (P 297) in Fascicle 12, for instance, a poem has no antecedent, hence no specified subject, when read as a poem outside the fascicle context. But it is explicitly defined within that context as the middle of three poems written within the same bifolium and on the same subject. "One Year ago—jots what?" (P 296)—the first poem of the fifth sheet—narrates the anniversary of the parting from a lover. "Alone, I cannot be—" (P 298, the third and last poem, on the verso of the leaf on which P 297 is written) represents the state of being haunted by the recollection of the lover's presence. Therefore *what* is like the light of "It's like the Light—" is the pain of separation attested by the first poem and said to be ameliorated in the third by the recollection of the lover summoned up as omnipresent. In between the memory of the parting and the reexperiencing of the memory as if it were a presence is the poem in question, which anticipates an ultimate cure—reunion after death—that will supersede the makeshift earthly one.

"I saw no Way—The Heavens were stitched—" (P 378), examined in the context of the fascicles, would also seem to illustrate that context clarifies. In fact this is a slightly more complex example, for reasons that will become apparent. Consider the poem as an isolated lyric:

> I saw no Way—The Heavens were stitched—
> I felt the Columns close—
> The Earth reversed her Hemispheres—
> I touched the Universe—
>
> And back it slid—and I alone—
> A Speck upon a Ball—
> Went out upon Circumference—
> Beyond the Dip of Bell—

Emily Dickinson's poem is gnomic, abstract, bereft of situation, without apparent subject. Or it is inventing a subject; specifically it is inventing a language for experience that is unrecognizable, hence incomprehensible, hence inhospitable to conventional description. This, at any rate, is what I once thought when I described the poem as a "leavetaking of the known temporal world," a poem in which "abstraction invests utterance with the foreignness of the venture." I elaborated as follows: "When Dickinson's poems go 'Beyond the Dip of Bell—,' as this one attempts to do, to excavate the territory that lies past the range of all phenomenal sense, they are haunted by the terrible space of the venture, as language is flung out into the reaches of the unknown in the apparent hope that it might civilize what it finds there" (*LT,* pp. 8, 9).

In that gloss of the poem, I understood the bizarre geographic, architectural and geometric images—"Columns," "Hemispheres," "Circumference," not least "the Dip of Bell"—as a direct manifestation of an experience which was not only undomesticated but *could* not be domesticated, since the situation had no experiential referent. Read thus—as an isolated lyric—the poem seems like an exercise in solecism, as well as solipsism, having not only no referent but also no context: barely comprehensible.

But to read the poem differently in the context of the poem that precedes it on the same bifolium in Fascicle 31 is to see that there could be a referent for the experience. For the first line of the previous poem, copied on the other side of the page of "I saw no Way" is "To lose one's faith—surpass/ The loss of an Estate—" (P 377), and this proximity, however loosely, establishes the poems in a relation to each other, suggesting that the cause of the disorientation might not be mysterious at all, but rather loss of faith. Moreover, to read "I saw no Way" in relation to yet a different poem, the first in the same bifolium, "The Soul's Superior instants" (P 306), is to see that it too represents a geography in which recognizable features of a scene are abolished, the speaker in "The Soul's Superior instants" being said to have "ascended/ To too remote a Hight/For lower Recognition"—to have ascended, in other words, to a sphere in which what occurs is called "Mortal Abolition," the abolition of the mortal world which is then replaced by an apparitional world not dissimilar to that in "I saw no Way."

Yet to establish a relation between and among poems is not yet to clarify it. Would, for instance, the epithet "Superior," which characterizes the moments of dissociation from the earthly world in "The Soul's Superior instants," equally apply to similar moments in "I saw no Way"? Or would it rather be the case that the exaltation and the despair of such alien moments were, in the two poems, being counterpointed to each other? Ultimately, in the second of the poems in the same bifolium ("Me prove it now—Whoever doubt" [P 537]) what is represented simultaneously is the immanence of a *speaker*'s death and the recollection of her lover's death. As "Me prove it now" precedes "To lose one's faith—surpass/ The loss of an Estate," would the lover's death in one poem be the cause of the loss of faith in the next, a loss of faith whose *consequences*, one could say, are demonstrated in the apocalyptic imagery of the poem, "I saw no Way—The Heavens were stitched—," with which we began? To ask these questions, as the poem read in the fascicle context makes it inevitable that we do, is not to arrive at a more stable interpretive situation, but it is to arrive at a different interpretive situation than that in which the poem is read elliptically as a decontextualized utterance. It is to be confronted by a different interpretive situation just to the extent that there are relations among poems that we cannot disregard and, as much to the point, that we do not precisely know how to comprehend.

To see a poem contextualized by a fascicle is sometimes to see that it has an altogether different, rather than only a relationally more complex, meaning when it is read in sequence rather than as an isolated lyric. For example, to read "Because I could not stop for Death—" (P 712) with reference to other fascicles and to other poems in Fascicle 23 is to see that the speaker's journey may not be solitary, not because she is accompanied by the abstract figures of death and immortality, but perhaps rather because she is accompanied by a lost lover here personified as death. This way of understanding the poem would be consonant with the many poems in the other fascicles and some of the poems in this one, poems in which a lover has died, and it would explain why in "Because I could not stop for Death—" death is figured as a lover or in any case as a suitor. Such a contextualization changes the sense of the poem. It changes it since the speaker's inability to imagine an end to the journey because death cannot be imagined (the conventional reading of the poem) is different from her inability to imagine death's end because she is not in fact dead. Reread in the context of the fascicles, "Because I could not stop for Death—" proposes a haunted relation to a death, which, though always there in memory, *cannot* deliver passage to eternity since, though death is always present, it is never, in fact, one's own.[18]

18. Other poems in Fascicle 23 about the apprehension of death ("The Whole of it came not at once—/ 'Twas Murder by degrees—" [P 762], "Presentiment—is

Yet if to read a poem in the fascicle context is potentially to domesticate it—to make it less uncanny than the conventional interpretation does—in other instances, poems read in the fascicle context call such a domestication into question. Thus in Fascicle 24 "This is my letter to the World/ That never wrote to Me—/ The simple News that Nature told—/ With tender Majesty" (P 441)—that poem anthologized in high-school textbooks to epitomize Dickinson at her most saccharine— is not necessarily a poem about a benign telling of nature's secret. Rather, at least with reference to surrounding poems in the fascicle, the secret being told is ominous. One poem in the same fascicle, for example, describes the earth as "A Pit—but Heaven over it—" (P 1712); in others, life extends without significance or value, one speaker explaining: "Therefore—we do life's labor—/ Though life's Reward—be done—/ With scrupulous exactness—/ To hold our Senses—on—" (P 443).[19] In still another poem, "It sifts from Leaden Sieves—" (P 311), nature in the form of a snowstorm obfuscates the visible, making it unrecognizable, as negation makes things unrecognizable. In context rather than in isolation, "This is my letter to the World" is not a benign telling of nature's story, but rather an account informed by the sinister aspects of the fascicle's other poems. For the letter to the world, its delivery to our "Hands," to hands the speaker "cannot see," is inescapably to be read as analogous to those stern communications the speaker has herself received.

But if reading poems in the fascicle context specifies subjects for

---

that long Shadow—on the Lawn—" [P 764], "He fought like those Who've nought to lose—" [P 759]) and about apprehension of another's death ("You constituted Time—/ I deemed Eternity/ A Revelation of Yourself—" [P 765]) substantiate that possible reading. For a recontextualization along similar lines, see the discussion below of "I read my sentence—steadily—" (P 412) in Fascicle 15.

19. Franklin claims that the lines I have quoted, while concluding "I tie my Hat—I crease my Shawl—," are separated from that poem by an intervening stanza which he says concludes "A Pit—but Heaven over it—," arguing that Dickinson used a single sheet on which to copy the conclusions to two separate poems (I:534). Despite the uncharacteristic line drawn between the stanzas which Franklin suggests belong to P 1712 and P 443, respectively—a line corroborating his sense that these stanzas complete separate poems—the quatrain attributed to P 1712 is metrically, imagistically, and thematically consonant with, as well as a direct continuation of the sense of, P 443. For the "them" who would be "start[led]" in the stanza said to conclude P 1712 are rather the ones for whom "calm" is being "simulate[d]" in the

poems and even in some cases their antecedents, it also raises problems about how the very groupings that contextualize poems are related to each other within the fascicles. I want now to sketch out these problems with respect to two particular issues: first, the way in which the pairings of poems within a fascicle govern lyrics not implicated in the pairing, and second, conversely, the way in which the central poem in a fascicle can be seen to govern poems that appear paired or clustered. I shall touch on the issues raised by Fascicle 15 and anticipate even more preliminarily issues raised by Fascicle 16—both considered in more detail in subsequent chapters.

By "paired" I mean the following: In several of the fascicles the first and last poem are either complementary or antithetical, or the poems are complementary *and* antithetical. In Fascicle 28, for instance, the first poem ("My period had come for Prayer—" [P 564]) and the last ("I prayed, at first, a little Girl" [P 576]) refute each other, in that while one suggests that prayer is transcended by worship, the other suggests that prayer is deflected by the impossibility of worship. In Fascicle 34 the first poem ("Bereavement in their death to feel" [P 645]) represents a speaker's experience of a death for which there is no recompense, while the last poem ("Essential Oils—are wrung—" [P 675]) represents consolation for death in the essence that survives it: "this" ["The Attar from the Rose"] "Make Summer—When the Lady lie/ In Ceaseless Rosemary—." In Fascicle 40, the last of the fascicles, the first and last poems ("The Only News I know/ Is Bulletins all Day/ From Immortality" [P 827] and "Unfulfilled to Observation—" [P 972]) represent speakers who perceive immortality and who, oppositely, are unable to do so. Thus the first and last poems of many of the fascicles, while differently related to each other, are undeniably linked, often by the reversal or countering of the idea in the initial poem. While outside of the fascicle context to see the same theme treated differently in disparate poems can seem an

---

previous stanza of P 443, and the suppressed "Bomb" in the stanza said to conclude P 1712 is in fact anticipated by the "Stopped. . .ticking" of earlier lines in P 443. Hence the "Therefore" of the line in that poem's final quatrain. Moreover, the meter of "I tie my Hat—" is composed of alternating lines of eight and six syllables, or seven and six; so is the meter of the disputed stanza (if one understands its first two lines as a broken unit of seven syllables). On the other hand, the meter of P 1712 seems based on six-syllable lines, framed by conspicuously irregular opening and closing stanzas.

accident resulting from arbitrarily placing these poems in proximity, within a fascicle context, in the instances I have described, it is impossible to see such conjunctions as arbitrary, since, placed by Dickinson at the beginning and end, they in effect frame what lies between them.[20]

Fascicles 15 and 16 exemplify the terms in which the phenomenon of pairing—and the heteroglossia made manifest in the pairing—is significant. Fascicle 15 contains paired poems governed by three sets of antithetical assertions: first, that madness can't be stopped ("The first Day's Night had come—" [P 410]) and that it *can* be ("We grow accustomed to the Dark—" [P 419]); second, that losing a lover—and therefore only having him speculatively—is unbearable ("It is dead—Find it—" [P 417]), and, conversely, that having him only speculatively is entirely bearable ("Not in this World to see his face—" [P 418] and "If I may have it, when it's dead" [P 577]); third, that direct knowledge is desired ("You'll know it—as you know 'tis Noon—" [P 420]) and, conversely, that oblique knowledge is superior ("A Charm invests a face/ Imperfectly beheld—" [P 421]). Moreover, these three, apparently unrelated topics may be seen to be connected because, in the fascicle context, through the proximity of the poems, antithetical attitudes toward madness and toward knowing are generated by the specific subjects of not knowing—

---

20. If in some fascicles first and last poems can be seen as paired to reveal disparate but related perspectives, in other fascicles—in Fascicle 5, for instance—a number of single lyrics each maintain two (paired) perspectives generated as if from one vantage. That is, the perspective gleaned from one place, emotion, or state illuminates not the site of its origin but the site of its reversal. "What Inn is this" (P 115) does so from the vantage of looking at earth from heaven, as the more conventional poems ("As Watchers hang upon the East" [P 121], for instance) do by looking at heaven from earth. Implicitly or otherwise, these poems insist that knowledge of one perspective depends on knowledge of its reverse (as in "Success is counted sweetest/ By those who ne'er succeed" [P 67] and "Talk with prudence to a Beggar" [P 119]). Yet that "For each extatic instant" (P 125) ends the fascicle suggests that the states the poems predicate as antithetical but entertain as equal are not in fact either, since the duration of one perspective (an "instant") is not equal to the duration of the other ("years"). Considered as a group, then, many of the poems in the fascicle attempt to see the "other" side—of pain, of poverty, of death—only to conclude in the intermediate poems, as well as in the ultimate poem, that there is only one perspective: that of pain, which is a constant, despite attempts to see it "differently." Here it could be noted that the doubleness ultimately refuted is the same as the doubleness initially predicated—with no acknowledgment that the relation is one of either refutation or predication. Hence it must be understood in terms of the heteroglossia discussed earlier.

and of not having—the lover. Therefore a narrative not suggested by any of the poems read singly is suggested by the poems read in relation, though not in chronological relation.

In Fascicle 15, as noted, the connections among paired poems also affect a reader's understanding of poems not implicated in the pairing. More, poems that are not part of a pair, and not apparently implicated in the concerns of any of the pairs, may seem to govern all of the pairs by applying, if only indeterminately, to even one of the three concerns they manifest. This is the case with "I found the words to every thought/ I ever had—but One—" (P 581), because *which* one—which thought— seems to refer to one of the fascicle's three central topics (not having the lover, not knowing [the lover], madness [because of not knowing or not having the lover]) without being definitively identified with any one of these. The indeterminacy has the effect of retaining the ambiguity of the one subject for which words cannot be found. Indeed it has the effect of heightening the tension around the poem's ambiguity since the possibilities are narrowed to three without being reduced to one. Similarly, "I had been hungry, all the Years—" (P 579), that poem which, even read singly, presents hunger as a conventional metaphor for desire, addresses, by changing the terms of, the three topics that dominate the fascicle. It does so because, as this is the last poem in the fascicle, "I had been hungry, all the Years—" would seem to advocate *not* having, *not* knowing, *not wanting,* except speculatively, the lover of whose presence the speaker had—in the paired antitheses—earlier been *deprived.* Thus the final poem in the fascicle, which in effect specifies a complicated connection between having and desiring, itself exists in opposition to the attitude toward desire expressed by the poems which have preceded it. They adopt various stances toward what the speaker desires but does not have. The final poem oppositely defines having as itself antithetical to desire.

That a fascicle's various paired antitheses should, by proximity or contiguity, be associated with each other; that poems unimplicated in any of the fascicle's antithetically paired poems should nevertheless seem to refer to them (as "I found the words to every thought/ I ever had— but One—" does); that a single poem should come into definitive antithetical relation to the series of paired opposites against which that single poem chronologically positions itself (as "I had been hungry, all the Years—" does)—in other words, that patterns discernible in some of the poems should inevitably affect a reader's perception of other poems ostensibly outside of that pattern—reveals yet another order a fascicle imposes on the poems within it. The order not of a narrative, and not of a single structure, it is, in the case of Fascicle 15, the order of antithetical perspectives that come to seem complementary, come even to seem unified when they are read in opposition to a poem—the last in the fascicle—whose assertions assault the supposition on which the oppositions are founded. It is the order of poems whose allegiances shift, and can be seen to do so.

In Fascicle 15, poems not part of pairings are nonetheless implicated in them. In distinction, Fascicle 16, first, seems ordered by a single poem that asserts authority over that fascicle's antitheses. Because the fascicle's oppositions concern a dominant theme in Dickinson's poetry (death) and a dominant question posed by that theme (whether death is to be understood literally or metaphorically) and even a second query that pressingly informs the initial question (whether death is desired or declined), the centrality of such a poem, which seems to legislate over these questions, promises to be informative.

Second: The poems in Fascicle 16 that could be described as representing death could also be differently described as representing choice, and, differently still, could be seen as representing stances toward vision. In other words, there are thematic clusters in Fascicle 16. These could be characterized as governed by the topics of death, choice, vision. What is interesting about the clusters is that poems understandable as governed by one topic can differently be construed as governed by another. For example, "Before I got my eye put out—" (P 327) can be conceived as a representation of an anticipated death; alternatively as a poem that represents choice; yet alternatively as a poem that represents discrete stances toward vision. In other words, the poems in Fascicle 16 fit simultaneously into disparate categories. Another way to say this is that there are no disparate categories to be connected.

Third: Certain ambiguities raised by reading the poems as isolated lyrics (Is death in poems like "'Tis so appalling—it exhilirates—" [P 281] literal or metaphoric?), while clarified by being read in the fascicle context, are replaced, when read in that context, by other, quite different ambiguities. Is vision (and in some cases, death) being chosen or rejected? It is difficult to answer the question because while in some poems death, for instance, is chosen, in others it is declined. And it is also difficult to answer because while the topics of choice, death, vision are in some poems treated as synonymous, in other poems they are treated as antagonistic. So the poems remain implicated in each other in ways that are at once redundant and contradictory.

Fourth: Some of these questions appear to be answered by an intermediate poem in the sequence, "When we stand on the tops of Things—", (P 242), a poem that I earlier called central because it transcends the partiality of any of the positions advanced in the other poems. Vision on the top of things, vision that looks down, is vision of "The smoke all cleared away from it—/ And Mirrorrs on the scene—." It is vision of a different order, say, of a totality, and it could be said to resolve the question of whether something is chosen or chosen against. It resolves this question because it implicitly rejects the partiality of perspective that would require such a choice. To the extent that the poem presents a vision of totality which heals the choices and divisions represented in the other poems, it seems to offer an alternative to the way they partialize the world. Of course totalizing itself is only another possibility. Totalizing, by excluding partiality, must itself be seen as partial. As if to make that point in different terms, to the extent that "When we stand on the tops of Things—" is itself a middle poem, asserting wholeness from only an intermediate position, it cannot possibly be said to offer an alternative to the divisions represented by the fascicle's other poems. In the following chapters I shall elaborate these and similar issues with respect to Fascicles 15 and 16, among others.

To exemplify, again preliminarily, the differences between reading in the fascicles and reading lyrics singly, consider the relationship—I shall ultimately argue it is more than a relationship—between two celebrated poems, "Of Bronze—and Blaze—" (P 290) and "There's a certain Slant of light" (P 258), that follow each other in Fascicle 13 (figs. 8–9), a juxtaposition which is fascinating for the disparate stances it offers toward the attempt to take loss impersonally, to reconstrue nature's manifestations of indifference to persons as benign. In "Of Bronze—and Blaze—" nature's indifference to us is what we are to cultivate in relation to ourselves. But if "Of Bronze—and Blaze—" records the indifference to the self that the self should and does adopt, "There's a certain Slant of light" cannot do this, the speaker there rather internalizing indifference as the difference that is betrayal—as a sign of despair and death. Fascicle 13 records a series of connected attempts to understand loss as natural, as a mere conversion, say, of day into night. To the extent that the speakers accept the impersonality of such a metaphor (as "Of Bronze—and

Blaze—" does), loss is inconsequential; to the extent that loss seems only alien, the speaker is afflicted by the difference that registers as internal ("Where the Meanings, are"). For with respect to the shifting light that "comes," that "goes," this shifting, when internalized, when taken in or taken personally, turns to despair. "Of Bronze—and Blaze—" does not, then, simply contextualize "There's a certain Slant of light"; it also changes its meaning, for when the two poems are read as retorts to each other, the second becomes a denial of the neutral perspective advanced as natural in the poem that precedes it. Or rather the second poem makes clear that the *natural* perspective is not the *person's* perspective, and cannot be made so. I shall return to this example.

In my preliminary discussion of Dickinson's fascicles in general and of these two fascicles in particular, I have raised questions rather than answering them: What is the difference between reading a poem in a fascicle context and reading it as an isolated lyric? What are the distinct ways in which poems are related in a fascicle? How do poems which seem grouped in clusters or pairs affect poems not ostensibly implicated in that grouping? How do single poems become central poems in the fascicle context? Finally, I would want to ask why these are not merely formal questions. Or in what way do formal questions have theoretical implications for rethinking the very nature and limits of form? I conclude this introduction by briefly taking up the last of these questions.

The fascicles invite us to read Dickinson's poems in the context of other sequences—Herbert's *The Temple*, Barrett Browning's sonnets, Tennyson's *In Memoriam*, Shakespeare's sonnets—which we can presume Dickinson had read.[21] Yet to place Dickinson's poems in the context of

21. Herbert was anthologized in Chambers's *Cyclopaedia of English Literature*, as he also was in Griswold's *Sacred Poets of England and America* (New York: D. Appleton and Company; dated 1849 on the title page and 1848 on the copyright page). Susan Gilbert Dickinson owned the 1844 edition of the *Cyclopaedia* published in Edinburgh by William and Robert Chambers; Edward Dickinson's copy was printed in Boston in 1847 by Gould, Kendall and Lincoln. A separate edition of *The Temple* was owned by Susan Gilbert Dickinson. Finally, although there is no proof that Dickinson read Shakespeare's sonnets, since her letters do not allude to them in particular, Edward Dickinson had a copy of the sonnets in his eight-volume 1853 edition of Shakespeare's *Comedies, Histories, Tragedies, and Poems,* which we know Dickinson had read, and which Richard Sewall tells us Edward Dickinson purchased in 1857. See Jack L. Capps's *Emily Dickinson's Reading 1836–1886* (Cambridge: Harvard University Press, 1966), pp. 12, 68–69; and *The Life of Emily Dickinson* (New York: Farrar,

other lyric sequences does not imply that we should read her poems only in sequence, or even mainly in sequence, rather than as isolated lyrics. Therefore, demonstrating that the poems can be read in sequence, and demonstrating the multiple ways in which sequences can be read (as in Fascicles 15 and 16), does not clarify whether the poems are to be read in sequence or isolation. But the reason it does not illuminate this, I shall argue, is that Dickinson herself was uncertain about how her poems should be read, an uncertainty demonstrated by the fact that she both sent her poems to friends as individual lyrics and also copied them in the fascicles in sequences. Or, to formulate the point more strongly, it is not merely that Dickinson was uncertain, but that she refused to make up her mind about how her poems should be read. This refusal—another aspect of what I have called choosing not to choose—is crucial to the problematic of reading her poetry.

Multiple ways of reading Dickinson's poems are consonant with the multiple variants in those poems; I have touched on this topic earlier. Interestingly, the variants have characteristically been understood as a nuisance by her readers. In 1890 Dickinson's first editors, T. W. Higginson and Mabel Loomis Todd, eliminated all variants when they made other substantive textual changes. In 1960 Thomas Johnson did the equivalent, as he chose among the variants he had recorded to make a reader's edition. In the years after 1981 Ralph Franklin, while seeming to reverse this decision, has in effect repeated it in his refusal to produce a transcript of the copies of the facsimiles. He has repeated it in practice, because few people will read the facsimile texts, and even most of those readers will not read these texts but will rather note the ordering of the fascicle's poems, which they will then read in the Johnson edition. But what if we are to see the variants interlineated in a poem as posing alternatives to given words, which—this is crucial—are part of the poem? What if what Dickinson has to teach us is the multiplicity of meanings that, properly understood, resist exclusion? In other words Dickinson

---

Straus and Giroux, 1974), II:467. See, too, Sewall's list of books in the Dickinson collection at Houghton Library, some of them, as indicated by the library's register, containing markings "probably" or "perhaps" by Dickinson (II:678–79). Dickinson mentions Tennyson and Barrett Browning in her letters, and the collections of their poems owned by the Dickinson family are in the Houghton Library.

appears to be understanding variants as non-exclusive alternatives—a phenomenon that would have analogues in Christopher Ricks's description of the anti-pun in which a poet "creates meanings which take into account those absent senses of a word which his verse is aware of fending off."[22] In Ricks's discussion of anti-puns, though, these senses are absent in the sense of being implied while also being precluded. They are incorporated, for instance, in the second sense of a word which is implicitly ruled out. In Dickinson's poems alternative senses are displaced but not decisively so because they remain ambiguously counterpointed to the word to which they stand in explicit juxtaposition, and to which they often stand in direct proximity on the manuscript page. Thus while in Ricks's notion of the anti-pun a second sense is entertained and then dismissed, in Dickinson's poems alternative words collide without particular words' being clearly made secondary or subordinate. For alternatives to various words are not treated in Dickinson's text as *other* than those words.

One way of understanding variants is that a reader is required to choose between them and there is even evidence for both choices. Preliminary dilemmas aside, one is supposed to choose, and, indeed, if one had the right evidence, one could make the right choice. There is nothing ontologically tricky about such a situation.

A second way of understanding the problem of two entities that look like variants is that while they look as if they require to be chosen between, they do not so require, because both are clearly part of the poem or of the single entity (as in the examples from Whitman's and Yeats's poetry). So not only is no choice required, but a choice would in fact be a mistake.

A third way of understanding variants—a way of understanding them necessitated by reading Dickinson's fascicles—is that they are meant to be experienced *as* variants, and so one is also meant to be experiencing the necessity of choosing between them. Thus the situation exemplified by Dickinson's variants is more like the first case than it is like the second. But it is different from the first case because there are no possible criteria that could enable one to choose. So in this third case, the reader experiences the necessity for choosing, without access to the criteria by which she could make a choice. In other words the problem is

22. "William Wordsworth I: 'A Pure Organic Pleasure from the Lines'" in *The Force of Poetry* (Oxford: Clarendon Press, 1984), p. 99.

not solved by having more evidence, because the problem is not raised as
a question of evidence. And in fact, as I shall argue in the following
chapter, there is no way that the problem posed by the imperative to
choose countered by the prohibition against choosing could be simplified
or solved.

One implication of not being able to choose among the variants is
that we would have only one adequate text of Dickinson's poems—that
of the facsimile—an unsatisfactory solution because in effect no one reads
this text. That problem would seem to be solved if the decision were
made to print a transcript of the fascicle texts, for then people would
read them. Yet even if a transcript of the fascicle texts were printed, such
publication would not address what I take to be the real problem: the
nature of the relation between poem and text. That is, there is the "text"
that is the document; there is the "text" that is the poem as the published
or, in Dickinson's case, publishable entity; and there is the more contemporary sense of "text," which is what the poem becomes as "read." In
Dickinson's case the contemporary or semiotic nature of "text" depends
on the text as document. It specifically depends on the felt ladenness of
the document's *alternatives* in some exacerbated way.

What is central here is the question of form. What the fascicles raise
is precisely a question about the relation between text and poem (about
the non-identity of text and poem), a relation shown to be problematic
by the fact that our difficulty of reading is not solved once one has chosen
which text (Johnson's or Franklin's) one is going to read. For once a text
has been chosen, if there are variants to that text, one has still not cleared
up the question of how to read the variants. The metrics of the poem
insist we choose only one of the variants. But the presence of the variants
insists on the impossibility of doing so. Another way to describe the
dilemma is that, since Dickinson refuses to choose among the variants,
she disallows us from doing so. The conventional interpretation of this
situation is that there are as many poems as there are variants. This is
precisely the wrong way to understand how words work in poems. The
variants exert pressure against each other in a *particular* poem and at
particular places *within* that poem. Since one cannot read the variants
simultaneously, with respect to the variants, noted as non-exclusive alternatives, Dickinson is unread because Dickinson is unreadable.

But if it is the case that there are variant meanings as well as variant
ways of determining meanings, then the problem posed by Dickinson's
poetry is not scarcity of meaning, not "leanness" at all, as Hartman and

other critics have suggested—the hyphen-hymen does not persephonate Emily—but rather an excess of meaning. (Here it would be correct to assess Hartman's vocabulary of leanness as implicitly gendered, reifying leanness with respect to Dickinson while it reifies sublime amplitude with respect to Wordsworth or Whitman. Harold Bloom's free-form rhapsodies about the American sublime writ large as instantiated by Emerson and miniaturized as instantiated by Dickinson reinforce the point.)

In the face of this excess—an excess which emerges because of the contextualization—a poem like "I saw no Way," read outside the fascicle context is sheer consolation, since it relieves us of a situation of reading in which options are provided without being specified. Here of course I am making two claims with respect to excess, one of which involves the variants and the other of which involves the fascicle groupings. To read a single lyric in relation to context, to other poems in the fascicle, is not necessarily the same as to read a lyric in relation to its variants. To read in these ways generates potentially different claims about how a text which we might have thought of as self-identical is disrupted. One is a claim about text and the other about context. But questions of context and of variants are inseparable in Dickinson's fascicles, first because only in the fascicle groupings is it fully apparent how the variants work, and second because, as I shall explain, only within the fascicle groupings do we see how what might have looked like a question of context (where a variant of a line in another poem seems also to pertain to the poem we are reading) becomes a question of text.

This situation of excess—too much meaning determined too many ways—is not particular to Dickinson. On different grounds Dickinson's contemporary and model, Ralph Waldo Emerson, comes to mind, for his essays—with their multiple and contradictory assertions, not to mention their performative rather than discursive means of advancing an argument; their frequent absence of persons, or their representations of persons as disarticulated body parts ("so many walking monsters,—a good finger, a neck, a stomach, an elbow, but never a man," as Emerson writes in "The American Scholar" [*RWE,* p. 54]); the atemporality they both advance and enact; their tonally levelled assertions in which disasters are recounted without as it were being registered—raise questions analogous to those raised by Dickinson's poems. In Emerson's case such questions are raised by the relation of single sentences or sections within a given essay, and by the relation of single essays to each other within a given volume. [23] In the case of Emerson criticism there are few formal readings of individual essays—few readings despite the fact that Emerson continues to be conceived as the cornerstone of American literature and his atypical essay "Self-Reliance" is said to epitomize his work (without such an assertion's being accompanied by a serious examination of that essay's putative status). Similarly, Dickinson continues to be read as one of the two central nineteenth-century American poets without being read. In the context of the situation posed by Dickinson's poems and Emerson's essays, the turn away from reading does not constitute a sophisticated rise above/beyond formalism. Rather it illustrates a refusal to consider the theoretical implications of a formal examination such as I have sketched above.

Blake systematized meaning. Spenser allegorized it. Whitman eroticized it. More than any other poet Dickinson economizes it: makes the question of its economy (how much or little) and the question of its relativity, its in(ter)determinacy (how much and how little in relation to what) central to the poetry. For while a first, cursory understanding of economy would endorse the ideology of leanness as an absolute condition of Dickinson's poems and of their meaning, in fact what Dickinson is ultimately always questioning is the economy according to which poems are written, as she is also always questioning the economies within them, endlessly raising questions of relation and magnitude. It is as if sense for

23. For example, the relation remains to be explored between "The Poet," in which the figure so named is said to be free and to make us free ("He unlocks our chains. . . ." [*RWE*, p. 463]) and two other essays, "Gifts" and "Nominalist and Realist," in which a poet is not an emancipator but exactly the reverse. "The magnetism which arranges tribes and races in one polarity, is alone to be respected; the men are steel filings. Yet we unjustly select a particle, and say, 'O steel-filing number one! what heart-drawings I feel to thee! what prodigious virtues are these of thine! how constitutional to thee, and incommunicable.' Whilst we speak, the loadstone is withdrawn; down falls our filing . . . and we continue our mummery to the wretched shaving" (pp. 576–77). In the face of these interpretive difficulties raised by Emerson's essays—whether to read an essayistic statement as subordinate, as central, in relation to the preceding sentence or to the preceding essay—it is no surprise there is a dearth of criticism in the form of close reading of Emerson's essays. In Dickinson's case there is a virtual critical industry, but it is based on a reading of the poems which excludes the reading of the variants and ignores questions about the multiple ways of reading made inevitable by the two contexts—of the fascicle and of the lyrics encountered individually—as I have tried to outline them.

Dickinson were defined in the tension between the too little and too much—specifically the tension occasioned by how subjects are construed, given delimited boundaries and related—that imperfectly regulates the experience of her poems. This too little or too much is easily recognizable in the thematics of her poetry, as in the disequilibrium of the "one Draught of Life" paid for by "existence—" (P 1725) or the temporal disequilibrium of "Transporting must the moment be—/ Brewed from decades of Agony!" (P 207). And there are other examples: "Because You saturated Sight—/ And I had no more Eyes/ For sordid excellence/ As Paradise" (P 640); "Why Floods be served to Us—in Bowls—/ I speculate no more—" (P 756); "I had not minded—Walls—/ Were Universe—one Rock . . . But 'tis a single Hair—/ A filament—a law—/A Cobweb—wove in Adamant—/ A Battlement—of Straw—" (P 398). But this too little or too much is also recognizable in the disequilibrium of excess—words crowding each other out in the displacements of variants that don't in fact displace each other, in alternative ways of reading that are not really alternative.

As this description implies, if Dickinson's poems economize meaning, in so doing they make it problematically relational, illuminating what could be described as a central discovery of Dickinson's poems, perhaps even the thing they most have to teach us: how relations specify subjects by obliquity and juxtaposition, and indeed specify subjects in the process of either evolving or shifting. I have now indicated preliminarily how this works in two fascicle contexts in which poems are paired in ways that are both antithetical and fluid. In conclusion I touch on how meaning is made relational in a single instance. For although one manifestation of Dickinson's presumed intention may be seen to confine the reading of poems to the fascicle, when lyrics are nevertheless read outside this context, the poems may newly be seen to reveal, perhaps by virtue of the fascicled reading, what the boundaries of their subjects are and how those boundaries must be seen to shift. Or perhaps it is the case that the multiple shifts that we see in the fascicles suddenly make sense of—even actually make visible—shifts that have always, albeit unaccountably, marked aspects of our reading of the poems considered singly.

At the end of "Because I could not stop for Death—" (P 712), the "Horses Heads" loom over the edge of the poem, claiming our attention, for these heads, which are regarded from the vantage of the carriage, block or obstruct. The "Horses Heads" are not, then, only a synecdoche for the horses, they are also, more precisely, a way of delineating that impediment to the speaker's vision: they are all she can see, or what she cannot see beyond. What I mean to emphasize in this familiar instance is the way in which the subject is made to change as the part subsumes the whole, or potentially does so—synecdoche being a governing as well as a topical issue—even while its unspecified relation to that whole remains insisted on, not only as in the vision of the "Horses Heads" that replaces the vision of "Death," but also as in "When we stand on the tops of Things—," which upstages by reinterpreting the fascicle's surrounding lyrics through its preemptive relation to them. The formal concerns raised by the fascicles duplicate the formal concerns raised by single lyrics, occasioning, not incidentally, questions that are not formal:

What is a subject? How is it bounded? What are the boundaries around what something is? Dickinson raises these questions because she writes into being subjects (in the sense of topics) that are conventionally written out of it. But she also raises these questions by reconstructing the subject as something that is at once economized and relational; by insistently treating the subject as something not given and also not single (one specific relation in question being that of part to whole); by amplifying the idea of a subject to include its variants as well as variant ways of conceiving it. Finally, Dickinson raises these questions by producing utterances that are extrageneric, even unclassifiable, and (for that reason, in a way that it seems to me no one yet has quite explained) untitled.

2

READING DICKINSON I

I. Amplified Contexts

༄✿༅

IN THE PREVIOUS CHAPTER I have written about the problems of reading Dickinson, about ways in which Dickinson is unread because Dickinson is unreadable. In the first section of this chapter I shall consider questions produced by the amplified contexts in which Dickinson's fascicles might be read. In subsequent sections and chapters I then turn to the fascicles themselves to examine how one of the concerns raised repeatedly by the texts—differently exemplified by the larger contexts discussed below—must be considered: the ways in which problems of reading and problems of choosing are inseparable in this poetry. But, first, to enumerate (and in some cases to reiterate) several distinct but related questions which Dickinson's fascicles, considered in a larger framework, generate:

1. The question of how the single poem is related to the sequence is also raised by the poetry of Herbert, Sidney, Shakespeare, Pope, Collins, Bradstreet, Whitman, Yeats, Pound, Williams, Lowell, Berryman—to take deliberately disparate examples.[1] With respect to this question, then, I am not making an exceptionalist claim per se for Dickinson. (One might, however, want to ask whether the fact that for the past hundred years Dickinson's work has been read in the form of the single lyric, rather than in the sequences comprised by the fascicles, does not legiti-

---

1. The case of Wordsworth's classifications, as discussed by Frances Ferguson, provides a more interesting analogy still, and perhaps even a parallel case. See *Wordsworth: Language as Counter-Spirit* (New Haven: Yale University Press, 1977) and especially the chapter "Wordsworth's Classifications of His Poems," pp. 34–95. Wordsworth created classifications for his poems that "order" how he intended them to be read; these arrangements are not unlike the orders discernible in Dickinson's fascicles. What, to my mind, is interesting about these classificatory structures is that (1) they supply interpretive categories which structure internally, so that, for instance, poems under the rubric of "Affection" are to be read differently from poems under the rubric of "Imagination." But (2) by virtue of these categories, according to Ferguson's account, poems are also to be read relationally so that, for instance, "Poems founded on the Affections" are in some sense opposed to "Poems of the Fancy" (p. 55). In fact, these distinct categories form something of a dialectic (p. 63) with respect to the understanding of metaphor. Yet even as these classificatory categories order from within and relate from without, they are not definitively binding, since, notwithstanding the classificatory structure, it is possible to see the lyrics

mate considering her poetry as a special case.) Indeed, with respect to two central concerns that emerge from reading the fascicles—the relation of lyric to sequence, and the relation of manuscript to print (issues that in Dickinson's case, as I shall suggest, only appear to be separate, since if Dickinson had published her poems, it is not clear whether she would have published single lyrics or sequences)—one of the questions that remains to be answered is: What would constitute the exceptionalist case?

Consider, for instance, the question of publishing. Particular examples clarify that authors do not publish for very different reasons. Herbert did not publish *The Temple* during his lifetime, and for Herbert the point of not publishing was to ensure that the poems *not* survive his death; we have his poems in violation of instructions requesting that the manuscripts be destroyed. There is no evidence that Shakespeare had anything to do with the publication of his plays during his lifetime (although he did publish two of his poems), perhaps because plays were thought of as a subliterary genre. Sidney did not publish his manuscripts, desiring to think of himself more as a patron than as a writer. For Sidney's wariness of publication was effectively the repudiation of his own writing, nothing specifically literary being published in his lifetime. Spenser circulated his manuscripts and subsequently published them— thereby complicating the notion which certain critics have developed that print in the Renaissance could never be a route toward the exclusive spheres of courtly patronage and preferment. In many of these cases, the investment in writing, and in some cases in printing, was not a professional investment. In fact in the Renaissance manuscripts circulated ex-

---

as individual, "microcosmic insets within the macrocosm of which they are a part" (p. 40). Thus the poems that are classified and structured can also be read as lyrics, and their structure can be understood still differently in relation to much larger structures: *The Prelude* and *The Excursion*. Finally, what is also provocative in Ferguson's account of Wordsworth's classifications—with an eye to its potential analogy with the Dickinson fascicles—is the way in which Wordsworth intended an order which would, for instance, consequentially read the "Intimations Ode" against "My heart leaps up"—an order that has been dismissed by Wordsworth's readers to just the extent it has been found to be so heterogeneous as to be unintelligible. In other words, Wordsworth's order is dismissed because it does not conform to the prescriptive critical sense of what an order should be. Susan Gilbert Dickinson's 1854 edition of *The Complete Wordsworth,* in the Houghton Library, contains two prefaces which discuss the classifications alluded to above.

tensively, and this became a normal mode of disseminating a text. The Renaissance had of course its distinctive literary protocols.

Yet not publishing, and circulating rather than publishing manuscripts, are phenomena that continue into the nineteenth century. For instance, Wordsworth did not publish *The Prelude* during his lifetime, among other reasons because its copyright protection would expire at his death if he did so. *The Prelude* was therefore published posthumously, at least partially so that his widow would have the benefit of copyright law. Lord Byron's aristocratic contempt for the nitty-gritty of publishing at the beginning of his career gave way under various pressures to a wholehearted involvement in all aspects of the publishing trade. And, under a still different set of pressures, Byron's indulgence in commercialism was itself metamorphosed, just before his death, into an ethical commitment to publish *Don Juan* without regard to either profit or reputation. Coleridge was an agent for the publication of Wordsworth's poetry and an eager promoter of his own poetry. On the other hand, any number of psychological reasons could be adduced to explain why Coleridge notoriously delayed the completion and publication of *Christabel,* but a full account of that withholding would have to engage the specific cluster of anxieties associated with the question of plagiarism as debated in the early nineteenth century—a debate that in this case involved something as circumscribed as meter. (In his Preface to *Christabel* Coleridge defended himself against charges that he was plagiarizing the meter of other poets, such as that of Walter Scott, which had been developed only after auditions of his own poem.) Thus even among contemporaries such as the English Romantics, there were specific motives and concerns that informed decisions about publishing.[2]

American examples are no less heterogeneous. Edward Taylor did not publish his poems, although he did transcribe *Gods Determinations* and *Preparatory Meditations,* as well as his minor poems, into four hundred manuscript pages of a leatherbound "Poetical Works," thereby suggesting that he wished these poems preserved.[3] They were not published

2. For an exhaustive account of Lord Byron's publishing, see Jerome Christensen, *Lord Byron's Strength: Romantic Writing and Commercial Societies* (Baltimore: Johns Hopkins University Press, 1992). I am indebted to a conversation with Jerome Christensen for the information about the debate over Coleridge and the meter of *Christabel.*

3. See Karen E. Rowe's introduction to Taylor in *The Heath Anthology of American Literature* (Lexington, Mass.: D. C. Heath and Company, 1990), I:342–46, and

until they were discovered almost three hundred years later in 1937 by Thomas H. Johnson. Anne Bradstreet's manuscripts circulated privately until her brother-in-law took them to London and had them published without her knowledge. It is not clear why Bradstreet herself declined to publish, although in "The Prologue [to Her Book]" she had declared "I am obnoxious to each carping tongue/ Who says my hand a needle better fits. . . . If what I do prove well, it won't advance,/ They'll say it's stol'n, or else it was by chance." After the London publication Bradstreet continued to write and, as persistently, declined to publish. When a 1678 Boston edition of her poems appeared, it was posthumous. It is the work published after her death that is distinctive. Henry Adams published *The Education* but, as he circulated only one hundred copies of it among his family and friends, *The Education* could be said to have been published semi-privately. It was in print, so it could not have been considered a manuscript, but it was not disseminated widely, so it could not have been considered completely or exactly public. In "not publishing" his *Education* Henry Adams might have been following John Adams and Thomas Jefferson, neither of whom wanted his memoirs or autobiography published, since in each case it was intended only for his family's reading. Henry James republished his novels in the *New York Edition,* thereby revising the terms in which, through the newly written Prefaces, he now wished them read—terms which substantially changed the understanding of the novels as initially published.[4] As the examples emphasize, to invoke any instance of why authors do or do not publish, or even of how they republish, is to see that all examples are historically particular.

Why didn't Dickinson publish? There are at least three ways of answering that question: She couldn't publish. She chose not to. Or she *couldn't* choose—that is, she couldn't choose how to publish her poems.

To amplify, briefly, each of these alternatives: She couldn't publish. Because "portfolio" poetry, as Emerson and, after him, Higginson, called it, was not traditional poetry, the fascicles could be considered a solution to a set of cultural prohibitions, or rather cultural prescriptions, which delineate certain features poems should have. Dickinson published her

---

Rowe's *Saint and Singer: Edward Taylor's Typology and Poetics of Meditation* (Cambridge: Cambridge University Press, 1986).

4. See "The Prefaces, Revision, and Ideas of Consciousness," in my *Thinking in Henry James* (Chicago: University of Chicago Press, 1989).

poems in manuscript rather than in print because in the case of those few poems that were printed in her lifetime, as well as of those of her poems which were printed posthumously, the conventions of print, reflecting the traditions of established poetry, violated the characteristics of *Dickinson's* poetry—its grammar, its syntax, its style, its capitalization, its variants, its insistent absence of titles. The handful of poems published in Dickinson's lifetime had their essential features altered. In the face of these constraints and violations, there is no way Dickinson could have printed her poetry in its uniqueness.

A second answer to the question, however, is not that Dickinson couldn't publish, but rather that, like Bradstreet and Taylor, she chose not to. "If fame belonged to me, I could not escape her," a letter written on June 7, 1862, to Higginson explains, obliquely addressing the issue. Earlier in the same letter she archly comments: "I smile when you say that I delay 'to publish'—that being foreign to my thought, as Firmament to Fin—."[5] Therefore she collected her poems privately. Her defiant letters to Higginson, in which she solicited his opinion only to challenge it, to argue with the literary conventions she claimed she wanted to learn, make it possible to suppose that her alternative way of writing poetry required a private space in which conventions could be revised without the revision's being contested.

In fact, one feature that distinguishes Dickinson's poetry is the way in which the notion of (anyone's) poetic sequences, with their attendant irregularities, is complicated by Dickinson's irregular and fractured notions of form. Dickinson, for example, is not writing sonnets. Her metrics are not standard, nor are her punctuation and rhyme. It may be, then, that formal inventiveness is something that writing in private allowed Dickinson to develop. For Dickinson the process of writing the manuscripts without circulating them opened the space of writing to incorporate the social into the private sphere. Or rather it resituated the social in a liminal space: readers, or potential readers, were established at the edge of the private. They were able to look at the fact of her writing, forced to look at it, while being essentially prevented from looking *into* it. For it was a well-known fact—well known to all who knew Dickinson—that Dickinson was a writer. Thus Dickinson created the public spectre of herself as a writer. But in not publishing her poems,

5. *The Letters of Emily Dickinson,* ed. Thomas H. Johnson (Cambridge, Mass.: Harvard University Press, 1958), II:408.

and in not circulating her manuscripts, with the exception of certain lyrics, she achieved the particular feat of writing in public while effectively exempting her writing from public legislation.

But there is also a third way of understanding the packets discovered in the bureau drawer. It is not that Dickinson couldn't publish, or that she chose not to. It is rather that she couldn't choose how to do so. She could not decide whether to publish her poems in sequences or as lyrics, just as where there were variants she could not choose among them. Moreover, at the level of whole poems Dickinson herself treated her manuscripts as versions of each other. She copied them as sequences in the fascicles while sending them as single lyrics to friends—a not exceptional practice among poets writing sequences, although most of the poets who circulated poems as single entities (Gray or Pope, for instance) subsequently published them in sequence. It may well have been the case that Dickinson did not publish her poems because she literally did not know whether to publish them as a sequence or as single lyrics. Or because she could not publish them in both forms at once.

In fact, were there an exceptionalist case to be made with respect to Dickinson, it might be founded on the unprecedented degree to which the formal and the professional are made inseparable in this poetry. Dickinson redefined the profession of the writer to just the extent that she redefined the non-exclusive relation among competing poetic forms. So doing, she misleadingly appeared to stand outside the profession, cherishing instead her vocation. The true writer, or rather the poet, then, was she who invited the comments about form which subsequent poetic form never registered. Dickinson's lyrics evaded the formal conventions Higginson would have imposed on them, and the form of the lyric was itself evaded by the fascicles' restructuring of relations among lyrics. And this defiant originality, this refusal to allow the original to be shaped by the conventional, could be seen to have depended *ultimately,* however negligibly it depended *initially,* on the principled refusal to publish. Thus Dickinson's poetry might be discovered to immortality rather than to the imperfect "professional" readers (Higginson, Samuel Bowles) whose friendship she welcomed but whose literary advice she ignored. In one of her celebrated lyrics on poetry Dickinson designates the poet as "Exterior—to Time—" (P 448). There are poems—I shall examine one of them—that confidently predict this outcome for her own work.

2. Even if there were no exceptionalist case, reading the fascicles in the context of other poetic sequences would clarify important features of

Dickinson's fascicles. The critical problems raised by reading Dickinson's poems are of course not unlike the problems raised by reading the poems of Whitman, Herbert, Shakespeare. In this respect, my attempt to re-contextualize Dickinson's lyrics is on one level formal. But to say that the attempt is formal is not to say that it is simple. Nor is it to say that what would count as formal is clear.[6] One can, for example, ask about how the narrative told by Dickinson's fascicles is related to other narrative groupings, such as Herbert's or Shakespeare's, which she can be presumed to have read. Such sequences tell similar stories about wooing and not getting. In distinction, however, as I shall elaborate, Dickinson likes to return to a situation in which a lover is dead, and she wishes that he weren't, or to a situation in which she finds a means to negate the consequences of the death. But, one is led to ask, is that the same kind of story—and is it even a story—as the one told in Shakespeare's sonnets?

To amplify the comparison: In a sonnet sequence there are stages, and the end is known. With Shakespeare, however tenuously, the grouping relates to the narrative, and there is a narrative structure. With Herbert, on the other hand, it is hard to claim a narrative even if there is an ending. Perhaps one should ask whether apparent fascicle sequences are more like sonnet sequences or devotional sequences. Such a distinction is suggested because, on the one hand, the speaker in Dickinson has lost the lover, as in many of Shakespeare's sonnets; on the other hand, she has not yet had the lover, but awaits precisely that union, as in Herbert's poems. In this respect the erotic dimensions of the love poem and the spiritual dimensions of the religious poem come together in Dickinson's fascicles because the erotic moment has been *de*-theologized or re-theologized. Even if such contextualizations suggest that Dickinson's groupings are more than chronological, it is important to consider why we should pay more attention to Dickinson's groupings than to those of other poets who reorder single lyrics—more attention to Dickinson's groupings than to regroupings of lyric poems by Whitman, Stevens, Yeats, Marianne Moore, or Williams, for instance.

One way of formulating a distinction between Dickinson's fascicles and other sequences is to say that what binds them together is not only or primarily chronology and theme, but rather a structural element. To

6. In fact, an adequate account of relations among poems would require an edition of them like Stephen Booth's edition of Shakespeare's sonnets, with its accompanying commentary.

begin to describe this element is to see something so idiosyncratic that it appears almost unprecedented in nineteenth-century American poetry. For if in Dickinson's fascicles there is a moment that obsessively occurs, the recurrence of this single moment raises the question of whether there is a narrative or whether narrative structures are invoked only intermittently. The moment obsessively returned to might operate more in the manner of a variant, a phenomenon I shall examine specifically with respect to Fascicle 20. It will further be seen that if there is a story in the fascicles, it is told discontinuously. In addition, because the poems that do not adhere to this story seem themselves amorphous in topic, the poems that *do* tell the story appear to dominate the fascicles. Yet since the story is also itself disrupted in the telling, even *by* the telling, it does not, I shall argue, function as a story. Rather, as suggested, these "returned to" moments function as variants of something, though what is being returned to and departed from is never, within the limits of one lyric entity, fully in view. The story is not fully in view precisely because there is no narrative structure that would sustain it from without, and also because as the speaker tells the story, she deflects from and subverts the story being told. Thus the discontinuity exists along the lines of a narrative that is broken from outside, or rather that is never fully established. But discontinuity also exists by virtue of the fact that the narrative is disrupted from the inside. Although the binding of the fascicles seems to promise continuity, seems to promise moments that are either connected or returned to, in Dickinson's fascicles these reiterated moments are not the same. But they are also not fully differentiated. Hence there is an apparent self-contradiction from "inside" the lyrics, which, I shall argue, must be understood in terms of the structure of the "variant." It is this combination of narrative discontinuity and displacement of narrative structures by variants which sets apart the kind of connections that link Dickinson's poems in the fascicles. They are thus distinguished from the connections made by Shakespeare on the one hand and Herbert on the other, even as the structure of the variant links the poems in the fascicles more than poems are linked in "books" by Stevens, Yeats, or even Whitman.

One might further ask how in Dickinson's sequences relations named as "antithetical" and "complementary," which function like variants, structure ostensibly discrete entities. Perhaps the relation between words in Dickinson's poems, as emblematized by the dash, is like the relation between poems—not unfigurable, but oppositely figurable: "I saw no

Way—The Heavens were stitched—"/ "I saw no Way the Heavens were stitched—." The double grammar of the poem's first line exemplifies at the smallest unit the undecidable meaning generated by the poem's internal relations as well as by its ambiguous relations to the surrounding poems in the bifolium. At a different level of formal connection, one might ask how the variants not only associate words within a poem, but also create antithetical and complementary associations between poems in the same fascicle, even when the poems are not placed in proximity. For example, in Fascicle 20, "Dare you see a soul at the 'White Heat'?" (P 365) and "One need not be a Chamber—to be Haunted—" (P 670) are connected by the first line of one poem and a variant of a line of the second poem. The "White Heat" in one poem, a metaphor for passion ostensibly refined, even purified, then repudiated by death, when encountered in the variant of the second poem as a specter called "That Whiter Host," inevitably, if subterraneanly, links the two poems, suggesting that the ghost who is feared is not generalized at all, but is rather some embodied vestige of a once familiar, now concealed, but still embodied, passion. I shall return to this example.

3. The previous remarks extend our consideration of the contexts in which to scrutinize the variants as discussed in chapter 1. I previously observed that we may see variants as raising not only a textual question but a question that is other than textual, and so not resolved by determining which edition one reads, because it has to do with the nonidenticality of poem and text. For, as I have noted, one can read the Franklin text, but where variants exist, the issue of how to choose among them is still unresolved. We may also see variants in an amplified context: displacing narrative structures as a means of connecting ostensibly discrete poems. We should, in addition, see the variants as raising a fourth concern, asking us to deliberate what not choosing means. For example, it would be interesting to ask whether the thematic problem of not being able to choose a single topic (to choose the lover, vision, death, as exemplified in Fascicles 15 and 16)—or a single relation to any of these topics—is connected to the textual problem of not being able to choose among the variants. Here the undecidability in the content of the poems could be seen to have consequences for their form. In these fascicles choice is being thematized, but it is also being superadded and embodied in the poem's textual manifestations. Thus the question of choice seems not just thematized but also formalized, although by broken form. And since alternatives to words are not treated as other than those words, the

existence of multiple variants may indicate how Dickinson might have regarded revision, as deflecting the necessity of choice; how she might have regarded revision in terms of amplification rather than of substitution, equivocation being played out in corollary thematic and formal terms.

4. Another issue raised by the fascicles is the way in which economy and gender are related to each other. As noted in the previous chapter, measurement is one of the ways in which Dickinson thinks of her project. She is asking: What is small and what is large, and how is the small unexpectedly potent? Dickinson may be raising these questions in a private space because there is no room to raise them in a public space. Transacted in this private space is a renegotiation of gender definitions as well as of poetic definitions. For not only are representations of women redefined in poems like "Title divine—is mine!" (P 1072) but perhaps also, albeit obliquely, is the representation of women poets, as in "I would not paint—a picture—" (P 505), where poetry and the speaker's relation to poetry are explicitly reconstrued. Since this poem redefines the relation of passivity and power, witnessing and creation, it also implicitly redefines whether the choice not to write poetry may be discovered—as in this poem—to be a subverted choice. I take such a subversion, in which choosing not to create is itself negated as a choice (since the poem that would not be written already *has* been) to be implicitly connected to the question of *who* can create (in the poem's last stanza, the question of who can write poetry), and, given the way in which poetry is shown to be received, also connected to the question of *how* poems may be written. Thus in "I would not paint—a picture—," discussed in chapter 4, the poem that is almost unrecognized by its author may be the poem that is almost unrecognizable, at least according to the conventions of how poems may be written. Poems like P 505 may implicitly redefine the kind of poetry that women may write. "Women's poetry" could in fact be published in the 1860s. Periodicals are filled with it. Such poetry is explicitly what Dickinson is not writing.[7]

---

7. See, for example, Richard Sewall's Appendix IV, "Popular Poetry from the *Springfield Republican,* 1858–62" in vol. II of *The Life of Emily Dickinson* (New York: Farrar, Straus and Giroux, 1974), pp. 742–50. The sample of sentimental poems provided by Sewall is written by both men and women. But Dickinson would also have read anthologies like Rufus Griswold's 1840 *American Women Poets.* For a discussion of poets Dickinson would likely have read, see also Cheryl Walker, *The Nightingale's Burden: Women Poets and American Culture Before 1900* (Bloomington:

5. In addition, albeit put too generally: In the nineteenth century structures, and not only poetic structures, are subject to construction. Consider Poe's *Eureka,* for instance; Melville's last three novels; Thoreau's *A Week on the Concord and Merrimack Rivers;* and Poe's "The Philosophy of Poetic Composition," a document that theorizes how the lyric should be structured. In Whitman's and Dickinson's cases poetic structures lie outside of the province of conventional genres. In the American nineteenth century, moreover, the cultural and the intertextual come together because American ways of addressing the problem of poetic structure seem to depend on models of federation. Ostensibly discrete poetic entities are at once independent and united. Though such a political model would more evidently pertain to Whitman than to Dickinson, the vexed connection between autonomous structures and dependent structures is analogously visible in the fascicles. And although the relation of single poems to the plurality of other poems is a specific problem with which all poets must contend, Whitman and Dickinson deal with this problem in a particularly repetitive way. Both of them, albeit differently, write new poems by rewriting the old ones, and they formulate the relation between old and new, different and same, private and public, in terms of generic inventions that simultaneously isolate and unite entities. Hence Whitman's invention of poetic clusters, which are defined in that they are

---

Indiana University Press, 1982). Walker argues that, in addition to Helen Hunt Jackson and Elizabeth Barrett Browning, mentioned by Dickinson in her letters, Dickinson was probably acquainted with the poetry of Maria Gowan Brooks, Lydia Sigourney, Maria Lowell, Caroline Gilman, and Amelia Welby. She had surely seen copies of magazines like *Godey's Lady's Book*. Walker writes: "At the age of fourteen, [Dickinson] mocks her tendency to become 'poetical' . . . 'you know that is what young ladies aim to be now-a-days.' For the rest of her life, [Dickinson] toyed in her poems with that stock character, the poetess, craftily using the conventions of the role to serve her own purposes and then rewriting the part to suit herself" (p. 87).

The topic of "secret sorrow" was, Walker argues, a convention of women's poetry that Dickinson adopted and transformed. I would specify the transformation to which Walker alludes as follows: Dickinson *celebrated* sorrow when it defied hypocritical secrecy, as in "I like a look of Agony,/ Because I know it's true—" (P 241). But celebrating the sorrow in Dickinson's poems is often a prelude to *contesting* the sorrow. (At the end of P 463, in which a speaker lives with the memory of a lover rather than with the lover, the summary personal assessment renders all but gratuitous the conventional theological one, claiming "That Life like This—is stopless—/ Be Judgment—what it may—.") In these two ways—celebrating the sorrow and contesting the sorrow—the convention of women's poetry is unabashedly reversed.

titled but amorphous, for the lyrics assigned to each cluster shift with successive editions and his reinvention of the so-called same poem. Hence Dickinson's fascicle structures, which seem alternative to wholly individuated lyric structures but are not in fact alternative.

Alternatives that are not exactly alternative can be viewed in the contents page of the deathbed edition of Whitman's *Leaves of Grass,* which provides titles for poems that lack them in the 1855 edition. Poems are in some cases differently titled in intermediate editions. Thus "Sun-Down Poem" of the 1856 or second edition becomes "Crossing Brooklyn Ferry" of the 1860 or third edition. "Repeated" poems are often reordered in successive editions. "There Was a Child Went Forth," the tenth poem of the 1855 edition, is ultimately placed in the cluster of poems titled *Autumn Rivulets,* even as poems in some editions (for instance, "By Blue Ontario's Shore") derive from the prose of other editions—in this case from the "Preface" to the 1855 edition, from which it takes more than sixty of its lines. Such equivocation about what a poetic entity "is," such reconstitution of the entity by virtue of its placement in a larger structure, so that the poem is not simply subordinated to other poems in the structure—in Whitman's clusters, in Dickinson's fascicles—but reformed as a different, dependent entity, is to be remarked upon. For by virtue of rearrangement the poem as delimited text is deprived of stable integrity.

The textual instability shared by Whitman and Dickinson—the way in which their poetic structures derive their elements simultaneously from variation and repetition, subordination and autonomy—is only one of many crucial features that draw the two poets together, despite the propensity of literary criticism to celebrate their differences. For instance, Whitman is understood to illustrate the inclusiveness of emotion, its embrace of everyone. Dickinson is understood to illustrate the exclusiveness of emotion, its singular choice of object and its pervasive rejections. In Sandra Gilbert's "The American Sexual Poetics of Walt Whitman and Emily Dickinson,"[8] characterizations like these are seen to typify the difference between "men's poetry" and "women's poetry," resulting even in the two poets' preferences for their respective genres. Yet the poetic features thus characterized as opposite are not in a most significant context opposite at all, because Whitman's fiction of non-

8. In *Reconstructing American Literary History,* ed. Sacvan Bercovitch (Cambridge, Mass.: Harvard University Press, 1986), pp. 123–54.

exclusivity and Dickinson's of complete exclusivity equally exaggerate, albeit in different directions, sentiments that cannot possibly be either all-inclusive or all-exclusive. In this respect the two poets are alike. Each espouses an opposite fantasy of self-conversion: completely to exclude the world, completely to incorporate it. Moreover, the two poets similarly imagine that the redeterminations of the boundaries of a poem could be made analogous to the redetermination of the boundaries of a self. In Dickinson's case, such redeterminations revolve around impossible partializations—of the self, of the poem—employed to make visible something like identity or essence. In Whitman's case, such redeterminations revolve around impossible totalizations—of the self, of the poem—also employed to make visible something like identity or essence. Thus to see beyond the conventional construction of the two poets is inevitably to observe that in each case similar choices appear to be made—and, consequently, structures to be respectively fractured and compounded—that "cannot" be real choices.

Finally, in one important sense, as Whitman does not choose—as the thematic principle of *Song of Myself* is one of inclusion, and the principle of successive editions is one of textual variation—so the identity of Whitman's texts, much like that of Dickinson's, must be understood in terms of those textual variants. Variants and variation are strategies for redefining the boundaries of a Whitmanian as well as of a Dickinsonian text. They seem strategies for making unresolvable the question of what lies outside the text. In Whitman's poetry, however, although unboundedness is thematized, although choices in the poems are explicitly declined, and although textual rearrangements of the ostensibly "same" poem seem continuously renegotiated, ultimately there is a terminus to the oscillations enacted by Whitman's successive editions of *Leaves of Grass*. For in the last of the editions overseen by Whitman, the borders of Whitman's texts, in some ways always fluid, in other ways are stabilized, even definitively fixed.

In distinction, Dickinson's texts remain permeable. I now turn to the fascicle texts to consider questions of permeability in relation to questions of choice—as choice is formalized in the variants, as it is thematized in the fascicles, as it unfolds in other contexts in which something (a person, a desire, an ability, even a second poem) appears to be eschewed and excluded, even as that thing is discovered to be included and incorporated in, sometimes even intrinsic to, the entity from which it was deceptively set apart. Thus I mean to consider, first, how we read the variants, proximate words that do not in fact displace each other; second, how we read poems that are proximate to each other; third, how we read connections among poems not proximate but in the same fascicle; and, fourth, how we must differently read single fascicles (16 and 20). Finally, in chapters 3 and 4, I shall consider implications of the fact that the problems of reading and the problems of choice are in this poetry inseparable.

II. VARIANTS

INITIALLY I PROPOSED WE CONSIDER the variants in a line as inclusive rather than as substitutive. Or I asked whether they might be so considered. But to look at the poems is to see that Dickinson's variants are often related in such different and multiple ways that no single characterization could adequately describe them. For example, in Fascicle 14, consider "The [maddest/nearest] dream—recedes—unrealized—" (P 319).[9] Both "nearest" and "maddest" are superlatives, but different kinds of superlatives:

> The maddest dream—recedes—unrealized—
> The Heaven we chase—
> Like the June Bee—before the Schoolboy—
> Invites the Race—
>
> Stoops to an Easy Clover—
> Dips—Evades—
> Teazes—deploys—
> Then—to the Royal Clouds—
>
> Spreads his light pinnace—
> Heedless of the Boy—
> Staring—defrauded—at the
> Mocking sky—
>
> Homesick for steadfast Honey—
> Ah, the Bee
> Flies not—that brews
> That rare variety!

1. maddest] nearest   11. defrauded] bewildered
9. Spreads] Lifts

9. The "variants"—which in this poem appear to have been copied at a different time, or at least a different moment, than the text—are placed above the word to which they offer an alternative: on the manuscript page "nearest" is above "maddest"; "Lifts" above "Spreads"; "bewildered" above "defrauded" (fig. 3). Where pertinent, in the examples which follow, I indicate the position of the variants on the manu-

In the context of the poem "maddest" and "nearest" seem to modify each other rather than to exist as alternative possibilities. Maybe the relation of the words is something like "maddest and nearest" or "nearest so maddest," even "maddest because nearest," the intoxication being caused *by* the proximity, not simply conjunctive but perhaps more strongly consequent. In a different causal connection, because proximity does not guarantee permanence, "nearest" could be seen to generate "maddest." And there may be a causal connection as well between the other variants in the poems. Thus the boy witnessing the disappearance of the bee/dream is "bewildered" because "defrauded." Causality may also be predicated in relation to another pair of variants, because the dream seems amplified as a consequence of its leaving. Hence although "spreads" first pertains to what the bee does to its wings, there is a second sense in which the verb describes what happens to the speaker's vision of the dream when it departs or "lifts." The dream grows more expansive as it disappears, *because* it disappears, as earlier that dream had maddened by its transient proximity.

But if it is possible to read the variants in this poem as causally related, in other poems variants can exist in differing stances of potential substitution—with substitution itself implied but not quite undertaken. For example, in a poem I shall return to in another context, "Of Bronze—and Blaze—" (P 290) in Fascicle 13, a choice is indicated which is not at first fully embraced, when the speaker, regarding the northern lights with an awe she finds herself incorporating, characterizes herself as taking "vaster attitudes/manners" ("manners" written below "attitudes"): "An Unconcern so sovreign/ To Universe, or me—/ Infects my simple spirit/ With Taints of Majesty—/ Till I take vaster [attitudes/ manners]—/ And strut upon my stem—/ Disdaining Men, and Oxygen,/ For Arrogance of them—" (fig. 8). In the stanza it would seem that "manners," or ways of appearing, are being transformed into "attitudes," or ways of thinking. Yet in this instance "manners" and "attitudes"— potentially synonyms—are related to each other without, it seems, replacing each other, since nothing is sufficient to suggest the transformation. Thus a choice is suggested that is not yet made. We are then

script page in a parenthesis directly following the affected text, as well as listing the variants at the end of the poem, as in the Johnson variorum.

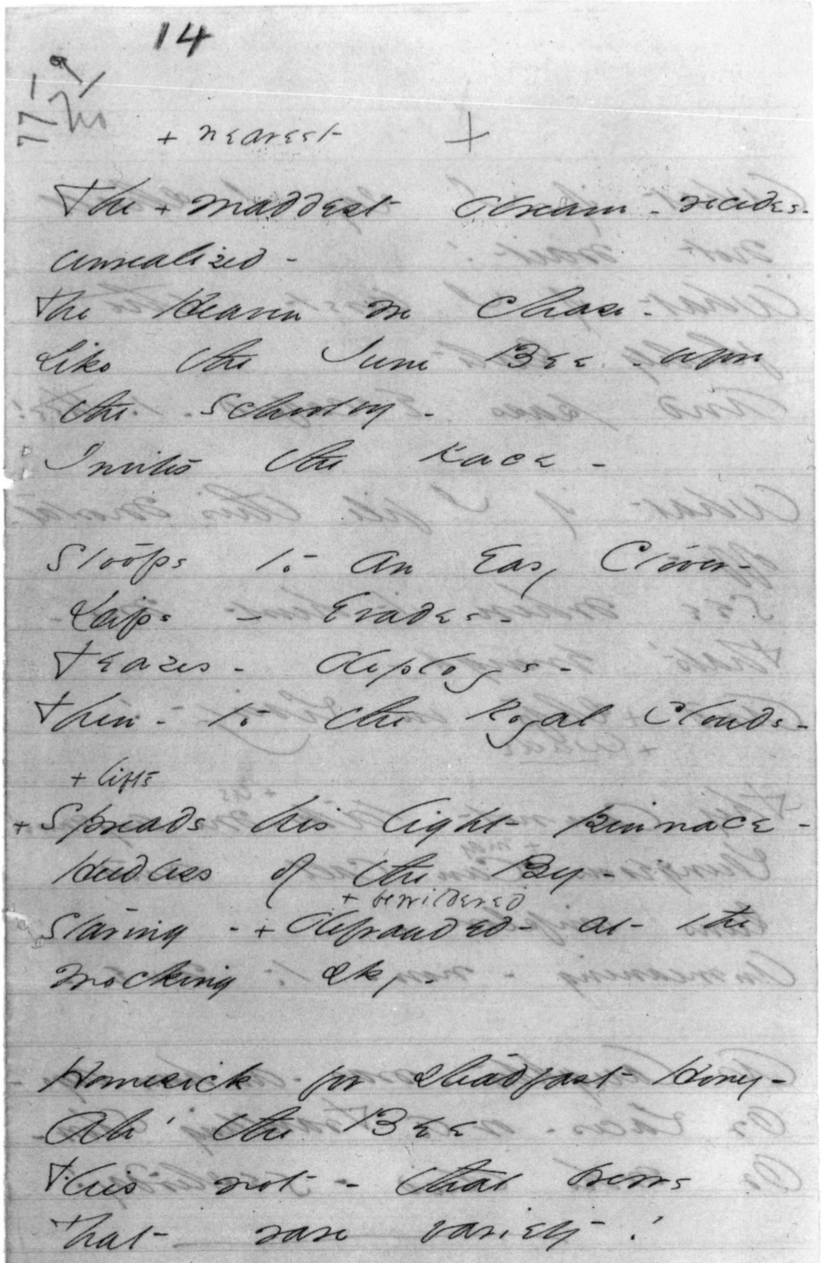

FIG. 3. Fascicle 14, bf1, 1st recto

required to assess the differences among the connotations of the words. This is a pertinent task since how the speaker is behaving and thinking— and how behaving *changes* in relation to thinking—is just what is being worked out as the northern lights are being envisioned. (One could also argue that "attitudes," in the sense of stances or postures, draws the word toward, rather than away from, the non-subjectivity of "manners." Maybe, then, what is insisted upon is precisely the fact that an ostensible difference between a subjective and a non-subjective position with which the poem *begins* is *by* the poem dispelled.) Yet if in this example substitution—of a way of thinking for a way of acting—is still only considered, in the two concluding lines of the same poem, where the speaker imagines herself dead, imagines herself as: "[An/Some—] Island in dishonored Grass—/ Whom none but [Daisies,/Beetles—] know" ("Some" at bottom of page; "Beetles" below "Daisies"), a substitution is exactly what is executed in the first of the variants. For there the speaker is conceiving herself as made dead and anonymous—"an" island with particularity become one without it—even as "Beetles" and "Daisies" which have no logical connection seem neither interchangeable, nor substitutive, nor in any other way related. Rather, in their unlikeness they seem only to co-exist—beings like the speaker (who earlier analogizes herself to a flower) and beings not like her, in the vision of her own death mingling indiscriminately.

Thus far I have described the variants as working in multiple ways. They may be connected in an implicit causal relation, as in "maddest because nearest." Or they may work in non-uniform ways within the same poem, the first variant in "Of Bronze—and Blaze—" implying a transformation from "manners" to "attitudes" that is suggested rather than negotiated; the second implying a transformation unambiguously enacted as well: "An Island" become "Some Island." In the same poem, with respect to the last of the variants, no transformation can be said to take place, since neither "Beetles" nor "Daisies" can be seen as logically prior or anterior. Thus they must co-exist. In implying substitution, in enacting substitution, in prohibiting the idea of substitution, in "Of Bronze—and Blaze—" the variants work in multivalent ways. In distinction, in the following example, P 580 (fig. 4), the choice between the variants enacts in another register the same conflict of the poem as a whole:

I gave myself to Him —
And took Himself, for Pay,
the solemn Contract of a Life
Was ratified, this way —

+ The Wealth might disappoint —
Myself a poorer prove
than this great Purchaser
suspect,
the Daily Own — of Love

Depreciate the Vision —
But till the Merchant buy —
+ Still Fable — in the Isles of Spice
the subtle Cargoes — lie —

At least — 'tis Mutual — Risk —
Some — found it — Mutual Gain —
Sweet Debt of Life — Each Night to owe —
Insolvent — every Noon —
+ Him all myself — + Hon — So —

FIG. 4.   Fascicle 15, bf2, 2nd recto

I gave myself to Him—
And took Himself, for Pay,
The solemn contract of a Life
Was ratified, this way—

The Wealth might disappoint—
Myself a poorer prove
Than this great Purchaser suspect,
The Daily Own—of Love

Depreciate the Vision—
But till the Merchant buy—
Still Fable—in the Isles of Spice—
The subtle Cargoes—lie—

At least—'tis Mutual—Risk—
Some—found it—Mutual Gain—
Sweet Debt of Life—Each Night to owe—
Insolvent—every Noon—

1. myself to Him] Him all   11. Still] How—/So—
   myself—

The poem deliberates an equivocal understanding of what is had and what is not. Is an exchange that looks mutual not in fact mutual? The first stanza suggests mutuality, but the middle stanzas, and the last two lines, contest it. They contest it because in the second stanza the speaker is shown to be poorer than the lover and because the exchange, far from being mutual, is, from one point of view, hypothetical ("The Wealth might disappoint—"). From another point of view, the exchange is only prospective and even conditional. The exchange is "till the Merchant buy—/ Still Fable—." Thus in these middle stanzas the inequality is reiterated, the fear being that what the speaker does not have is the very contractual love said to be "ratified" in stanza one. Maybe the contract is ratified in supposition or in vision, as in the vision of a dream. That, at any rate, is what the last stanza implies. Or it is one way to read the last two lines of that stanza, in which having and not having are connected to different temporal states—suggesting that the speaker "owe[s]" each night because each night she dreams she has the lover (Donne's "So, if I dream I have you, I have you"), but is daily "insolvent" or impoverished because she wakes to see the vision was a dream. Italicizing this doubleness, the boundary between the two senses of "owe" (to "own" or "possess" and to "stand in debt") seems deliberately blurred in line 15.

Say, then, the speaker is impoverished of the lover (contrary to the first stanza, he is not in fact taken). But she is also impoverished of herself—the "Pay" that presumed the purchase (giving herself to him) does not in fact secure it and is also not, apparently, returned. In various ways, then, the poem asserts an equal exchange which—also in various ways—is shown not to be equal. The exchange is not equal because it is hypothetical. It is not equal because even in prospect what is imagined is inequity ("The Wealth might disappoint—/ Myself a poorer prove"— poorer than she was; poorer than she supposed; poorer than he). The exchange is not equal because the vision is "Depreciate[d]" and depreciated by the waking reality in which nothing is owned, though all has been paid out. The exchange is not equal because it is not mutual, not "Mutual—Risk" and, in addition, not "Mutual Gain," "Some— found it" perhaps only implying that *he* finds it so while she does not. In either case it is not equal because what from the vantage of desire is bounty to be paid for is from the vantage of reality insolvency to be recompensed.

And in this poem the variants (both copied at the bottom of the page) precisely reiterate the questions raised about what an exchange is and about whether this *is* an exchange. They do so since the poem raises the question, What is the nature of the economic exchange? Is it equal or mutual, as the first stanza implies? (Does what is *owed* purchase something that is ultimately *owned?*) Or is it unequal, as the last stanzas imply? Just this question (equal or unequal, mutual or not)—and importantly just this inability to answer the question—is reiterated by the first variant: "I gave myself to Him/ I gave Him all myself." For the two ways of formulating the gift (specifically its amount) are themselves not equal. One could further say that the speaker's inability to calculate the precise economics of the exchange is not simply repeated and embodied but also underscored by the variants. It is underscored in the first variant, which draws the disparity into view, and in the second variant, which calls attention to the consequences of that disparity. For if the first variant reiterates questions about inequity, the second dwells on, by marginally elaborating, the *status* of the exchange understood as unequal: "Still/ How—/ So—Fable."

Thus the margins are made central, and are also brought into relation with the center. For such an exchange is "Still Fable"—still *only* fable—a state that could be said not yet to have changed. With emphasis placed on the connotation of "still" as "arrested," it is a state that is not *ever* going to change. It is "How—Fable," in the sense that the condition of fable is recognized and identified. It is "So—Fable"—fable to the extent that the lack of mutuality determines the lack of reality. Thus the differences among the variants in the third stanza call to mind questions of status ("How—Fable"), of temporality ("Still Fable"), and of degree ("So—Fable"). These are all consequences (albeit different consequences), as I noted earlier, of assessing, as both the poem and its first line's variant do, the crucial discrepancy between "gave myself to Him" and "gave Him all myself." The variants in the poem replicate its double economics and elaborate the conclusions that arise from refiguring the exchange in terms of the inequity expressed by the way in which "gave Him all myself" is not only an alternative to the first way of wording the assessment, but also a rebuke to it. For one way to understand the variant in the first line is as a *correction* to a fantasy of mutuality.

But if what I am suggesting is the case, the poem unfolds its meanings both elaboratively and dialectically. The dialectic occurs between the two economic constructions. But it also occurs between the poem and its variants, as the variants elaborate the economics of scarcity rather than of plenitude. What the poem as a whole reiterates, then, is also specified at pivotal moments in the poem. We see these moments as punctuated by the "variants." But it is important to recognize what they are variants of. For we must read the variants not only in relation to the choices proposed within a given line (as variant choices of words) and not only in relation to the poem as a whole, but also in relation to each other. The variants in the first and third stanzas inevitably modify each other. Having done so—since the points touched on by the variants are also the points contested by the poem—they modify, in a second sense, the whole poem once again, insisting that only in fantasy is this an exchange. It will become clear why to read in these ways—for reading here is plural—in effect revolutionizes what reading is. For we are reading in several registers simultaneously, and reading several kinds of revision: of words in particular lines; of the way in which the variant in one line affects our choice of how to construe variants in another line; of disparate, if related, emphases; of the way in which variants read in relation to each other create a corrective reading of the poem. In addition, and as a consequence, we are also reading revision as a phenomenon complexly *integral* to the poem, rather than anterior or exterior to it.

Revision has a different relation to an interior in "If I may have it, when it's dead" (P 577), also in Fascicle 15 and bound two bifolia after "I gave myself to Him—." Ten lines in this poem have variants; in the transcript they are listed below the poem:

> If I may have it, when it's dead,
> I'll be contented—so—
> If just as soon as Breath is out
> It shall belong to me—
>
> Until they lock it in the Grave,
> 'Tis Bliss I cannot weigh—
> For tho' they lock Thee in the Grave,
> Myself—can own the key—
>
> Think of it Lover! I and Thee
> Permitted—face to face to be—
> After a Life—a Death—We'll say—
> For Death was That—
> And This—is Thee—
>
> I'll tell Thee All—how Bald it grew—
> How Midnight felt, at first—to me—
> How all the Clocks stopped in the World—
> And Sunshine pinched me—'Twas so cold—
>
> Then how the Grief got sleepy—some—
> As if my Soul were deaf and dumb—
> Just making signs—across—to Thee—
> That this way—thou could'st notice me—
>
> I'll tell you how I tried to keep
> A smile, to show you, when this Deep
> All Waded—We look back for Play,
> At those Old Times—in Calvary.

Forgive me, if the Grave come slow—
For Coveting to look at Thee—
Forgive me, if to stroke thy frost
Outvisions Paradise!

2.	so] now—	21.	notice] speak to—
6.	Bliss] Wealth I cannot weigh/Right	25.	come] seem
		26.	Coveting] eagerness—
8.	own] hold	27.	stroke] touch/greet
14.	Bald] Blank—	28.	Outvisions] [Out] fables—
20.	across] it seemed		

In the poem death is actively craved because death is understood not to be death insofar as the speaker in that state gets to possess the lover. In fact, the anticipated possession so completely transforms death back into life, disembodied "Bliss" into an embodied lover (the "It" of stanza one to the "Thee" of stanza three), a prospective moment into a retrospective one (for in the sixth stanza the united lovers reminisce about life before the grave, here called "those Old Times—in Calvary"), that the vision seems confident and assured. But just that confidence is undermined by the variants, particularly the last two. For in the variants the life so rapturously anticipated in the poem undisturbed by its margins is suddenly blurred and put at risk. We have a glimpse of the unclarity earlier in the poem, where several of the variants imply different purchases on the future (figs. 5–7). In the second stanza, for instance, does the speaker "own" the key or does she merely "hold" the key to the lover in the grave (as the variant placed to the right of the line suggests)? Does she merely have access to him, or does she more fully possess him? Is the "Bliss" she awaits something that cannot be calculated, or something that *is* calculated as an inestimable "Right" or inestimable bounty here called "Wealth I cannot weigh" (as the variants at the end of the poem propose)? This repeated equivocation about the future, or about the future with him, is also reiterated by the variants to the poem's last lines.

More specifically, the positions of the words and their variants on the manuscript page have palpably ambiguous implications, in that (in "Forgive me, if to stroke thy frost / Outvisions Paradise!") "touch" and "greet" are below the line on which "stroke" occurs and, therefore, also *on* the line on which "thy frost" is. Thus it visually appears as if "stroke," "touch," and "greet" are alternative ways of indicating how the dead lover will be caressed, felt, or, more formally, only welcomed. The variants thus make interrogative the nature of an encounter earlier attested as

If I may have it -, when it's
dead, -
I'll be Contented - so - + now -
If just as soon as Breath
is out -
It - shall belong to me -

Until they lock it in the
Grave.
'Tis + Bliss I Cannot weigh -
For tho' they lock thee in -
the Grave.
Myself - Can + own the Key - + hold

Think of it Lover! I and thee
Permitted - face to face to be -
After a Life - a Death -
will say -
For Death was that -
And this - is thee -

FIG. 5. Fascicle 15, bf4, 1st recto

I'll tell Thee All—how Bald
it grew—   + Blank—
How Midnight felt, at first—
to me—
How all the Clocks stopped
in the World—
And Sunshine pinched me—
'Twas so Cold—

Then how the Grief got sleepy—
some—
As if my Soul were deaf and
Dumb—
Just making signs + across—
to Thee— + it Seemed
that this way Thou Could'st
notice me— + Speak to +

I'll tell you how I tried to keep
A smile, to show you, when
this Grief

FIG. 6.   Fascicle 15, bf4, 1st verso

All wasted - we look back
for Play,
At those Old Times - in Calvary.

Forgive me, if the Grave come⁺
slow - + turn
⁺or Coveting to look at thee -
+ Eagerness.
Forgive me, if to + smoke
the Frost - + touch + your-
+ Out-visions Paradise!
+ parts. + Wealth I cannot weigh
+ Right

FIG. 7. Fascicle 15, bf4, 2nd recto

definite and comprehensible. Crucially, these variants question not the fact of the encounter, but the degree of its intimacy. They question whether there can be intimacy with a lover in some imagined place of death. And this question—Can one revive the dead, or can death reverse the loss, and, if so, at what proximity and expressed by what terms of palpability?—is reiterated in the final variant. There "Outvisions" is contrasted to "[Out]fables" ("fables" written below "visions") as something clairvoyantly seen is contrasted to something only supremely imagined. Thus if in "I gave myself to Him—" the variants *reiterate* and make a hierarchy of the poem's own double economics, in "If I may have it, when it's dead" the variants *undermine* the future affirmed in the poem. Yet if the variants of "I gave myself to Him—" *clarify* its ambivalent figuration, and if the variants in "If I may have it, when it's dead" *create* ambivalence that undercuts the poem's certitude, the two poems are drawn together by the same central point, made in each case by the countervoice of the variants (indeed by the fact that the variants produce versions of the *same* word, "fable"). For the variants ask whether what is had in one poem and anticipated in the other is "fable" or "vision."

In "I gave myself to Him—/ I gave Him all myself—" the variants *recapitulate* the poem's two economies, becoming an integral part of the poem whose double vision they repeat.[10] In "If I may have it, when it's dead," the variants *contradict* and raise questions about the vision of the poem. At issue in both cases is whether vision is only fable. The question is raised by the different relations of the variants to each of the poems.

10. Similarly, in the last two stanzas of the following poem, we see the variants work as amplifications of the poem's meaning. In Fascicle 20, directly after "One need not be a Chamber—to be Haunted—," on the second recto of the same bifolium is P 302 (fig. 23): "Like Some Old fashioned Miracle—/ When Summertime is done—/ Seems Summer's Recollection—/ And the Affairs of June—. . . . Her Blossoms—like a Dream/ Elate us—till we almost weep—/ So [plausible/exquisite]—they seem. . . . Her [Memory—/Memories] like Strains—[enchant/Review]—/ Tho' Orchestra—[be/is] dumb—/ The Violin—in Baize—replaced—/ And Ear, and Heaven—numb—."

The questions raised by the variants are: Is the speaker afflicted by a single memory or by memories? And what is the relation between the one and the many they generate? How, further, is "review[ing]" a memory like being "enchant[ed]" by it? These seem as though they might be successive rather than substitutive activities. Finally, is the memory "exquisite" or only "plausible"? Or is this precisely what the speaker can't understand, the relation between the "exquisite" and the "plausible"— specifically the question of whether the exquisite is or can be plausible? In this way (as in "I gave Him all myself—") the variants suggest not only alternatives, but

And it is raised by the way in which the poems are drawn together by the centrality of "fable." They are drawn together by the same word voiced in one case from the poem and in the other from the margins of the poem.

But if the ways in which variants work in relation to poems can connect those poems (questioning whether certain suppositions about reality are vision or fable), it is also the case that different poems in the same fascicle can, through their verbal echoes, be construed as variants of each other, making such poems seem comments on—even incompletely understood, if attenuated, continuations of—each other. Such a relationship is suggested by an example I touched on earlier, the following two poems from Fascicle 20, in the second and fourth bifolia, respectively (P 365 and P 670; figs. 14–15 and 21–22).

> Dare you see a soul at the "White Heat"?
> Then crouch within the door—
> Red—is the Fire's common tint—
> But when the quickened Ore
>
> Has sated Flame's conditions—
> She quivers from the Forge
> Without a color, but the Light
> Of unannointed Blaze—
>
> Least Village, boasts it's Blacksmith—
> Whose Anvil's even ring
> Stands symbol for the finer Forge
> That soundless tugs—within—
>
> Refining these impatient Ores
> With Hammer, and with Blaze
> Until the designated Light
> Repudiate the Forge—

4. quickened] vivid   6. She] It
5. sated] vanquished

---

additions, questions, and amplifications in a complex weave of incorporation that disables hard and fast distinctions between the "inside" of the poem and its "outside," its center and its margins.

One need not be a Chamber—to be Haunted—
One need not be a House—
The Brain—has Corridors surpassing
Material Place—

Far safer of a Midnight—meeting
External Ghost—
Than an Interior—Confronting—
That cooler—Host.

Far safer, through an Abbey—gallop—
The Stones a'chase—
Than Moonless—One's A'self encounter—
In lonesome place—

Ourself—behind Ourself—Concealed—
Should startle—most—
Assassin—hid in our Apartment—
Be Horror's least—

The Prudent—carries a Revolver—
He bolts the Door—
O'erlooking a Superior Spectre—
More near—

4. Material] Corporeal	19–20] A Spectre—infinite—
8] That Whiter Host.	accompanying—
17. The Prudent] The Body	He fails to fear—
17. a] the	19–20] Maintaining a Superior
	Spectre—
	None saw—

In "Dare you see a soul at the 'White Heat'?" the soul that has "vanquished Flame's conditions"—given up passion or, with reference to the fascicle context, given up the reciprocity of passion—is left with passion still, as "sated" implies. ("Vanquished" is written above "sated." For the position of other variants on the page, see figs. 14–15.) With reference to the second variant it is not, then, clear whether the "quickened Ore" has defeated flame's conditions, as "vanquished" and the isolated poem imply, or whether it has caused a surfeit which remains as excess, as "sated" and the fascicle context imply. For while read as a single lyric this poem seems to dramatize a Blakean refinement of spirit, what differently seem at issue in the fascicle context, where surrounding poems represent the death of a lover, are two kinds of passion: the fire's "common tint" of passion which is shared or mutual, and the white, "unannointed Blaze," in which passion is unconsecrated because solitary, in which, that is, it is only interior. These differences notwithstanding, both are figured in terms of light, as are both ways of quenching passion. The refining "Blaze" marks the self's attempt to purify passion, and the "designated Light"—death—exemplifies that final purification of passion which makes human efforts superfluous. If in this poem kinds of passion are discriminated—the "Fire's common tint," say, from "the 'White Heat'" of passion sustained through memory or obsession—and if the discrimination insists that both can be refined, finally the distinction does not matter, as the refinement is shown to be insufficient. The refinement is insufficient because the passion cannot really be refined, though it can be repudiated by the "designated Light" of death.

Or can it? For if the poem seems to propose two kinds of passion, one of which is distilled from, so that it also survives, the other, and if the end of the poem then stresses death as a purifying force which exceeds the efficacy of human effort, the variants in "One need not be a Chamber—to be Haunted—" make a corrective statement. They correct the idea that even death can purify passion. The two poems are connected because both represent the self as an enclosure (a furnace and a chamber) and equally because a variant of the second poem, "That Whiter Host," is, as mentioned, an inescapable verbal echo of "the 'White Heat'" of the first. "That cooler—Host," the phrase for which "That Whiter Host" is a variant, supplies a mediating term, like the ashes of "Heat" or passion to which the ghost succeeds. Yet read as a comment on the first poem the variant suggests that passion cannot be purified, even by death. It further intimates that the ghost that is feared is no general ghost/host—something preying upon the speaker—but is quite specifically the host of passion. Thus the horror represented by the second poem is a consequence of meeting with a passion first thought to have been refined, and later thought extinguished or dead.

Who or what has died? This question is raised because in "Dare you see a soul at the 'White Heat'?" it had appeared that the person harboring the passion—and therefore the passion—had died. In this poem, however, nothing is dead, though everything is concealed. One of the things that is concealed is something more pernicious, therefore more proximate, than an "Assassin." Again, the variants are clarifying. For to "O'erlook" "a Superior Spectre" (to see it is inside with you) is different from the spatial relation implied by merely being "accompan[ied]" by that spectre. Yet to read the variants in relation to each other is to see that what the speaker views or "overlooks" is the fact that she has been "accompanied" from within by what she cannot therefore exclude or close out. What she overlooks (views) is that she had overlooked (missed) something like the spectre's accompaniment of her. Since the ghost is discovered to be inside, the boundary between inside and outside ceases to be significant. And in fact part of the effect of the line and its variant is to suggest the lexical interiority of "host" to "ghost."

At the moment when the ghost is apprehended as present, even proximate, the distinction between the spectral and the material, stressed earlier in the poem, also becomes negligible, for when the spectral is discovered it is *as,* if not in, a manifestation of corporeality. (I shall return to a question raised by the last of the variants, which calls into question who or what is occupying the body/house.) Finally the palpability and ultimate visibility of the spectre calls into question whether the revolver can be trained on the spectre as it would have been on the assassin. For once the spectre is manifest, it could also be argued that it is mere susceptible corporeality.

Albeit in different ways, both poems raise the question of what an interior is; of what transpires in an interior—purification or murder; of whether purification or exorcism (of the passion ["the 'White Heat'"], of the ghost ["That Whiter Host"]) is a consequence of death in one case, or of a contemplated murder in the other. Both poems raise a question about the relation between death and murder. They do so in the context of a fascicle whose poems explicitly record the phenomenon of a lover who has died but nonetheless lives on ("Over and over, like a Tune—/ The Recollection plays—" [P 367]). These poems ask what sense, given that fact, it makes to say that death has any finality, has—most to the point—any efficacy to obliterate the passion of the one still living, or even to obliterate the one still living. Finally, other poems raise the question of whether the one left living can herself kill the passion not otherwise made dead.

What is an interior? What work is done there? How is an interior redefined with respect to what was thought to lie outside of it? These questions are reiterated, even reconstituted, by the fact that the entity of the single poem is itself reconstituted in relation to another structure, which must ultimately be seen not as "other" at all but as an integral part of the poem. So the variant to one poem becomes an additive part of the other, structurally relating the "outside" of one poem (its marginal variant) and the "inside" of the other—exteriorizing the inside by narratively unfolding it so that two poems are drawn together even as this process interiorizes the variants.

In the most extreme instance variants are not "outsides" working in relation to "insides" (as in "I gave Him all myself—/ I gave myself to Him—"). Nor are they alternatives to insides (as in "touch/greet/stroke thy frost"). Nor are they extensions of insides (as "One need not be a Chamber—to be Haunted—" could be said to be an extension of "Dare you see a soul at the 'White Heat'?"). Rather, as in the case of the following two lyrics—one published as the last poem, P 446, in Fascicle 16, the other sent to Susan Dickinson—they are two discrete wholes which, although both do not appear in the fascicle context, must, it might seem, also be considered as variant to each other:

> He showed me Hights I never saw—
> "Would'st Climb"—He said?
> I said, "Not so."
> "With me"—He said—"With me?"
>
> He showed me secrets—Morning's nest—
> The Rope the Nights were put across—
> "And now, Would'st have me for a Guest?"
> I could not find my "Yes"—
>
> And then—He brake His Life—and lo,
> A light for me, did solemn glow—
> The steadier, as my face withdrew
> And could I further "No"?
>
> 11. steadier] larger—

and to Susan Dickinson:

> I showed her Hights she never saw—
> "Would'st Climb," I said?

She said—"Not so"—
"With *me*—" I said—With *me*?
I showed her Secrets—Morning's Nest—
The Rope the Nights were put across—
And *now*—"Would'st have me for a Guest?"
She could not find her Yes—
And then, I brake my life—And Lo,
A Light, for her, did solemn glow,
The larger, as her face withdrew—
And *could* she, further, "No"?

Because these poems do not appear together as part of the fascicles, they provide a test case for what "variants" are. Equally they measure those limits around a poetic structure conventionally understood to ensure its integrity. For one way to consider these two poems is as variants of each other. But since the category of the fascicle is required to produce poetic identity, the more accurate way to describe the poems is as different (although similar) poems rather than as variants of the same poem. With the other poems I have been examining, the variant pushes us to decide which is the proper text, even as it problematizes our ability to choose, even, that is, as it opens up the boundaries between and among texts. With similar, albeit different, texts—like these poems—we do not experience the same pressure to choose. For here we have *versions* rather than *variants*. Thus the two texts raise questions about what happens when the same and similar words do not result in the same poem.

We could nonetheless enumerate questions about the two versions. Both raise the question of "choice"—here dramatized negatively ("'Would'st Climb'—He said?/ I said, 'Not so'"), then indeterminately and interrogatively ("A light for me, did solemn glow—/ The [steadier/larger], as my face withdrew/ And could I further 'No'?"). Finally, the version sent to Susan Dickinson dramatizes choice which is exteriorized, attributed to another, and passively viewed: "And *could* she, further, 'No'?" Moreover, the two texts raise questions about how to account for the change in pronoun. Does one poem conceal the feminine gender of the lover? Or from the perspective of a different poem, does the feminine gender rather conceal the fact that this is a love poem? In the version sent to Susan Dickinson, the woman is refusing the light and withdrawing from the overture extended by the speaker. For in this poem, as in its counterpart, the "glow" of the light and that of the refused love are indistinguishable, but in the version in the fascicle it is rather the speaker who is refusing the light/love—"I could not find my 'Yes'—." Thus the poem in its two versions is related to the crossed imperative advocated by Fascicle 16 as a whole: the inability to see ("I could not find my 'Yes'—") and the refusal to see ("'Would'st Climb,' I said?/ She said— 'Not so'—"). I have claimed that the fascicle as well as the two versions presents a double impulse: the desire for vision and the negation of vision. To the extent that both the fascicle's first poem ("Before I got my eye put out—" [P 327]) and its last poem ("He showed me Hights I never saw—") insist on the negation, the refusal—framing, as it were, the whole fascicle—could be said to have the last word, to counter the ambivalence about vision displayed in the intermediate poems.

In chapter 3 I shall look more closely at the structure of Fascicle 16, which "He showed me Hights" concludes, but preliminarily to anticipate some of the questions raised by that fascicle: Can vision grasp the dead as "Of nearness to her sundered Things" (P 607) implies? Or do the dead fall short of such vision, as "How noteless Men, and Pleiads, stand" (P 282) implies? Are vision and death identical, as "'Tis so appalling— it exhilirates—" (P 281) implies? Or antithetical, as "I felt a Funeral, in my Brain" (P 280) implies? Are vision, death, a lover, being chosen or declined? And why is the choice "to see" here made equivalent to the choice to take a lover? (The last two questions are specifically raised by the two versions of the poem I have been considering.) How are the ambiguities of choice differently settled by the opposite visions articulated in the two versions, "I showed her Hights she never saw—" and "He showed me Hights I never saw—"? And settled (differently still) in "When we stand on the tops of Things—" (P 242), which, with respect to the question of choice, should be regarded as a variant of "He showed me Hights"?[11] In reading between the two versions, does the question of

---

11. As noted earlier, vision "on the tops of Things" is vision that illuminates a totality which renders choosing gratuitous. Here is the poem in its entirety:

When we stand on the tops of Things—
And like the Trees, look down—
The smoke all cleared away from it—
And Mirrorrs on the scene—

choice really conceal the question of gender? For if Dickinson chooses not to choose about sexuality—chooses not to choose whether a he or a she is desired—she does so here in two discrete poems, however the poems make one wonder, when they are viewed conjunctively, whether the he in other poems is a cover for a she, or vice versa.

There are different ways to understand how choice in these poems is ultimately determined. Thus, with respect to "He showed me Hights I never saw—" in the fascicle context, if this last poem is understood as a definitive poem, the speaker is not choosing, or she is doing so negatively. If, however, one reads "When we stand on the tops of Things—" as the poem that controls the fascicle's meanings (its status conferred by its centrality), the speaker is seen not to *need* to choose, as the act of totalizing always obviates choice's necessity. Still differently, if one reads the variants, whether within an individual poem or between two poems become variants of each other, there is no way to choose—the choices, as I have described them, interpenetrating one another. Thus the question of choice is insistently reiterated by the variants, only to be left insistently unsettled.

In concluding this section I want to touch briefly on a related issue. "I showed her" and "He showed me" are two different poems, because, as

---

Just laying light—no soul will wink
Except it have the flaw—
The Sound ones, like the Hills—shall stand—
No Lightning, scares away—

The Perfect, nowhere be afraid—
They bear their dauntless Heads,
Where others, dare not go at Noon,
Protected by their deeds—

The Stars dare shine occasionally
Upon a spotted World—
And Suns, go surer, for their Proof,
As if an Axle, held—

7.	shall stand] stand up—	11.	go at Noon] walk at noon—
8.	scares] drives—	16.	an Axle, held] A Muscle—
10.	dauntless] fearless—		held
	/tranquil—		

noted, the category of the fascicle is required to produce poetic identity. By the logic which reveals that the integrity of an entity is dictated by the fascicle binding, the same words copied in *different* fascicles must be understood to constitute two discrete poems. This difference is reflected in the disparate constructions of the meaning of the two utterances that become available. For instance, in Fascicle 1 "The feet of people walking home" (P 7), copied in 1858 and then bound, exists in a grouping that asks about the relation between nature, death and immortality. Specifically, the fascicle asks: Is death part of nature or does it mark the end of nature? Can death be redeemed in nature or can it only be rectified by immortality?

Poems which question the relation between death, immortality, and nature begin the fascicle. Poems in which love, in the form of the naturalized self, is presented to a dead person conclude it. (In "When Roses cease to bloom, Sir" [P 32] the speaker is handing the dead person a flower, but in "Summer for thee, grant I may be" [P 31], the speaker *is* the flower she is handing to the dead person. Or she is the season that allows *him* to live and flower: "For thee to bloom, I'll skip the tomb/ And row my blossoms o'er!") As a consequence the fascicle seems to have the following argument: Poems which raise questions about death and immortality exist to enable the concluding answer; thus love is immortalized in the form of the self presented to the lover as if the self had been naturalized. And if the immortality of the naturalized self is ultimately questioned, as it is in the fascicle's last poem, the naturalized self is nonetheless the means of associating with the lover who, dead, is imperturbably being courted. In this context "The feet of people walking home" (where home is immortality) must be understood as an allegory about how such connections are negotiated. "The feet of people walking home" is an intermediate poem which makes of death itself an intermediate state ("Death, but our rapt attention/ To Immortality"), as in the succeeding poems in the fascicle the naturalized self will also do.

The same words of "The feet of people walking home" appear in Fascicle 14 (which attempts to regulate distance), surrounded by poems like "The [maddest/nearest] dream—recedes—unrealized—," "'Heaven'— is what I cannot reach!" (P 239) and "More Life—went out—when He went" (P 422). The *same* words result in a *different* poem, whose meaning is constructed according to other understandings: that there is *no* immortality; or if there is, it cannot be found in nature; or if there is, it can only be inferred; or if it can be more than inferred, if it can be gotten, it must be gotten *out* of nature—by coercion and regulation. In both fascicles immortality is said to be unknown. But in Fascicle 1, it is shown to be possessed, when at all, not elsewhere than in nature. It is shown in effect to be naturalized, whereas in Fascicle 14 "The feet of people walking home" is only a variant expression of distance that must be coerced precisely because it *cannot* be naturalized.

Another way to understand the different meanings of the two poems is to speculate that what organizes the poems in Fascicle 1 is *only* a chronology. Hence this fascicle contains no variants. For one way of explaining the virtual absence of variants in the first ten fascicles is to say that initially Dickinson was understanding her poems *only* in terms of chronological collections. In Fascicle 14, where the same words are recopied to make a different poem, what organizes the poems *are* the variants—specifically variants concerned with how to regulate distance.

Similarly in Fascicle 14 another poem, "Ah, Moon—and Star!" (P 240) is a version, rather than a variant, of "Ah, Moon—and Star!" in Fascicle 11. In both fascicles the poem represents a response to distance. But in Fascicle 11 "Ah, Moon—and Star!" could be said to represent the intractability of distance, whereas in Fascicle 14 the poem participates in a debate about whether, and how, such intractability can be regulated. While these particular examples may not be poetically interesting, the theoretical point they illustrate is. What they exemplify is the way in which the fascicle rather than the single lyric determines a textual identity in which the latter only participates. Given such an understanding it is clear that the same words in the two different fascicles could not constitute the same poem or predicate the same matrix of meaning.

Finally, if poems that appear in different fascicles contain the same words without being the same poem, how shall we understand virtually the same words copied in two different places in a *single* fascicle? I am thinking of the case of "Portraits are to daily faces" (P 170), copied in the second bifolium of Fascicle 8, and "Pictures are to daily faces," copied in the fifth and last of the bifolia of that same fascicle. Here what differs is a single word, as well as the two placements of the whole. As a consequence of such differences, and in line with the discrimination between "versions" and "variants," do we here have versions or variants, and according to what criteria? It seems to me that how one answers the question depends on the terms in which one understands repetition. One way to understand the phenomenon is to say that because something is being narrated, the double instances *cannot* be seen as variants: the poems differ not with respect to a single entity but with respect to their temporal sequence and dispersion. An alternative way to understand the same phenomenon is to view the poems not in terms of narrative but rather in terms of refrains, albeit variant ones. I shall say more about variants in relation to narratives in my discussion of Fascicle 20.

III. Proximities

༄༅

VARIANTS, USUALLY OF WORDS but sometimes of whole poems,
call into question the existence of single meanings isolated from alternatives, although how these alternatives work is not—it will have become
clear—uniform. In addition, I have been arguing, as in "I showed her
Hights"/"He showed me Hights," there may be no way to presume or
assert priority among these alternatives, a phenomenon disturbing just
to the extent that either the meanings are antithetical or, as in "I could
not find my 'Yes'—,"/ "She could not find her Yes—," they reassign, even
reverse, agency. As I have argued, since these versions are not in the same
fascicle, there is also no imperative to attribute priority to one of the two
poems. However, when variant poems exist in the same fascicle (as in
"When we stand on the tops of Things—" and "He showed me Hights I
never saw—"), or when variant words occur in the same poem, choice is
simultaneously demanded and prohibited. At the metrical level, one
word *or* another must be chosen: "maddest" or "nearest." At the semantic
level, complying with this imperative is impossible. The relation among
variants is that of proximity on the fascicle page—proximity in which
aspects of the same thing are ambiguously multiple, and therefore critically problematic, even when they are not contradictory.

The relation between poems on a fascicle sheet is also one of proximity. In the case of poems on the fascicle page, however, variants are not
apparently at issue, because sequentiality assumes the existence of separate entities. Yet, in the fascicles, it is unclear what it means for one
poem to follow another as a discrete utterance on a sheet. If poems are
not presumed to be variants—if the "same" thing is not being differently
rendered—what are the relations of entities we call discrete? I examine
this question with respect to the last two, celebrated poems in the third
bifolium of Fascicle 13. To do so is to consider how, in Dickinson's copying on a single leaf, a reader is to understand proximity and sequence.
On the third bifolium, the second recto (P 290; fig. 8):

X

Of Bronze - and Blaze -
the North - Tonight -
So adequate - it forms -
So preconcerted with itself -
So distant - to alarms -
An Unconcern so sovereign
to Universe, or me -
Infects my simple spirit -
with Taints of Majesty, -
till I take vaster Attitudes -
And strut opon my stem -
Disdaining Men, and Oxygen,
for Arrogance of them -

My Splendors, are Menagerie -
But their Competeless Show
Will entertain the Centuries
When I, am long ago,
+ An Island in dishonored
Grass -
whom none but Daisies, know.
Beetles -

+ some -

FIG. 8.   Fascicle 13, bf3, 2nd recto

Of Bronze—and Blaze—
The North—Tonight—
So adequate—it forms—
So preconcerted with itself
So distant—to alarms—
An Unconcern so sovreign
To Universe, or me—
Infects my simple spirit
With Taints of Majesty—
Till I take vaster attitudes—
And strut upon my stem—
Disdaining Men, and Oxygen,
For Arrogance of them—

My Splendors, are Menagerie—
But their Competeless Show
Will entertain the Centuries
When I, am long ago,
An Island in dishonored Grass—
Whom none but Daisies, know.

10. attitudes] manners   19. Daisies] Beetles—
18. An] Some—

and, following, on the back of that leaf, that is, on the second verso
(P 258; fig. 9):

There's a certain Slant of light,
Winter Afternoons—
That oppresses, like the Heft
Of Cathedral Tunes—

Heavenly Hurt, it gives us—
We can find no scar,
But internal difference,
Where the Meanings, are—

None may teach it—Any—
'Tis the Seal Despair—
An imperial affliction
Sent us of the Air—

When it comes, the Landscape listens—
Shadows—hold their breath—
When it goes, 'tis like the Distance
On the look of Death—

As I noted in chapter 1, to read the two poems in proximity is to see that something is being worked out with respect to alternative claims. The distance in "Of Bronze—and Blaze—" is the distance on the look of death that effectively trivializes it, whereas the distance in "There's a certain Slant of light" magnifies the look of death, even personifies it, in a personification that is made lifeless—neither representationally credible nor, implicitly, even able to sustain itself ("When it comes, the Landscape listens—/ Shadows—hold their breath—"), since the shadows will lose their substance when they flatten into darkness.

The question of how distance comes into being in the first of these poems, and of how it is regarded, is raised most fundamentally by the grammar of the initial lines, in which a speaker is describing the forming of night, the turning of the bronze and blaze of the northern lights into night. "Of" might thus indicate a place of origin, so that where the night is coming from *is* bronze and blaze. (With respect to a reiterated concern with origin, we could note that "*Of* Bronze—and Blaze" in this poem is related to the "affliction" "Sent us *of* the Air" in the poem that follows it.) But I think it makes more sense to see the grammar of the first line as a partitive genitive, the sense being "The northern night sky is something made of bronze and blaze," as opposed to night's being a place of bronze and blaze. Even constructed thus, the grammar is still parallel to that in the following poem. The light, the "imperial affliction," is made "of" an aspect of air, as night is made "of" an aspect of bronze and blaze. In each case where light comes from seems subordinate to what it is made out of. This primary sense is to be emphasized because in both cases the literal color is a figure for the emotional color—the emotional color itself being "Taint[ed]" as well as "Slant[ed]" by the visual color.

Adequacy in the first poem comes from the night's being viewed as previously arranged: "preconcerted with itself." It is arranged prior to the speaker's existence and, as much to the point, without reference to it. In the poem "Unconcern," indifference, "adequa[cy]" and "Majesty" are in fact contingent. Thus indifference is associated with "Majesty" as a manifestation of the latter. And this observed stance is also something the speaker desires to internalize. Therefore nature's "Unconcern" toward it-

There's a certain Slant of light,
Winter Afternoons.
That oppresses, like the Heft
Of Cathedral tunes.

Heavenly Hurt, it gives us.
We can find no scar,
But internal difference.
When the Meanings, are.

None may teach it. Any.
'Tis the Seal Despair.
An imperial affliction
Sent us of the Air.

When it comes, the Landscape listens.
Shadows. hold their breath.
When it goes, 'tis like the Distance
On the Look of Death.

FIG. 9.   Fascicle 13, bf3, 2nd verso

self and toward the speaker is imitated or emulated, so that the speaker is, as it were, naturalized, regarding herself with the same "Unconcern" with which she sees herself regarded. In other words, the emotion of the lights, the emotion the lights are imagined to have—itself distanced through watching them—has been imbibed. And then an analogy is made. The splendor of the northern lights is understood to be as distant from the speaker, and she from it, as she is going to be distant from her own life, and her life's work, when *she* is dead. What is incorporated, then, is distance from the life as well as from the lights. What is internalized is distance, unconcern, even indifference—attitudes thus associated with immortality. In this way the speaker regards herself as dead without caring about the death. For the death pertains only to materiality, which some immortal part of her is understood to survive. To be "Infect[ed]" by the light is to be first naturalized and then immortalized. It is to be taught the difference between the material and the immortal. This "vaster attitude" is differentiated, as noted in my discussion of the variants, from a "manner" or a pose. Thus the speaker's vision—first of the northern lights and then of the life—is negotiating a conversion from a stance, a mere manner, to an attitude or way of thinking. Precisely this way of thinking, in which the self can replicate nature's indifference to it, leads to immortality.

In the poem the axis of vision is vertical, the speaker looking first up at the lights, then down at the grave. But it is also horizontal or temporal, with that specific temporality which enables the speaker to think prospectively about death from a vantage imagined as retrospective. She is imagining of her own "Splendors"—her immortal life or her immortal work—that "their Competeless Show/ Will entertain the Centuries/ When [she is] long ago,/ [An/Some—] Island in dishonored Grass—/ Whom none but [Daisies,/Beetles—] know." Although the ground is said to be dishonored, because so much time is imagined to have passed that the graveyard has lost its identification as a graveyard, is hence no longer hallowed, the work is still identified as that which, like the lights, endures. It is "Competeless"—without comparison. And, implicitly, by association, it is also identified with that which is "com*plete*less"—not susceptible of completion, without the liability of being finished or finite.

Dickinson never sent this poem about the immortality of the work to anyone, a fact that might seem surprising but for the vantage suggested by the poems themselves. For the immortality of the work is negotiated outside the human sphere, to which it is not in effect subject. Or, to put this another way, the influences on the work, the domain seen to affect it, is that of lights, beetles, daisies rather than that of persons. To take these influences literally, as the poem instructs us to do, is to have another explanation for why Dickinson did not publish her poems—the transaction with immortality lying outside the public, because outside the human, domain.

Conversely, in "There's a certain Slant of light" the human world is everywhere apparent, as finitude is everywhere apparent. The consequence is oppression. The human world manifests itself in the experience of division, the division of the heavenly from the earthly as well as of the internal from the external. It further manifests itself in the production of "Meanings," and in the concern with how meanings are produced. And as division itself might be regarded as a master trope of the human world, division is no less apparent in the indirectly voiced desire to make meaning visible—to externalize meaning where it is imagined meaning could have form that might be recognized, apprehended, even possessed, as objects are apprehended and possessed. Finally, the human world is apparent in the serial manifestations of indirection, of affliction, of personification, of death. In these various ways, the poem is saturated with finitude, as the preceding poem was purified of it.

The personification of the landscape is an alternative, as it were, to the naturalization of the self. And such an inversion of the previous poem, this rejection of its terms, is apparent in the fact that light waves become sound waves, which become waves of heaviness and pain. Thus everything is personalized, translated to the person, and then confined or trapped there, as in the previous poem liberation from personhood was precisely what was celebrated. Yet whatever invades the speaker is also perceived as alien to her even as it is seen to penetrate her. So the indifference—the "sovreign" "Unconcern" of the previous poem—becomes the "internal difference" of this one. In fact, light is cast down and codified as the "Seal Despair," which itself hardens further into "the look of Death." One way to understand such causality is to say that the light, internalized, registers as despair and is understood as death. Another way to understand it is to see that this figure in the poem—this making of death into a figure that cannot be dispelled—is what death looks like when it is personified, when it is made to have a meaning as small as a person's meaning. In line with the trivialization, "the look of Death" does not quite displace the anthropomorphic "face" of death (as in the previous poem "Competeless" does not quite displace "completeless"). For death in "There's a certain Slant of light," reduced to human size, is almost given a countenance. Thus "the Distance" from death or from the "look of Death" (from how death appears when it has a "look," almost a demeanor or expression) is no distance at all.

I have noted that something is being worked out in the two poems about an ability to adopt nature's indifference to the self (with the consequence of immortalizing the self) and an inability to adopt that indifference which results in death's personification. But what shall we further say about the proximity of these poems? Is one a repudiation of the other? Does the second more neutrally correspond to the other as an opposite point of view? And how can these poems so closely identified be read as anything but retorts to each other? Or would it be more accurate to say that they are in effect two parts of the same poem? For as distance is experienced in the first of the poems, distance and hence immortality, distance is denied in the second of the poems. Hence death is regarded. In the context of the whole fascicle, the poems reiterate in various ways the questions: Can loss be naturalized or always only personalized? How is the recompense for loss to be conceived? From the vantage of "Of Bronze—and Blaze—," there *is* no recompense and no necessity for recompense, nothing—or nothing worthwhile—being understood to be lost. From the vantage of "There's a certain Slant of light," everything is determined to be lost, as anticipation or anxiety determines it, even as *what* exactly is feared lost is unspecified, and impossible to specify. It is impossible to specify since there is no distance on the experience as well as no specified distance on the look of death. Thus in some crucial way, clarified only by the fascicle context, the poems in proximity illuminate distance, making distance the subject—as it is achieved by the speaker in one poem, as it fails to be achieved by the speaker in another—a subject that can only be seen to unfold across the space of two poems no longer understood as discrete. For the poems represent different understandings of what distance is—when it is achieved and when it fails to be achieved—making everything that follows (the experience of loss, the anticipation of death, internality itself) functionally, and therefore radically, subordinate to this subject which it is the task of the poems in conjunction to redefine. Such a redefinition is no small accomplishment, for it transforms the poems taken singly—as Romantic "insight" poems—into representations that probe the conditions and consequences of perception, giving conditions and consequences governance over all. Then perception itself and the celebrated "internality" of "There's a certain Slant of light" are only a consequence of a certain way of seeing, of a certain vantage, that can in fact be regulated and that, when regulated, (savingly) dehumanizes. With reference to such regulation, the mechanistic rhetoric of the fascicle's last poem (P 292), "If your Nerve, deny you—/ Go above your Nerve . . . Lift the Flesh door—," can no longer be seen as enigmatically self-annihilating. For, like "Of Bronze—and Blaze—," it proposes an escape from the mortal position seen in both cases to be a diminutive position to which there is a *real* alternative. So a rereading of two poems in proximity within the fascicle, poems no longer quite discrete, requires a rereading of all the poems in the fascicle and of the fascicle as a whole.

Before examining how poems not directly contiguous are nonetheless associated, I look briefly at three more instances of manuscript proximity: two poems in the same bifolium; a poem that ends one fascicle and the poem that begins the following fascicle; and finally at two proximate fascicles.

In Fascicle 15 "If I may have it, when it's dead" (cited earlier) precedes "I read my sentence—steadily—" (P 412). The two make up a whole—the fourth—bifolium:

> I read my sentence—steadily—
> Reviewed it with my eyes,
> To see that I made no mistake
> In it's extremest clause—
> The Date, and manner, of the shame—
> And then the Pious Form
> That "God have mercy" on the Soul
> The Jury voted Him—
> I made my soul familiar—with her extremity—
> That at the last, it should not be a novel Agony—
> But she, and Death, acquainted—
> Meet tranquilly, as friends—
> Salute, and pass, without a Hint—
> And there, the Matter ends—

Read as belonging to a single lyric the contradictory pronouns have been explained in terms of a grammar devised to represent a self that is partialized, as, for instance, the one who simultaneously experiences, survives, and records the sentence of death might be figured as partialized. But read in relation to the poem which has preceded it in the bifolium—where death, though *another's* death, is also anatomized—the contradictory pronouns, one designating the soul as masculine, the other as feminine, are rather more logically explained by the presence of two persons ("Think of it Lover! I and Thee/ Permitted—face to face to be—/ After a Life—a Death—We'll say—/ For Death was That—/ And This—is Thee—"). In fact, if in the first of the poems "to stroke thy frost/ Outvisions Paradise!," then in the second of the poems, "there, the Matter" doesn't end. The end of matter as earthly materiality is not the end of matter as an issue. Nor is it the end of materiality at all, since only after death can the lovers be bodily united. And this would explain the tranquillity with which death is encountered and the pun delivered. For if *her* sentence is *his* death, but his death, and ultimately her own, are conditions for *their* union, then the conclusion of his life, and eventually of hers, is requisite for that state in which immortal selves can meet as mortal ones could not. Such a state—subjunctive, even unimaginable—continues to *be* imagined throughout the course of "If I may have it, when it's dead," for the condition of death becomes the occasion for union. Only in this state of canceled (earthly) materiality is this "Bliss/Right/ Wealth I cannot weigh"—to reiterate the first poem's variant names for such consummation—anticipated as possible.

Yet the "extremity" of the second poem on the sheet might differently be understood to record the cost of union so conceived. As such it might be a corrective of sorts to the ebullience of the earlier statement. We do not, then, know whether to read the multiple pronouns of "I read my sentence" as clarified, even unified, by attributing the two pronouns to two discrete persons who will be posthumously joined, as in "If I may have it, when it's dead." Or whether, conversely, to read the schism of the self registered in the second of the poem's multiple pronouns—the "I," "she," "him," "her"—as a retort to the representation of unity, here not reiterated but perhaps contested, much as I have argued the variants to "If I may have it, when it's dead" contest the idea of union.

Such questions about how to read poems in relation to each other—relations that treat poems as parts of the same entity, insisted upon by their thematic connections as well as by their manuscript contiguity—are raised again by a different kind of proximity, exemplified by the poem that ends Fascicle 15, "I had been hungry, all the Years—" (P 579), and

the one that begins Fascicle 16, "Before I got my eye put out—" (P 327).
I have briefly discussed the role the poem that concludes Fascicle 15 plays
in relation to the poems copied earlier in that fascicle. To reiterate: While
the earlier poems in the fascicle express antithetical stances to what the
speaker desires but does not have, this poem defines "having" as itself
antithetical to desire.

> I had been hungry, all the Years—
> My Noon had Come—to dine—
> I trembling drew the Table near—
> And touched the Curious Wine—
>
> 'Twas this on Tables I had seen—
> When turning, hungry, Home
> I looked in Windows, for the Wealth
> I could not hope—for Mine—
>
> I did not know the ample Bread—
> 'Twas so unlike the Crumb
> The Birds and I, had often shared
> In Nature's—Dining Room—
>
> The Plenty hurt me—'twas so new—
> Myself felt ill—and odd—
> As Berry—of a Mountain Bush—
> Transplanted—to the Road—
>
> Nor was I hungry—so I found
> That Hunger—was a way
> Of Persons outside Windows—
> The Entering—takes away—

7. Wealth] Things   19. Persons] Creatures—
8. for Mine] to earn

Consider, then, its different relation to the first poem in Fascicle 16:

> Before I got my eye put out—
> I liked as well to see
> As other creatures, that have eyes—
> And know no other way—

But were it told to me, Today,
That I might have the Sky
For mine, I tell you that my Heart
Would split, for size of me—

The Meadows—mine—
The Mountains—mine—
All Forests—Stintless Stars—
As much of noon, as I could take—
Between my finite eyes—

The Motions of the Dipping Birds—
The Lightning's jointed Road—
For mine—to look at when I liked—
The news would strike me dead—

So safer—guess—with just my soul
Upon the window pane
Where other creatures put their eyes—
Incautious—of the Sun—

15. Lightning's jointed
    Road] Morning's Amber Road—

The two states recorded in "I had been hungry" are those of imagining
and having, although the latter is refused. More complexly, three states
are represented in "Before I got my eye put out—": having, imagining,
and refusing to have again. Thus the poem predicates an implicit history
for its negative choice—the possession of sight preceding the loss of
sight. It also predicates a complex way of understanding that event, since
in the ambiguity of "got," blindness that is willed reinterprets blindness
that has been imposed. Moreover, as if reiterating the confusion between
what is chosen and what is inflicted, between cause and effect, vision,
were it to be restored, is prospectively thought to be the *cause* of something worse than the blinding (here anticipated as dying), as well as the
object of the blinding.

Yet has the speaker in fact been blinded? Such a question is raised
because, if the economy of "I had been hungry, all the Years—" results
in the choice of scarcity over plenitude, the economy of "Before I got my
eye put out—" seems to belie the forfeiture of vision ostensibly narrated.
It does so because the poem is resplendent with a dazzling countervision.

For not only is the soul upon the pane an instrument of vision that perfectly registers the seeing ostensibly renounced, but, in addition, the detail of the poem repeatedly suggests that sight is actually intensified at a deeper level. Then perhaps this poem offers an alternative to the scarcity in the poem that ends Fascicle 15, suggesting not deprivation at all but something like surfeit. So it would appear from lines like: "The Meadows—mine—/ The Mountains—mine—/ All Forests—Stintless Stars—/ As much of noon, as I could take—/ Between my finite eyes—," where everything there *to be* seen already *has been* seen. In these lines soul-vision does not simply compensate for eye-vision but seems definitely superior. (Such a replacement would be stressed by an elision that makes us hear in "Forests—Stintless Stars" the hint "tintless stars," evoking not only white eyes but also some kind of seeing independent of the eyes—the latter suggestion reiterating that mere eyesight is ruled out for the visionary.)[12] If plenitude is refused in "I had been hungry, all the Years—" and if plenitude cannot be refused in "Before I got my eye put out—," then do these poems predicate alternative economies (as never having had in "I had been hungry, all the Years—" is an alternative to having had too much in "Before I got my eye put out—")? Or do the poems rather predicate complementary economies, suggesting that to separate the options as the poems initially separate them (refusing plenitude in the first of the poems and being deprived of it, but without consequence, in the second of the poems) is false? Is the plenitude imagined in "I had been hungry" remembered in "Before I got my eye put out—"? Or does it not require to be remembered because, contrary to the claim at the conclusion of the latter, it has never in fact been forfeited? In other words, as the covetousness indicated by the reiterated possessive of the middle stanzas of "Before I got my eye put out—" suggests: When we consider the proximity of the poems, we are made to wonder whether such a separation of imagining, having, remembering—of dispossession and possession—and such a separation of the poems themselves, is itself a false way to economize consciousness.

Since Dickinson did not number her fascicles it can only be speculated that 15 preceded 16, or that 13 preceded 14. Thus the proximate

---

12. For the theory that discovers and explains such drifts and elisions, and to which I am here indebted, see Garrett Stewart's *Reading Voices: Literature and the Phonotext* (Berkeley and Los Angeles: University of California Press, 1990).

association I have discussed can only be hypothetical. Still, even if it were not the case that 15 preceded 16, the two poems invite the kind of inquiry initiated above, since each represents a relation between having and repudiating, or between having and appearing to repudiate, that half-corroborates, half-contests an aspect of the other, as a variant would. The question of whether the first poem in one fascicle follows from the last poem in the previous fascicle makes inevitable another, perhaps prior question: Can one whole fascicle be said to follow from another?

Again, such a question presupposes a hypothetical chronology. In fact more than chronology is at stake—chronology being an accidental rather than an essential feature of connection. For the fascicles' relation to each other is like that of the variants. In other words, the question of how one fascicle is connected to another is more fundamental than chronology alone could explain, though chronology would be required to establish Dickinson's association of these poems through manuscript proximity. The fascicles' relations are, more importantly, like those of the variants, which do not depend on a chronology, or sequentiality, per se; rather, their potentially canceled boundaries—that is, the possible emergence of new identities or configurations—derive not from continuing or narrating but from varying. Such an identity would emerge as a consequence of the blurred line between two discrete structures, in this case, two fascicles, which, as it happens, are presumed to be chronologically proximate. The point about the proximity is not, however, that something is being continued, but rather that something is being "repeated."

In that light consider Fascicles 13 and 14. In a third of the poems in Fascicle 13 the speakers attempt to naturalize loss. "Of Bronze—and Blaze—" is an example. But so are "She sweeps with many-colored Brooms—" (P 219); "How the old Mountains drip with Sunset" (P 291); "Blazing in Gold—and" (P 228); "Delight is as the flight—" (P 257); and "There's a certain Slant of light" (P 258). Moreover, the fascicle, considered as a whole, could be said to ground, by specifying, the source of the despair in "There's a certain Slant of light." For with reference to "There came a Day—at Summer's full—" (P 322, on the fifth bifolium), the source of the despair is the loss of a lover which in earlier poems is displaced onto multiple disappearances of natural phenomena. The poem that ends Fascicle 13, "If your Nerve, deny you—" (P 292), proposes terms of recompense: Oxygen will be found in death. With reference to the surrounding poems, it will be found in the restoration of the lover who has been taken. In fact, one could observe variant expressions, if not actual progressions, in the fascicle: from the prevalence of loss; to the naturalizing of loss; to the personalizing of loss; to the idea of its recompense. Naturalizing and personalizing loss are exemplified by "Of Bronze—and Blaze—" and "There's a certain Slant of light," discussed earlier at length. In proposing such thematic variation, Fascicle 13 seems complete. Yet if in Fascicle 13 loss is being acknowledged so that loss can be negotiated as natural, in Fascicle 14 this tacit acceptance is dramatized only to be negated. For Fascicle 14, as I shall argue, rejects the analogy of loss as natural, even as it tries to reclaim the lover that is lost by means that could be called supernatural. To put this another way: If Fascicle 13 establishes the existence of loss as a natural phenomenon, Fascicle 14 explores its felt manifestations—its manifestations for persons who contest it.

One fascicle suggests that loss can be negotiated, even naturalized, but the other suggests the impossibility of such a negotiation. What is significant about such oscillation is not that a prior view about loss is succeeded by a second, but that the conflict about whether loss can be negotiated by naturalization is integral to the single framework within which the contest about loss articulates itself. That two proximate fascicles should seem component parts of a single entity is the consequence of a juxtaposition. In this way a boundary that seemed fixed is suddenly rendered fluid, because what is proposed within each ostensibly discrete structure operates as a variant to what is proposed within the other.

3

Reading Dickinson II

I. Displaced Variants

I WISH NOW TO CONSIDER how we are to understand associations within fascicles where poems are not physically proximate—a question related to the cognate issue of conceivably non-contiguous but still topically sequential fascicles discussed in the preceding chapter. I shall consider this question at some length and with disparate examples. For what is of note about the way in which connections are established is that non-proximate poems are nevertheless related as variants of each other. Such poems do not exactly develop from each other so much as they repeat and modify aspects of each other. Two poems in Fascicle 15 illustrate. The first, P 410, is the initial poem in the fascicle:

> The first Day's Night had come—
> And grateful that a thing
> So terrible—had been endured—
> I told my Soul to sing—
>
> She said her Strings were snapt—
> Her Bow—to Atoms blown—
> And so to mend her—gave me work
> Until another Morn—
>
> And then—a Day as huge
> As Yesterdays in pairs,
> Unrolled it's horror in my face—
> Until it blocked my eyes—
>
> My Brain—begun to laugh—
> I mumbled—like a fool—
> And tho' 'tis Years ago—that Day—
> My Brain keeps giggling—still.
>
> And Something's odd—within—
> That person that I was—
> And this One—do not feel the same—
> Could it be Madness—this?

In the first two stanzas of the poem, the experience is thought to have been endured because it is thought to have been completed. In the third stanza, however, it becomes apparent that the experience recollected is the experience perpetuated, even amplified, in the repetition. Thus the poem charts divisions between discrete temporal moments: the end of the terrible experience thought to have been endured; its reemergence as a recollection—but one that looms and accentuates what might only have been rehearsed; and, finally, in stanza four, the identification of madness not with the initial experience but rather with the moment when it first took the form of recollection. For "that Day," demarcating madness in the fourth stanza, echoes not the "first Day's Night" of the initial stanza, but more exactly the "Day as huge/ As Yesterdays in pairs" of the third. In effect the disoriented sense of time in that stanza ("'tis Years ago—that Day") is a distortion that arises from the disorder of repetition. Thus if the initial experience breaks the soul ("snap[s]," rends and stuns it), the damage is understood as still susceptible of being mended. And this possibility is explicitly opposed to the condition described in the third stanza where the split cannot be healed because, when "a Day as huge/ As Yesterdays in pairs,/ Unrolled it's horror in my face—/ Until it blocked my eyes—," experience and the experiencing self are alike made unrecognizable. For this reason the recollection of the terrible event supersedes and takes priority over the originary experience. In these differentiations the poem implicitly asks about the relation between psychic and temporal splits, raising the question of whether the genesis of madness is in the occurrence; in the recollection of the occurrence as its repetition; or in the interpretation of the occurrence, that is, in the last line's naming or identifying it.

Beginning the next bifolium (with "The Color of the Grave is Green—" intervening) is P 414:

> 'Twas like a Maelstrom, with a notch,
> That nearer, every Day,
> Kept narrowing it's boiling Wheel
> Until the Agony
>
> Toyed coolly with the final inch
> Of your delirious Hem—
> And you dropt, lost,
> When something broke—
> And let you from a Dream—

As if a Goblin with a Guage—
Kept measuring the Hours—
Until you felt your Second
Weigh, helpless, in his Paws—

And not a Sinew—stirred—could help,
And sense was setting numb—
When God—remembered—and the Fiend
Let go, then, Overcome—

As if your Sentence stood—pronounced—
And you were frozen led
From Dungeon's luxury of Doubt
To Gibbets, and the Dead—

And when the Film had stitched your eyes
A Creature gasped "Repreive"!
Which Anguish was the utterest—then—
To perish, or to live?

At the end of the second stanza ("When something broke—/ And let
you from a Dream—") the speaker seems to escape from the experience.
But much as at the end of the first stanza of "The first Day's Night had
come—," where enduring the experience and completing the experience
were falsely equated, the escape is an illusion, and this speaker too is
condemned to reexperience a torture that appears to have no terminus.
Because she is condemned to reexperience it, the question at the poem's
end ("Which Anguish was the utterest—then—/ To perish, or to live?")
cannot be a real question, since the reprieve has not in the past been a
real reprieve. It cannot be understood as a real reprieve, since other seeming moments of conclusion (at the end of the fourth stanza as well as at
the end of the second) are not conclusions at all. Here then, repeatedly,
the experience's being over is, as in the first poem, only a prologue to the
experience's *starting* over. In fact one could argue that the "end" of the
first lyric in the fascicle is only a momentary cessation of a process reani-
mated in this lyric. For much about the two poems—the experience's
continuing to *seem* over when it continues not to *be* over (as exemplified
by the similes of the second poem that describe three separate beginnings
and ends for what continues to inflict itself); the rhetorical questions that
conclude the final stanzas of each of the poems; the temporal stages in

each that signal extremity—makes them inexact counterparts. Thus to read "'Twas like a Maelstrom, with a notch" in the fascicle context is to discover the antecedent for "it" inside another poem or in the particularizing word of another poem: the "Madness" of "The first Day's Night had come—." But if this association is correct, then in the second of the poems perhaps madness is itself *repeated,* rather than newly represented, in the unstoppability of torture. This appears to be the case because madness in one poem and torture in the other are constituted by repetition, as if to suggest that repetition itself is the *cause* of the torture.

These poems, then, seem variants of each other in that both dramatize an experience of ending, whose contingent and illusory status they reciprocally clarify. Yet if the two poems are variants of each other, it is unclear how both are related to the poem which intervenes, "The Color of the Grave is Green—. . . The Color of the Grave within—/ The Duplicate—I mean—" (P 411). That poem (along with "If I may have it, when it's dead," "It is dead—Find it—" [P 417], "Not in this World to see his face—" [P 418], and "I read my sentence—steadily—") apparently specifies a more precise cause for madness and torture. The cause is death by light of some of these poems, and *his* death by light of others. Finally, if, in the two poems examined, the torture, like the madness, or the torture of the madness, lies in the repetition, it is then unclear how the first poem in the third bifolium (P 419) should be seen. For "We grow accustomed" could be regarded as a compliant response to "The first Day's Night had come—."

> We grow accustomed to the Dark—
> When Light is put away—
> As when the Neighbor holds the Lamp
> To witness her Goodbye—
>
> A Moment—We uncertain step
> For newness of the night—
> Then—fit our Vision to the Dark—
> And meet the Road—erect—
>
> And so of larger—Darknesses—
> Those Evenings of the Brain—
> When not a Moon disclose a sign—
> Or Star—come out—within—

The B[r]avest—grope a little—
And sometimes hit a Tree
Directly in the Forehead—
But as they learn to see—

Either the Darkness alters—
Or something in the sight
Adjusts itself to Midnight—
And Life steps almost straight.

This vision, fitted to the dark rather than mired in it, is an antithetical response to those "Evenings of the Brain" in "The first Day's Night had come—" ("Evenings" and "Day's Night" recalling each other like slant verbal repetitions). It is also an antithetical response to "'Twas like a Maelstrom, with a notch." For in the earlier poems horror is not simply perpetuated but is also amplified through time. In distinction, in "We grow accustomed" the mind "adjusts" to "Midnight." It "adjusts" and remains intact. Then what ties "The first Day's Night had come—" to "'Twas like a Maelstrom, with a notch" is repetition, specifically the repetition of remembering, retelling, reenacting. Oppositely, what liberates the speaker in "We grow accustomed to the Dark—" is the breaking free of repetition. Something "alters" (either the darkness or the vision of darkness) so that an experience, not repeated, is rather genuinely left behind. Thus "We grow accustomed to the Dark—" represents an ending that is retrospectively seen in the other poems as only initially mimicked closure.

In Fascicle 15, then, madness expressed through repetition is itself the mechanism that connects the discrete poems. In Fascicle 14, poems are oppositely associated by their variant understandings of how to coerce proximity from distance, because the cause of the speaker's pain is the disappearance of a phenomenon, event or person that *cannot* be repeated. Thus what links the poems are the ways in which a vanished proximity is coerced and regulated throughout the fascicle. In the context of negotiations that attempt to restore what has disappeared, the poetic variants, discussed earlier, to the fascicle's first lyric, "The [maddest/nearest] dream—recedes—unrealized—," are *governing* variants, coordinate points, differently brought together in the range of poems that constitute this poetic sequence.

For example, in the fascicle's first poem, "The [maddest/nearest] dream—recedes—unrealized—," what is initially nearest is ultimately evasive. "Nearest" becomes "farthest"—here called "maddest" ("maddest" being the variant actually written on the poetic line; fig. 3) as the response to the disappearance. "Nearest" and "farthest" are spatial superlatives. That "maddest" should implicitly appear to subsume "farthest," as if it were a synonym, suggests the fusion of the adjective designating the extremity of the speaker's response to the dream's withdrawal, as narrated by what follows, with a word that denotes the dream's intrinsic extravagance. For the colloquial sense of "maddest," as most outrageous, most unthinkable or "far out," is implied, but so is "maddest" as designating the wildness of response provoked by the trauma of the dream's departure. To recall the earlier gloss on the variants' relations: The dream is "maddest" because initially "nearest." Thus the displacement of the dream (now no longer "nearest") is attended by the displacement of the word for the extremity connected with its vanishing. As I have noted, "maddest" appears to subsume "farthest" as if the characterizations—of the dream, of the distance, of the subsequent effect of the dream's disappearance—were superimposed or condensed in the poem's first adjective as a consequence of a transit which the lines that follow the adjective depict more linearly: "The [maddest/nearest] dream—recedes—unrealized—/ The Heaven we chase—/ Like the June Bee—before the School-boy—/ Invites the Race—." In P 319 the dream, disappearing, provokes and entices. In the second poem in this fascicle, "What if I say I shall not wait!" (P 277), the heaven that recedes is the one whose reclamation is willed: "What if I burst the fleshly Gate—/ And pass escaped—to thee!/ What if I file this Mortal—off—/ See where it hurt me—That's enough—/ And [step/wade] in Liberty!"

In the violence of the expulsion of the self from mortality, "nearest" and "maddest" are no longer allied, for what has escaped along with the body in "What if I say I shall not wait!" is also that association. "Maddest" disappears as a variant of the initial experience, almost as if it could also be canceled as a variant to the earlier poem. In the subsequent respatialization, what is *farthest* is only bondage, which the speaker and (given the subsequent variant's correction of singularity) also her lover are both spared. The bondage could be said, therefore, to be trivialized: "They cannot take [me/us]—any more!/ Dungeons [can/may] call—and Guns implore/ Unmeaning—now—to me—." Yet in the poem that follows, "Ah, Moon—and Star!" (P 240), just this escape is again deemed

impossible, distance prohibiting rather than inciting escape: "But—
Moon—and Star—/ Though you're very far—/ There is one—farther
than you—/ He—is more than a firmament—from me—/ And I cannot
go!"

Thus Fascicle 14 establishes a pattern of vacillation in which the negation of escape and the embrace of escape, the impossible and the tran-
scendence of the impossible, the far and the near, alternate. But whether
the poems endorse a perspective in which heaven disappears or one in
which it cannot do so because life is dispensed with so that this heaven
may be secured, what is repeatedly reiterated is the equivocal association
of variants like those examined initially: "maddest" and "nearest." In
P 582 we are told: "Inconceivably solemn!/ Things so gay/ Pierce—by
the very Press/ Of Imagery—"; and in P 239: " 'Heaven'—is what I
cannot reach!/ The Apple on the Tree—/ Provided it do hopeless—
hang—/ That—'Heaven' is—to Me!"

In the last two examples, then, and in the fascicle as a whole, what
might be alien is in different but related ways asserted to be proximate
or associated, as "solemn" and "gay" are, or as the " 'Heaven' " that is
"hopeless" is. For in the first example the "gay" is made "solemn," because as it approaches, even enters, the eyes, its pressure becomes painful. The "Press/ Of imagery" "pierce[s]," suggesting a penetration in
which feeling is inflicted, even intensified, when it is dislocated from
what prompts it. Thus, things are no longer "gay" but painful when they
are incorporated, and this transfer of location changes the status of what
is transferred. In the second example, although heaven is experienced as
far or unattainable, the speaker characterizes its relation ("hopeless") to
herself as near—as, in fact, interior. "Hopeless" and " 'Heaven' " are,
then, in some sense slant coordinates, one word denoting a desired object, the other an emotion about its unavailability. In this way it could
be said that the alien thing is made sense of—in fact, here defined—only
as relational. It is defined specifically by the relation of desire to an object
that is inaccessible (" 'Heaven' "), or by the relation between objects that
are exterior ("Things so gay") and a discrepant affect which is interior.
Two points are to be emphasized: that the "near" and "far" are differently
but repeatedly made coordinates, and that when their relation is regulated—because the near is made far or vice versa—the thing being regulated is in fact transformed.

This conjunction of the alien and the proximate (as in "maddest" and
"nearest," as in "solemn" and "gay," as in " 'Heaven' " and "hopeless") is

reiterated at several levels in Fascicle 14. It is even apparent at the manuscript level because, uncharacteristically, poems from disparate years—
from 1861, 1858, and 1862—are copied and bound together. It is exemplified by the fact that two of the poems copied in this fascicle are also
copied in two *other* fascicles: "The feet of people walking home" and "Ah,
Moon—and Star!" (in Fascicles 1 and 14 and Fascicles 11 and 14, respectively), contesting the idea of a single association of just these poems.
For, given the fact that the poems are also copied in two other fascicles,
to understand the poems in "context" is to understand them also *outside*
of this particular fascicle. It is to understand the difference between versions and variants. The conjunction of the alien and the proximate is
operative in the fact that although the poems are consistently about
loss—of a dream, of a lover—death is reconstrued as a way to overcome
the loss, providing access to the object despaired of as inaccessible. The
conjunction of the alien and the proximate has, then, as its goal an ultimate retrieval which cancels the initial displacement. We have seen how
displacement works at the smallest unit of the variants: "maddest/near-
est." What is displaced is the "dream" of the first poem. And that displacement signals a second one, in which the antithesis of nearest ("farthest") is at once implied and dislodged by a nomenclature by which one
word, "maddest," incorporates the spatial and the emotive. But displacement itself serves a purpose, for oppositions, not treated as oppositions—indeed not even always formulated as such, as in "nearest/mad-
dest"—become the site of transition, as in the following instance:
"Night is the morning's Canvas/ Larceny—legacy—/ Death, but our
rapt attention/ To Immortality" (P 7). What the fascicle most hyperbol-
ically represents is neither loss nor its contestation but a strategy for
overcoming what is implicitly posited as definitive, whether it be absolute bliss, its absolute loss, or, as in the previous poem, death—which is
not definitive at all, "but" only (in the line's dismissive grammar) a prelude to immortality.

What displacement represents in the fascicle as a whole—within, as
well as among, the poems—is regulation itself. Thus "maddest/nearest"
adjusts perspective by making the two words equivocally relational. I
have noted that "farthest" is absorbed by "maddest," so that the latter
means the former, or so that the two are inseparable, since it is by virtue
of the dream's being farthest that "nearest" is translated to—takes as its
variant—"maddest." A similar negotiation can be seen in the relation of

"Larceny—legacy," words which could be regarded as variants *within* the line of the stanza quoted previously: "Night is the morning's Canvas/ Larceny—legacy—/ Death, but our rapt attention/ To Immortality." The "dream" in the fascicle's first poem is said to recede, to become inaccessible. The rest of the fascicle reassesses, manipulates, and *regulates* the relation of objects as initially stipulated. In one of the most extravagant transformations, the life that is initially lost in "More Life—went out—when He went/ Than Ordinary Breath—" (P 422) becomes not life lost for the speaker but rather life that could potentially erupt *from* her. We see this in the image of the self analogized to a volcano ("Popocatapel" or "Etna") whose "Peat life," though dormant, is "amply vivid" and ultimately explosive. *His* life, extinguished, is not life that is gone. Rather, in the psychic economy of the poem, which measures *how much* and maps *whose* life is where, it appears that *his* life gone out is life transferred to *her.*

Thus what links the poems in Fascicle 14 is neither their proximity per se nor their thematic consistency (indeed consistency within or between poems is just what they do *not* exemplify), but rather the strategy of regulation and transfer; it is, moreover, a strategy whose manifestations are incommensurate and unpredictable—whether exemplified in Dickinson's grouping of these poems from different years; in overturning a poem's initial definitive claim; or in the absent but implicit transitions between individual variants to a line and between the poems in a fascicle. These poems advance sometimes antithetical, more often apposite, propositions, as in " 'Heaven'—is what I cannot reach!"; "The Heaven we chase—. . . Invites the Race—"; "Death, but our rapt attention/ To Immortality"; "What if I file this Mortal—off—. . . And [step/*wade*] in Liberty!"

Regulation is required to pry apart the variants "maddest" and "nearest." To separate the attributes is to cancel the disappearance. In "What if I say I shall not wait!" the disappearance can be canceled by the speaker's escaping to the one who has escaped. Or in "More Life—went out—when He went" it can be canceled by imagining a transfer of the life that is extinguished to the one who witnesses the extinction and absorbs the life released. Or it *cannot* be canceled as in the poems that record stasis: " 'Heaven'—is what I cannot reach! . . . That—'Heaven' is—to Me!" But regulation is dramatized more ostentatiously as a movement than as a topic—specifically, as a movement from poems which record loss (record the transit from "nearest" to "maddest") to those which obviate loss and those which despair of obviation. Then regulation is what is thought—"ponder[ing] how the bliss would look—" (P 271). Or regulation is what cannot be controlled by thought. For if the fascicle's first poem "Invites the Race—," invites thought to come, suggests that *thought* can regulate, the last extant poem copied into it, "Give little Anguish,/ Lives will fret—/ Give Avalanches,/ And they'll slant" (P 310), suggests that thought, under duress, cannot do so. Thus regulation associates the poems in this fascicle. What is rewritten is the relation between the alien and the proximate. The variants themselves, especially the initial one—"nearest/maddest"—are ways of establishing and maintaining perspectival, as well as linguistic, instability, instability itself facilitating change. To move from one position to its antithesis, from the "nearest" dream to the one that "recedes," or from a poem advancing one position (the dream cannot be reclaimed) to a poem advancing the opposite position (the dream/the lover *can* be), or to move from a superlative that registers proximity ("nearest") to one that characterizes an emotive state ("maddest") is to employ regulation to *change* unchangeable states and, even more, as in the last instances, to *equate incomparable* states.

This Fascicle 14 does. Among its erasures of inequality the fascicle treats variants *to* lines as commensurate with variants *within* lines. For example, the relation of "maddest" to "nearest" is analogous to that of "Larceny—legacy"—both pairings indicating transitions from one position or state to another which would appear to be the structural antithesis of the first, but which is not. In the case of "Larceny—legacy," the latter implies a specificity that "Larceny" does not. "Legacy" is not just a gift— which *would* be opposite to a theft—but a gift that is a bequest. Asymmetries like this, refusals of equivalence without true antithesis, derail opposition per se. Displacement occurs at the smallest unit of the variants, structurally set against each other without being opposed. And displacement is functional. It is the ground where inequalities are first recorded, then measured, then redressed. So gains and losses are not neutrally registered, but registered in order to be economized and readjusted.

In summary: I have been discussing poems in Fascicles 14 and 15 which are not physically proximate as variants of each other. In Fascicle

15, poems are variant presentations of the phenomenon of repetition—specifically, the repetition of remembering, reexperiencing, and retelling a terrible event. In these poems madness lies not in the terrible event, but rather in its repetition, in the reenactment in time of something presumably finished. For in Fascicle 15 a terrible event is made more terrible in its repetition. It is made so terrible that it raises questions about the status of the recurrence, or of the mind rehearsing it ("Could it be Madness—this?"); the event repeats itself in that mind as if in an eternal present.

In Fascicle 14, conversely, poems are variants on the idea of a present that is feared not to recur, of a present moment or event made distant, and of a speaker who undertakes the transgression of that distance. Thus "the Distance/ On the look of Death" observed in Fascicle 13 becomes, in the poetic sequence that arguably follows it, distance repeatedly traversed by a foreshortening or elision of space. For in poems like "What if I say I shall not wait!" or "Ah, Moon—and Star!" or " 'Heaven'—is what I cannot reach!" or "The feet of people walking home," impossible distances are charted and imagined as possible to navigate. Thus "nearest" becomes "maddest" only when the "dream" it modifies, initially proximate, escapes, becoming something like "farthest." And the association between "nearest" and "maddest"—the proximity of the two words, one impinging almost inexplicably on the other—depends on the degree to which the speaker's distance from what she has lost can be staved off. The words are liberated from association when—as in "What if I say I shall not wait!"—the life that has been lost is again secured ("What if I burst the fleshly Gate—/ And pass escaped—to thee!"). Or her distance from the loved object is differently staved off, as in "More Life—went out—when He went," because the life lost to *him* is life gained by *her*. In this way poems not proximate to each other are nonetheless poems about proximity. In fact it might even be argued that the distance physically separating the poems is requisite for associations to be made among them, since these associations depend precisely on the temporal and spatial gaps which are marked and spanned respectively.

If in Fascicle 15 time is repeated, and in Fascicle 14 space is repeatedly traversed, in Fascicle 20 repetition is thematized specifically as obsession. In turning to Fascicle 20, I want, however, to speak not simply about poems in a fascicle which, though not proximate, are indeed associated, but also about fascicles as discrete entities. I shall be claiming that the fascicles give the poems within them identity, even consistency, but that neither is necessarily conferred by the chronological order of the poems as determined by their binding. Thus we read connections, even equivalences, sometimes by appeal to proximity but sometimes by non-contiguous associations similar to those I have been considering. I turn first to Fascicle 20 and then to Fascicle 16.

II. FASCICLE 20: CHOOSING

POEMS IN FASCICLE 20 (for the facsimile text, see Appendix B, figs. 11–28) advocate a personal criterion—often a *person*'s criterion—for what is chosen and deemed acceptable, in opposition to a theological or social one. In fact I shall argue that in this fascicle the personal, the theological, and the social are first substituted, then equated, and then treated as interchangeable. We see this equivalence in "Mine—by the Right of the White Election!" (P 528; fig. 26) in the fascicle's last bifolium, whose leaves are no longer conjugate. While conventionally "Election" is a word that designates God's choice to save a given person, in Dickinson's poem "Election," exemplified by the reiterated possessive, connotes a human, even personal, claim, although the poem also deliberates the efficacy of this transfer, deliberates whether a person, rather than God, *can* elect.

> Mine—by the Right of the White Election!
> Mine—by the Royal Seal!
> Mine—by the Sign in the Scarlet prison—
> Bars—cannot conceal!
>
> Mine—here—in Vision—and in Veto!
> Mine—by the Grave's Repeal—
> Titled—Confirmed—
> Delirious Charter!
> Mine—long as Ages steal!

4. Bars] Bolts   9. long as] while
8. Good affidavit—

In the defiance of the last line absolute claim seems guaranteed by absolute certainty of dispossession. For consonant with the reversal discussed above—where election is not predicated on the guarantee of God's mercy—here election is rather predicated on the guaranteed violation of a woman's asserted right. But election is also predicated on the speaker's reiterated right to own what she is dispossessed of. The relation between the two final variants dramatizes the double nature of the claim. For if "while" implies "for the duration, during the time of," "long as" is more active, implying stamina or endurance that half-suggests a confrontation between the connotations of the two variants, between *enduring* and *contesting,* as well as between the stealing of the ages and the steeling of the speaker. And indeed to read as triumphant the stronger variant "long as," predicating insistence from the center, is to see the dominance of the speaker's will over the mere temporality she is resisting. For if "while" connotes duration, that time in which the ages steal, "long as" connotes waiting it out, hence attributes to duration a limit. Thus in the "Vision" of the poem, definitively enacted by the heteroglossia of the last two variants, what will ultimately be "Veto[ed]" is not the speaker's claim, but rather, subversively, the endlessness of her dispossession. Such transformations and reversals are reiterated in the fascicle's other poems. In "The Soul selects her own Society—" (P 303), it is again the soul, rather than God, that elects: "I've known her—from an ample nation—/ Choose One—/ Then—close the Valves of her attention—/ Like Stone—." I shall return to this and other substitutions enacted in the poem. First, however, salient aspects of the fascicle require description.

Notable in the poems of Fascicle 20 is their explicit sexuality. Sexuality is underscored by the fact that it is not diminished, and is even apparently awakened, by a lover who ought to be represented as bodiless because he is characteristically represented as dead, as in the last stanza of "Departed—to the Judgment—" (P 524; fig. 12), in the first bifolium:

> Departed—to the Judgment—
> A Mighty Afternoon—
> Great Clouds—like Ushers—leaning—
> Creation—looking on—
>
> The Flesh—Surrendered—Cancelled—
> The Bodiless—begun—
> Two Worlds—like Audiences—disperse—
> And leave the Soul—alone—

3. leaning] placing	7. disperse] dissolve—
5. Cancelled] Shifted	/withdraw—/retire—
7. Two] the—	

"The Bodiless—[is] begun" in that the body is "Cancelled" for the lover and "Surrendered" by the speaker, who has lost the lover's body. Yet throughout the fascicle that loss appears not to register. Or when it does, it is repeatedly, unmistakably, and palpably reversed—a reversal preliminarily signalled by the variants in the poem's seventh line, which explicitly raise a question about the nature of the other's disappearance. Namely, is something being "dissolve[d]," "withdraw[n]," "disperse[d]," or merely "retire[d]"? Questions about the ultimate status of the loss are reiterated in the variants to the first line of the second stanza. For it is one thing to understand the flesh as "Cancelled" as the word on the line does. It is another to understand the flesh as "Shifted," as I shall argue the other poems in the fascicle and the fascicle as a whole do.

By light of other poems in the fascicle the soul is not alone, at least the *speaker*'s soul is not. Although "Two Worlds—like Audiences—disperse—" designates a separation between the speaker and the lover, both of whom stand witness to a death that should absolutely sever one body from another, the first two stanzas of P 366 (figs. 18–20) reconstruct, even reincarnate, the body in their speculations about the speaker's subjunctive ministrations to the lover and his very flesh:

> Although I put away his life—
> An Ornament too grand
> For Forehead low as mine, to wear,
> This might have been the Hand
>
> That sowed the flower, he preferred—
> Or smoothed a homely pain,
> Or pushed the pebble from his path—
> Or played his chosen tune—

The previous supposition about what the speaker might have done for the lover is replaced in the poem below (P 368; fig. 25) by a more than spectral supposition. For whether the speaker in these poems recalls, hallucinates, or imagines a presence, this presence is so thoroughly infused with "body, wholly body" as to leave no doubt that it is not the lover merely, but more specifically the lover's body, that is reincorporated:

> How sick—to wait—in any place—but thine—
> I knew last night—when someone tried to twine—
> Thinking—perhaps—that I looked tired—or alone—
> Or breaking—almost—with unspoken pain—

And I turned—ducal—
That right—was thine—
One port—suffices—for a Brig—like *mine*—

Our's be the tossing—wild though the sea—
Rather than a Mooring—unshared by thee.
Our's be the Cargo—*unladen—here*—
Rather than the *"spicy isles—"*
And thou—not there—

If, then, the lover's flesh is "Cancelled" in reality, it is not canceled in recollection or reconstruction of the reality. And the reconstruction—unequivocal, repetitious, atypically unparadoxical—replaces the idea of "bodilessness" narrated by "Departed—to the Judgment—" with "the Cargo—*unladen—here*" of this poem. Thus the body that has died becomes the body reincarnated. It is absent but anticipated or, if gone for good, still treated as a presence. Though "Our's be the tossing" refers to the speaker and her "Brig" (to the speaker and her body), the reiterated possessive ("Our's be the Cargo") also inescapably applies to the speaker and her lover, to the lover and *his* body. The speaker has allied herself with the lover in the narrative of the poem, independent, as it were, of the conditions stipulated there. Since *his* port is her respite, the turning from all others amounts to a re-turning to him. Moreover, since turning back to him is not simply possessive, but more directly sexual, the presence of his sexuality, the "Cargo—*unladen—here*," seems a promise of the cargo's ultimately *being* unladen. As much to the point, it seems a promise that sexuality will be sustained until the speaker actually possesses what she now abundantly has in mind. Thus sexuality, *hers*, is linked to *his*: "*That* right—was thine—." And since the lover is not in fact present to claim what he owns, what she possesses and is possessed by is his sexuality—purified of its embodiment but not, for all that, understood to have disappeared.

More than any other, then, this fascicle could be said to produce a narrative. In the narrative,[1] a lover dies, but his sexuality survives the

---

1. The narrative is attested to by the first four poems copied in the first bifolium: "I took one Draught of Life—" (P 1725), "A train went through a burial gate" (P 1761), "The Morning after Wo—" (P 364), and "Departed—to the Judgment—" (P 524). As suggested in the Textual Note, although the bifolium has a missing first leaf, Franklin speculates convincingly that the poems on that sheet are almost cer-

death. It may be hypothetical, unsituated, even inaccessible. But for all that it is no less reconstructed as corporeal. Given the premise of corporeality, the idea of reward in some other life is narrated as trivial, and a counter-criterion for reward in the present—an absolute claim in *this* life based on the obduracy of obsession—is advanced. Hence the dismissive concluding stanza of "I reason, Earth is short—" (P 301; fig. 16), the last poem in the second bifolium of Fascicle 20: "I reason, that in Heaven—/ Somehow, it will be even—/ Some new Equation, given—/ But, what of that?" When the idea of recompense elsewhere is not dismissed (as it is not in "Although I put away his life—" [P 366]), it is only entertained with bitterness.

In the last three stanzas of "Although I put away his life—" a promise is exacted: that the speaker after death may attend the lover. But the point of the promise, and of the anticipated fulfillment, seems itself overwhelmed by a gratification so delayed that its achievement is insignificant next to the recollection of its absence. Deprivation, and the lover's imputed agency in it, are finally subject to the speaker's accusation. Consider the last three stanzas of the poem:

> Your Servant, Sir, will weary—
> The Surgeon, will not come—
> The World, will have it's own—to do—
> The Dust, will vex your Fame—
>
> The Cold will force your tightest door
> Some Febuary Day,
> But say my apron bring the sticks
> To make your Cottage gay—
>
> That I may take that promise
> To Paradise, with me—
> To teach the Angels, avarice,
> You, Sir, taught first—to me.

Thus, in "Although I put away his life—," a plea or a hope turns into a threat. And the conclusion of the poem, in which desire ultimately fulfilled is still desire that has for so long remained *un*fulfilled, is not effec-

---

tainly the first two enumerated above. However, for obvious reasons their sequence cannot be specified. See *The Manuscript Books,* I:434.

tively different in its dismissal of the posthumous fulfillment from the conclusion of "I reason, Earth is short—." For in both poems the speaker insists of the fulfillment, "But, what of that?" Although ultimate fulfillment may be imagined in "Although I put away his life—," immediate fulfillment seems almost always to supplant it in the obsessive recollections by which the speaker is haunted and inhabited in the fascicle's other poems.

In fact the insistence of obsession, its repetition as a topic, binds the fascicle together, replacing the idea of death, introduced at the fascicle's beginning, with an idea like this one in P 367 (fig. 20):

> Over and over, like a Tune—
> The Recollection plays—
> Drums off the Phantom Battlements
> Cornets of Paradise—
>
> Snatches, from Baptized Generations—
> Cadences too grand
> But for the Justified Processions
> At the Lord's Right hand.

Obsession, introduced in the previous poem, is renewed in the first and last stanzas of P 302 (fig. 23):

> Like Some Old fashioned Miracle—
> When Summertime is done—
> Seems Summer's Recollection—
> And the Affairs of June—
>
> . . . .
>
> Her Memory—like Strains—enchant—
> Tho' Orchestra—be dumb—
> The Violin—in Baize—replaced—
> And Ear, and Heaven—numb—

13. Memory] Memories   14. be] is
13. enchant] Review—

Noteworthy about "Over and over, like a Tune—," as about the first and last stanzas of "Like Some Old fashioned Miracle—," is not only the obsessive repetition which keeps the past in the present by constant rehearsal, but also the coordinate fact that, especially in the first of these poems, what is recollected is simultaneously transformed into sounds that are divine. Thus the profane "Drums" and "Cornets" of that poem's initial stanza become first "Snatches" and then "Cadences" of the second stanza. They are specifically cadences of salvation, understood ceremonially as "the Justified Processions/ At the Lord's Right hand." In fact salvation seems conferred not by anticipation but by the potency of mere recollection. Thus recollection is analogous to salvation because the qualities that attend it, the quality *of* it, are only comprehensible in terms of that superlative, ultimate state.

Moreover, if in the first of the poems the present is replaced by recollection, earthly music by cadences of salvation, such cadences themselves, in the second poem cited, are replaced by "Memory/Memories." The latter are not *of* strains, but are rather said to be "like Strains"—the "Memory/Memories" *being* the music rather than being *of* the music. These strains replace instruments ("The Violin [is put] in Baize"), as well as stilling the instrument of hearing (the "Ear"), and they even quiet what had appeared to be the object of listening—the heavenly sounds initially attended to. In fact "Heaven" made "numb" pertains not simply to the divinity of that which is initially recollected ("Heaven" here understood colloquially), but also to the speaker's imperviousness to anything outside of memory (including "Heaven" understood as a presumed destination). For memory is the ultimate standard; indeed, it is made in this poem the *only* standard. Thus in both poems everything is rendered silent and insensate by the workings of the mind.

I shall eventually ask what these substitutions and displacements mean. But first I want to consider the relation between how narrative functions in this fascicle and how variants function in it. Narrative would seem one way of bringing the variant into the poem without problematizing the poem's identity, since the narrative allows one to have both poetic entities the variants produce by first having one and then having the other. Thus it could be argued that the narrative is a complementary strategy for choosing not choosing. But I think that in this fascicle, and in the fascicles as a whole, there is a tension between narrative and variants.

In Fascicle 20, for example, a story is ostensibly being told about the death of a lover. Yet the narrative never really advances, because variant moments stall its progression in the recalling. Some of these moments register the impossibility of forsaking the lover who has forsaken the speaker; others register the inevitability of returning to the lover. Thus the story of loss being told—the ostensible narrative—is not being told. It is rather disrupted by variant claims about the impossibility of leaving and losing the lover who, the narrative claims, has been left and lost. Another way to put this is that if the narrative tells the story of death and loss, the variants contradict that story, creating a counter-story of their own that is the antithesis of the narrative. In fact, as I shall argue, the variants characteristically do more than simply disrupt the narrative continuity; they also, more importantly, disclaim the difference (between the moments preceding the death and the moments rectifying it, between the person of the lover and the person of the speaker) that would make sense of the narrative ostensibly being told. We shall see how variants, in disclaiming that difference and in themselves articulating identity within difference, exist in tension with the narrative. Because these variants contest the fact of loss that requires rectification, with reference to the variants the lover who has died has not really died. The speaker separated from the lover is not really separated, because any distinction between the two is, as I shall explain, rendered immaterial, even as it is registered in variant terms across several poems.

The question of displacement has arisen previously, at least by analogy, in the discussion of variants to two poems in this fascicle. Thus I have suggested that the "'White Heat'" of "Dare you see a soul at the 'White Heat'?" reappears in the variant to a line in a poem copied two fascicle sheets later, "That Whiter Host" of "One need not be a Chamber—to be Haunted—"; not incidentally, this echo connects the two poems as well as the specific lines that seem variants of each other. The point about the recurrence is not simply that in the second poem the self is haunted by the very passion of which, in the first of the poems, death was said definitively to rid it. The point is also that this passion is apparently (in the second poem) something embodied—albeit concealed *in* the body, perhaps even *as* a body in the physiognomy of that poem. In other words, the death that implicitly concludes "Dare you see a soul at the 'White Heat'?" does not, as that poem had claimed, "Repudiate the Forge" (does not repudiate the soul, or the body housing the soul which is being refined). Rather, the second poem gives this soul habitation in another body. Or if "the Forge" is understood as an emblem for the body, rather than the soul, that body is itself revived. Death makes material in the second poem what was spectral in the first (P 365 and P 670; figs. 14–15 and 21–22). I quote both poems again:

Dare you see a soul at the "White Heat"?
Then crouch within the door—
Red—is the Fire's common tint—
But when the quickened Ore

Has sated Flame's conditions—
She quivers from the Forge
Without a color, but the Light
Of unannointed Blaze—

Least Village, boasts it's Blacksmith—
Whose Anvil's even ring
Stands symbol for the finer Forge
That soundless tugs—within—

Refining these impatient Ores
With Hammer, and with Blaze
Until the designated Light
Repudiate the Forge—

4. quickened] vivid   6. She] It
5. sated] vanquished

One need not be a Chamber—to be Haunted—
One need not be a House—
The Brain—has Corridors surpassing
Material Place—

Far safer of a Midnight—meeting
External Ghost—
Than an Interior—Confronting—
That cooler—Host.

Far safer, through an Abbey—gallop—
The Stones a'chase—
Than Moonless—One's A'self encounter—
In lonesome place—

Ourself—behind Ourself—Concealed—
Should startle—most—
Assassin—hid in our Apartment—
Be Horror's least—

The Prudent—carries a Revolver—
He bolts the Door—
O'erlooking a Superior Spectre—
More near—

4. Material] Corporeal	19–20] A Spectre—infinite—
8] That Whiter Host.	accompanying—
17. The Prudent] The Body	He fails to fear—
17. a] the	19–20] Maintaining a Superior
	Spectre—
	None saw—

The "'White Heat'" of the first poem—ostensibly canceled by the "designated Light" of death—is, as I have noted, not canceled at all. With reference to the second poem, it is only submerged and concealed. It is submerged in the transformed line of the variant "That Whiter Host," and is differently concealed as a hidden entity, "Ourself—behind Ourself," which resides within the person/chamber. For this entity is neither fully identical with nor fully differentiated from the speaker, a fact that the repeated pronoun makes clear. "That Whiter Host" is also neither fully spectral nor fully material. For although called "a Superior Spectre," it is sufficiently corporeal to be shot by a "Revolver" as something palpable could be.

The transformation of that "'White Heat'" to "That Whiter Host" is of interest not only because it reverses the idea of death's finality in the first of the poems (much as obsession in the poems discussed earlier reverses death's finality by replacing bodilessness with images of recollected corporeality). The transformation is also of interest because of the inevitable, if initially improbable, specific association of "That Whiter Host" with the Eucharist. This association, though oblique, is nevertheless implied, first of all by the stressed connotations of the word itself, for the spirit that departs in "Dare you see a soul" is resurrected, a half-mental, half-material presence—its menace a consequence of its evasive palpability. Thus, in one sense, the "Host" is so named because it occupies the body-house claimed as its own. It is the dubious welcomer of the self who becomes its guest. But in another sense the "Host" is named as such because it enigmatically resides, or incarnates itself, in the speaker's body. For if, on the one hand, the contested ownership of the dwelling is at issue (whose chamber is this?), on the other, the identity of those contesting ownership is also and no less at issue. (Whose self is internalized? How exactly do we understand the incorporation of one self in another, even in the corridors of that other's brain?) The psychological way to understand incorporation, strongly implied by "Ourself—behind Ourself—Concealed," seems insufficient, given the double connotations of "Host" and the surrounding poems in the fascicle context.[2] Hence it needs to be complemented by the religious way of understanding the incorporation, although to see the "Host" as a figure for the lover's body rather than for God's is so radically to transform that immediate context as to make it virtually unrecognizable. Other poems (for example, "I cannot live with You—" [P 640] in Fascicle 33, discussed in my conclusion) will make the association between Christ and a dead lover as overt as it may here seem speculative.

The beginning of Fascicle 20 makes and insists upon the connection between the one who has died and the Christ that is crucified. In suggesting that the parodied or imitated religious context could complement the psychological one in "One need not be a Chamber—to be

2. Recall the speaker's comparison of her plight to that of Christ in the first poem (P 527; fig. 17) in the third bifolium of Fascicle 20: "To put this World down, like a Bundle—/ And walk steady, away,/ Requires Energy—possibly Agony—/ 'Tis the Scarlet way/ Trodden with straight renunciation/ By the Son of God—/ Later, his faint Confederates/ Justify the Road—/ Flavors of that old Crucifixion—/ Filaments of Bloom, Pontius Pilate sowed—/ Strong Clusters, from Barabbas' Tomb—/ Sacrament, Saints {partook/indorsed} before us—/ Patent, every drop,/ With the {Brand/Stamp} of the Gentile Drinker/ Who {indorsed/enforced} the Cup—."

The road trodden by "the Son of God" is also apparently the road trodden by the dead lover. Or so it would appear in "The Morning after Wo—" (P 364; fig. 11) on the first bifolium of Fascicle 20. There nature, epitomized by birds, is said to mock the speaker's sorrow by its "utter Jubilee": "The Birds declaim their Tunes—/ Pronouncing every word/ Like Hammers—Did they know they fell/ Like Litanies of Lead—/ On here and there—a creature—/ They'd modify the Glee/ To fit some Crucifixal Clef—/ Some Key of Calvary—." In this way the connection between the one who has died and the Christ who has been crucified is made, is insisted upon, at the fascicle's beginning.

If in the first instance the "straight renunciation" is experienced by the speaker, in the second its cause—another's death presented as analogous to Christ's—cannot be overlooked as random. For the way that Christ is said to make himself material is similar to the way in which the dead lover appears to and in the speaker. Thus I take literally the analogy of the first poem: "Sacrament, Saints {partook/indorsed} before us—/ Patent, every drop." However blasphemously, something like the sacrament of the Eucharist is being imitated.

Haunted—," I seem to be claiming that the internalized "other" is both an aspect of the self and the corporealized lover—the lover corporealized as God was. It will become clear why the claim that an entity is both a self and an other is, in the poems in this fascicle (and, I shall argue, in Dickinson's poems more generally), not in fact contradictory.

It is not in any of the poems taken singly, but in all the poems of Fascicle 20 taken together, that we see that the lover whose death is represented in many of the poems is like the "Lord" of "Over and over, like a Tune—." The lover is like the Lord not only because recollections of him associate him with divinity—not only, in other words, because he is worshiped—but more radically because he has no body. Or because the body that he has ("That cooler—Host/That Whiter Host") is a *symbol* of the body, a "Superior Spectre," not fully spectre or ghost but also not fully body. In fact what makes the poem a horror poem is precisely the indeterminate status of what haunts the speaker—spectre or body. "How does a spectre become a body when a lover has died?" is precisely the question that seems asked in all the poems in Fascicle 20. "Spectre or body?" is reiterated as one of the central Christian mysteries—when God first becomes flesh and then relinquishes it, electing to die. That sacrifice is half-parodied, half-imitated in the bodilessness of a poem like "Departed—to the Judgment—," which the subsequent lyrics in the fascicle convert back to body, much as God, through the Eucharist, is said to be made again corporeal. Finally, with respect to theology, this question—spectre or body—is reiterated when Christ's body is taken into the human body as the Eucharist.

We see the confusion of the spectral and the bodily, of the secular and the sacred, in "Mine—by the Right of the White Election!" where the speaker, claiming her right (albeit to what is indeterminate), seems to insist she possesses something like a lover (for what object but a lover would generate the passion of this disputed property?). Say, then, the speaker understands that the body of the lover, like the body of the Lord, is the body with its palpability first sacrificed and then assured. In the case of God, palpability is assured after death through the promise of the resurrection and through Christ's explanation of how to take the Eucharist: "Take, eat; this is my body." In the case of the lover, palpability is assured because it is conversely, in the first stanza of P 370, constructed *mentally:*

Heaven is so far of the Mind
That were the Mind dissolved—
The Site—of it—by Architect
Could not again be proved—

Heaven is "of" the mind, in the sense of "in" the mind. For "so far of the Mind" implies "so completely made out of its substance," rather than invoking any operable sense of "far" as "distant." These transformations (of dispossession to claim, of the spectral to the bodily, of heaven as a site to heaven as a construct) and, in the case of "That Whiter Host," this transubstantiation attend the fascicle as a whole. They attend the fascicle as a whole because they chronicle the fact that a lover has died, that his death can be rectified and salvation still imagined by analogy to the narrative of Christ, who, though sacrificed, is then embodied in the Eucharist. Thus what is substituted in the fascicle is life for death, and concomitantly sexuality for bodilessness. The substitutions depend on a paradigm that shocks even as, in its various reiterations, it explains and situates.

But if the lover is reembodied—is turned from a spectre into a body—the speaker is, conversely, turned from a body into a soul in P 303 (fig. 24) as the speaker betrays in her self-designation:

The Soul selects her own Society—
Then—shuts the Door—
To her divine Majority—
Present no more—

Though the speaker's obsession returns her lover to a hallucinated and (in the case of "One need not be a Chamber—to be Haunted—") feared materiality, still life *has* been sacrificed. As it happens, *hers*. Since the speaker is given back her recollection of the lover's body, her own body takes on the attributes of (*his?*) soul. In analogous substitutions alluded to earlier—substitutions that (in "Over and over, like a Tune—") replace the actual with the recollected, which is then analogized to the heavenly, and that (in "Like Some Old fashioned Miracle—") replace the strains of music with the strains of memory, which silence the music by being superior to it—the entities displaced and left behind are nonetheless left intact.

Conversely, in the substitution enacted by "The Soul selects her own Society—," as I shall explain, the other's body is left intact, although the speaker forfeits *hers*. This is perhaps what is meant by the variant in "Departed—to the Judgment—" when "Flesh," first said to be "Cancelled," is alternatively said to be "Shifted." In the economy of the poem's exchanges, when the body is returned to the lover, the speaker seems to relinquish her body, even as, so doing, her soul is made sufficiently palpable to have welcomed his body—as to a dwelling. Or say the speaker remains sufficiently palpable to have ushered his body (the "One" of the poem's concluding stanza) into an enclosure fronted by a door, which then closes behind him. Which then closes him in. Herself without a body, herself represented as if the materiality of body had been exchanged for the materiality of a dwelling (the structure of the self in this poem being analogous to that of the self in the haunted brain poem), the speaker has the curious capacity to receive (or refuse to receive) *other* palpable bodies, here called "Society." For although the speaker's soul seems to have no palpability of its own, it nonetheless exhibits the capacity to adjudicate others' palpability, to *regulate* her relation to it. So "The Soul selects her own Society—" continues:

> Unmoved—she notes the Chariots—pausing—
> At her low Gate—
> Unmoved—an Emperor be kneeling
> Upon her Mat—
>
> I've known her—from an ample nation—
> Choose One—
> Then—close the Valves of her attention—
> Like Stone—

> 3. To] On   8] On [her] Rush mat
> 4. Present] Obtrude   11. Valves] lids—

The fascicle as a whole, like the poem just cited, insists on the association of the divine and the earthly, for again the soul that selects is like the God who elects. Such an association is based on remembering as embodying, an incorporation repeatedly made equivalent to salvation itself. The association of the divine and earthly is based on a parody of the Eucharist because, although spirit is embodied, embodiment itself is regarded as a haunting—the incorporated body being the body that is sometimes hunted down (as in "One need not be a Chamber—to be Haunted—") as well as the body that is venerated (as in "The Soul selects her own Society—"). It is based on certain substitutions which reiterate death's inevitable sacrifice of corporeality but do so by displacing or "shifting" it. In this displacement, as I have argued, the lover is pure body and the speaker is pure soul. Finally, incorporation is based on the doctrine of election, drawn on but reversed so that the election is not God's to save man, but rather a woman's to wrest/save/steal, or (in "The Soul selects") merely to usher in the "One" who embodies "All." That last superlative is not random. For at the beginning of another of Dickinson's poems, "The Missing All, prevented Me/ From missing minor Things" (P 985), the "All" that is missed is specified as neither the lover nor salvation. Nevertheless, "All" seems to refer to entities as comprehensive as the lover or salvation. In the context of Dickinson's poems it may refer to the lover who *would have* been salvation. As *he* was "missed," or as *it* was "missed," either can only be designated by a superlative and totalizing abstraction. Thus a poem like "The Missing All" exacts a price, specifically the sacrifice of particularity. For the "All" is designated but is deprived of distinct form. It is, oppositely, discrete and distinctive form—the *embodiment* of the "All"—that Fascicle 20 understands as compensation.

In Fascicle 20, remembrance—understood in terms of salvation, and more specifically redefined by a dead lover's being corporealized—is being chosen. The determinacy of this choice is to be distinguished from the situation in Fascicle 16, where the problem of choice is consistently reiterated and as consistently evaded. I shall turn to this second fascicle in a moment, because in counterpoint to Fascicle 20, it illustrates, even emblematizes, what is revealed when choice is not, as here, regarded as a problem of substitution. (To reiterate the argument, the substitution revealed is the body for bodilessness, and her body for his.) Before leaving Fascicle 20, however, I want to make five concluding observations pertinent to the fascicle, and indeed to Dickinson's poetry as a whole.

1. There is a consistency to what this fascicle claims, even among poems not directly related to its theme of the lover's death and his ghostly repossession. Thus, for example, "I think the Hemlock likes to stand" (P 525; figs. 13–14) does not represent death, but does represent solitude; represents, arguably, a condition of nature's "Austerity" similar to that severe deprivation recorded elsewhere in the fascicle as a direct consequence of death. While the source of the strenuous conditions in the poem are unspecified, their consequences are familiar from other

poems in the fascicle. Apparently consoling by the analogy of its endured hardship, the hemlock "satisfies an awe/ That men, must slake in Wilderness—/ [And/Or] in the Desert—cloy—/ An [instinct/hunger] for the [Hoar,/drear—] the Bald—/ Lapland's—nescessity—." Thus in that same bifolium, "To hear an Oriole sing" (P 526; figs. 15–16), espousing an individual criterion for assessing what is being heard, is allied with "The Soul selects her own Society—," for both advocate the individual perspective as interpretively governing, as ultimate: "The Fashion of the Ear/ Attireth that it hear/ In Dun, or fair—." "To put this World down, like a Bundle—" (P 527) does not explicitly connect the sacrifice it records to the rejection of this world in favor of the one now occupied by the lover (as "How sick—to wait—in any place—but thine—" [P 368], for example, does). But there is an implicit connection between the two poems—as well as an explicit connection between "To put this World down, like a Bundle—" and the poems in the same bifolium ("Although I put away his life—" and "Over and over, like a Tune—," discussed earlier). That connection is made in the cool description of the pain occasioned by the sacrifice:

> To put this World down, like a Bundle—
> And walk steady, away,
> Requires Energy—possibly Agony—
> 'Tis the Scarlet way
>
> Trodden with straight renunciation
> By the Son of God—

Finally, "She lay as if at play" (P 369; fig. 27), while about the death of a woman rather than of a man, seems, like the poems that represent or refer to the death of a man, to focus on the absoluteness of the condition from which there is no apparent escape.

In the poems I have discussed, as in those to which I have summarily alluded, there is no escape for the dead person. But, repeatedly, desire provides an escape for the person left alive. Hence the poem that ends the fascicle (P 370; fig. 28), quoted in full below, concludes by respecifying *what* a superlative is by respecifying *where* that superlative is:

> Heaven is so far of the Mind
> That were the Mind dissolved—
> The Site—of it—by Architect
> Could not again be proved—

'Tis vast—as our Capacity—
As fair—as our idea—
To Him of adequate desire
No further 'tis, than Here—

2. "Adequate desire," then, is what the fascicle as a whole consistently represents. But this topic (desire's defining itself as adequate in the face of death) is precisely what is disconcerting about Fascicle 20 in particular and about certain features of Dickinson's poetry in general, which the fascicle exemplifies. "Adequate desire" is a consequence of a disencumbered soul's confronting a palpable body. That a death should precede such a representation of desire seemingly explains one person construed in terms of body and a second person construed in terms of soul. Yet what renders the partialization of body and soul extraordinary—not at all explicable by the circumstances fleshed out in the fascicle—is the fact, repeatedly noted, that the one who is rendered in terms of corporeality is the one who is dead. The speaker, the one alive, is, in these representations, characteristically reduced to impalpability.

3. In the partialization of body and soul represented throughout the fascicle, where the features of body are ascribed to one self while the properties of soul are ascribed to the other, we can see that scarcity or economy *does* punctuate this poetry, though not in the deconstructive terms to which the first chapter refers. In the economy of these representations, the poems divide persons into body and soul, as death presumably does, even as they reverse the conventional way of allocating body and spirit in that division.

Such a reversal crucially addresses a characteristic of Dickinson's poetry that remains as enigmatic as it is uncommented upon. It is a commonplace that Dickinson's speakers are frequently minds, souls, entombed consciousness. Or, as a poem like "A nearness to Tremendousness—" (P 963) claims, they are *un*entombed consciousness, not incorporated at all, but rather defined by "Illocality." Fascicle 20 explains the origin of such isolated and partial entities. For as noted earlier, it is the dead lover who is accorded the body, while the speaker becomes (with reference to "Heaven is so far of the Mind") pure mind and (with reference to "The Soul selects her own Society—") pure soul. In the economy of these divisions sacrifice *is* exacted. But, as the poem at the start of the fascicle tells it, the speaker pays its price: "I took one Draught of Life—/ I'll tell you what I paid—/ Precisely an existence. . . . They . . . handed me my Being's worth—/ A single Dram of Heaven!" Thus the poems economize life since what is paid and its recompense are compared and assessed as unequal. But the poems also economize life because they literally partialize it, according a body to the lover and an immaterial part—a consciousness, a soul, a mind—to the speaker.

4. Although the cost as initially stipulated is blatantly unfair, something is imagined as lavishly compensatory. For if the speaker is all soul, as the lover is all (imagined) body, logic suggests that only in a reunion would the self/selves be whole. This compensation involves something returned, but also something added. For since the body of the lover has been severed from the soul of the speaker—since death has rendered him all body as his death has rendered her all soul—in the reunion of body and soul lies personal wholeness, a wholeness restored *to* the person, made literally inseparable from a union *of* persons. The self cut off from the lover is also the self cut off from the body, from her own body redefined in these poems as indistinguishable from his.

Thus, although the first-person pronoun in the phrase "I've known her" in "The Soul selects her own Society—" suggests a separation between the speaker and the soul that selects, the poem's readers correctly equate the "I" and the "she." The soul, insufficient to represent itself, requires double pronouns. It does so because the soul, for the reasons I have specified, lacks encasement. It has no "outside" or body, hence no manner of socially representing itself. Without autonomy, the disembodied soul must be spoken for.

And this way of understanding loss—and, more to the point, this way of understanding its potential rectification—makes sense, as I think nothing else does, of a defining aspect of Dickinson's poetry: the way in which it repeats—outside of the fascicle context, almost incomprehensibly—the division of body and soul. Similarly it makes sense of Dickinson's numerous self-reflexive poems (poems like "Like Eyes that looked on Wastes—" [P 458] or "I live with Him—I see His face—" [P 463]), which both demand and foil explanation. They seem at once to dramatize as split the self's relation to itself and *simultaneously* to dramatize the inadequate separation between a self and an other. For in these poems a self's relation to itself *is* that self's relation to another, who is logically indistinguishable.

5. Finally, this way of understanding the separation of body and soul (as self-referential *and* as referential to another) would clarify what "The

Soul selects" calls "Society," for from the *self*-division, the division *within* the other, and the division *of* the self from the other, something is produced that is rightly understood as plurality.

To conclude the discussion of Fascicle 20, and its implications for Dickinson's other poems, I quote from a poem (P 458) outside the fascicle, a poem in which the other who is alien is the other who is internalized, and I quote whole this time "The Soul selects her own Society—," in which, oppositely, the soul receives the other as a self-completing entity:

> Like Eyes that looked on Wastes—
> Incredulous of Ought
> But Blank—and steady Wilderness—
> Diversified by Night—
>
> Just Infinites of Nought—
> As far as it could see—
> So looked the face I looked upon—
> So looked itself—on Me—
>
> I offered it no Help—
> Because the Cause was Mine—
> The Misery a Compact
> As hopeless—as divine—
>
> Neither—would be absolved—
> Neither would be a Queen
> Without the Other—Therefore—
> We perish—tho' We reign—

> The Soul selects her own Society—
> Then—shuts the Door—
> To her divine Majority—
> Present no more—
>
> Unmoved—she notes the Chariots—pausing—
> At her low Gate—
> Unmoved—an Emperor be kneeling
> Upon her Mat—

I've known her—from an ample nation—
Choose One—
Then—close the Valves of her attention—
Like Stone—

3. To] On   8] On [her] Rush mat
4. Present] Obtrude   11. Valves] lids—

In the first of these poems, to *see* the self is problematically to be connected to the self as an insufficiently differentiated other. In the second, to see the other, to select the other, is to be closed to all others, but to be completed by the single other as the body completes the soul or as society completes the individual. For the chosen one, the one within—within the door, the valves, the lids, the enclosure—embodies all others so that those outside are others who are gratuitous. (In "lids," the variant to "Valves," that incorporation is represented as manifestly bodily and literal.) Further, in the perspective of exchange regulated by the poem, the Emperor's kneeling alone reveals that those "outside" are made solitary, as the soul, having chosen, is conversely made social.

In Fascicle 20, then, what appears to be rethought is the status of personhood. The lover seems physically whole; the speaker, as in the two poems quoted above, seems partialized. And such a division is made sense of in terms of fantasies of *completion* that first require fantasies of *substitution*. In the fascicle the substitutions that have been made throughout are: the speaker's election for God's; the soul for the body; the self's corporeality for the lover's. The attendant sacrifices notwithstanding, what is represented in this fascicle—as opposed, I shall argue, to Fascicle 16—is the insistence on recompense. For the sequence of choice (election/selection) and then substitution involves giving things up in order to get things back. If to choose means recompense, what does it mean not to choose? The latter question is raised by Fascicle 16. For if in Fascicle 20 what is chosen can in part be described as substitution itself and, however paradoxically, consequent wholeness, Fascicle 16 illustrates what happens when choice is eschewed, when choice *cannot* be chosen.

III. FASCICLE 16: NOT CHOOSING

WHEN THERE IS NO CHOICE, there is no substitution, hence also no wholeness. In such a situation, poems in the fascicle, much like the words recorded in the margins as non-exclusive alternatives, are themselves variants of each other. This is the case because poems in Fascicle 16 reiterate the same terms, thereby suggesting that they are, however loosely or obliquely, bound to each other. But they do not reiterate the same relation to those terms. Therefore, when one reads through the fascicle, it ultimately becomes unclear what those terms are, or how the relation of the poems to one another should in fact be understood. Consider, for example, the first six poems of Fascicle 16. I have already cited the poem that begins the fascicle, "Before I got my eye put out—." In that poem the refusal of a certain kind of vision is made synonymous with the refusal of death. In the poem that directly follows, to the contrary, what is embraced is a vision of death akin to the one decried as dangerous in "Before I got my eye put out—." For in "Of nearness to her sundered Things" (P 607) a speaker predicates too intense a fascination with others who are dead. This fascination confers death on the living by confusing the dead and the living, or rather, by the speaker's exchanging, in her attention, the living for the dead. As a consequence of her intimacy with the latter, they have the vitality of the living and she has the inertness of the dead:

> Of nearness to her sundered Things
> The Soul has special times—
> When Dimness—looks the Oddity—
> Distinctness—easy—seems—
>
> The Shapes we buried, dwell about,
> Familiar, in the Rooms—
> Untarnished by the Sepulchre,
> The Mouldering Playmate comes—

In just the Jacket that he wore—
Long buttoned in the Mold
Since we—old mornings, Children—played—
Divided—by a world—

The Grave yields back her Robberies—
The Years, our pilfered Things—
Bright Knots of Apparitions
Salute us, with their wings—

As we—it were—that perished—
Themself—had just remained till we rejoin them—
And 'twas they, and not ourself
That mourned.

8. The] Our

I have suggested that the poem represents too intense a fascination with the dead. But the poem could equally be described as representing choice—specifically the speaker's preference for the dead over the living, in distinction to the prior poem which declined a comparable choice. Or "Of nearness to her sundered Things" could be described as a poem representing vision, for it deliberates over the question of which are more vivid: the dead or the living. And these three topics—of death, of choice, of vision—as well as the speaker's different relations to these topics are explored throughout the fascicle, as if each of the poems were part of a single entity. Yet confusing such an idea of totality is the fact that vision, choice, death, while implicated in all of the fascicle's poems, have, in any one of them, a different hierarchical relation to each other— the topic of vision, for instance, sometimes predominating over the topic of death, and sometimes vice versa.

Moreover, if the association of the poems, dictated by Dickinson's copying and reiterated by the repetition of certain themes, requires us to read the poems as in some sense continuous, the continuity is also disturbed because we are prohibited from seeing strict allegiances or oppositions between and among the poems' representation of the same issues. For example, "Of nearness to her sundered Things" contradicts the perspective of "Before I got my eye put out—" (the previous poem in the fascicle's first bifolium). It does so because "Of nearness to her sundered Things" chooses sight rather than blindness. Indeed, as if to oppose the choice of vision to that made in the previous poem—made inevitably rather than arduously—we are told "Distinctness—easy—seems—."

Yet if the choice made by the two poems looks neatly antithetical, that antithesis is confounded in the following ways. In "Before I got my eye put out—" vision (and therefore life) is painful because *too* vivid. In "Of nearness to her sundered Things" pain is occasioned by the fact that the speaker's vision of life is *insufficiently* vivid. Thus, although death is avoided in one poem and chosen in another, each poem constructs the factor determining choice—vision—in terms that court comparison even as they refuse it. For terms that seem oppositional in one context (in "Of nearness to her sundered Things" death is chosen; in "Before I got my eye put out—" it is avoided) in another context seem analogous. Specifically, the different choices notwithstanding, both poems equate vision and death. Moreover, while in "Before I got my eye put out—" the speaker chooses not to see, in "Of nearness to her sundered Things" agency is more complex than "choosing" or "choosing not to see" implies. In the latter it is the dead who seem to choose the speaker—"Bright Knots of Apparitions/ Salute us, with their wings—"—rather than the other way around.

In the first of the poems the speaker negates vision, and that negation, it is claimed, wards off death, whereas in the second poem the speaker *does* see, and her assent allies her with the dead. But it allies her with the dead made live, or more alive than the living. (In a similar paradox, discussed earlier in this chapter with respect to "Before I got my eye put out—," while vision is apparently eschewed, its absence is made immaterial, since soul-vision replaces eye-vision, even appearing superior to it.) Thus, repeatedly, poems make ostensibly opposite choices and, just as repeatedly, ostensible oppositions do not work as oppositions. Say (as the poems I have examined may prompt us to assert, even categorically) that death is allied with vision. Death is avoided in the first of the poems and solicited in the second. But the fascicle as a whole advances no summary position about whether death is being warded off or welcomed, even as it keeps producing the expectation of such a conclusion by arranging each poem's restatement of the question as if, in relation to the surrounding poems, that question were, and continued to be, a conflicted one.

The third poem in the fascicle, "Tie the Strings to my Life, My Lord" (P 279), addresses the question of choice—specifying the question of death as if *it* were a question of choice. For the third stanza of this poem represents the ride to death, here called the "ride to the Judgment," in terms of an election:

> But never I mind the [steepest/Bridges]—
> And never I mind the Sea—
> Held fast in Everlasting Race—
> By my own Choice, and Thee—

Why choice should be asserted in the face of death, should continuously be asserted (albeit in different manifestations, since to choose death as the speaker in the previous poem does is not the same as to choose how to figure or characterize death), is a question to which I shall return. Of course to claim death as a choice is to obviate its power, although, even preliminarily, that explanation does not account for the disparate terms in which the poems relate choice and death. In the poem that directly follows, the relation is causal. Death is chosen because it exemplifies truth. But, at the same time, death is said to obliterate vision (at least that of the dying person): "The Eyes glaze once—and that is Death—" (P 241), even as it appears to sharpen and satisfy the vision of the one who *observes* the dying person:

> I like a look of Agony,
> Because I know it's true—
> Men do not sham Convulsion,
> Nor simulate, a Throe—
>
> The Eyes glaze once—and that is Death—
> Impossible to feign
> The Beads upon the Forehead
> By homely Anguish strung.

As the first four poems in Fascicle 16 make clear, then, although death, vision, and choice are somehow associated, the terms of that association change in each of the poems, making it appear that in some poems death is chosen, while in others it is declined. Moreover, in "Before I got my eye put out—," to see is to die. Hence vision is avoided. In "I like a look of Agony," the vision *of* the dead (rather than the vision that the dead have) is the ultimate indication of what cannot be feigned. Hence vision is courted. Both in "I like a look of Agony" and in "Of nearness to her sundered Things," it is the dead who are seen, but in "Of nearness to her sundered Things" seeing the dead allies the speaker *with* the dead, whereas in "I like a look of Agony" she is separated from them. Differently still, in the seventh poem in the fascicle, "How noteless Men, and Pleiads, stand" (P 282), which I shall quote in sequence, death and the dead are what cannot be seen, being categorically described as "O'ertakeless." And these shifting claims, and shifting ways of representing claims, suggest a fundamental ambivalence about whether death is desired and about how choice and vision are implicated in that desire.

The ambivalence I am describing is explicitly taken up by the next— the fifth—poem in the fascicle, P 280:

I felt a Funeral, in my Brain,
And Mourners to and fro
Kept treading—treading—till it seemed
That Sense was breaking through—

And when they all were seated,
A Service, like a Drum—
Kept beating—beating—till I thought
My Mind was going numb—

And then I heard them lift a Box
And creak across my Soul
With those same Boots of Lead, again,
Then Space—began to toll,

As all the Heavens were a Bell,
And Being, but an Ear,
And I, and Silence, some strange Race
Wrecked, solitary, here—

And then a Plank in Reason, broke,
And I dropped down, and down—
And hit a World, at every plunge,
And Finished knowing—then—

19. plunge] Crash—   20. Finished] Got through—

I have written elsewhere of this poem that it represents the making of a thought unconscious (*LT,* pp. 96–98). The poem cannot represent a

As all the Heavens were
a Bell,
And Being, but an Ear;
And I, and Silence, some
strange Race
Wrecked, solitary, here—

And then a Plank in
Reason, broke,
And I dropped down, and
down—
And hit a World, at every
+ plunge,
And +finished knowing— then—
Rash— +Got— through—

FIG. 10.   Fascicle 16, bf2, 2nd verso

literal funeral, since people do not feel funerals, they attend them. They also do not feel funerals in the brain. Moreover, here the funeral seems to precede the death as well as the burial of the thing which is ceremonially presided over. Since what is in the brain that can be buried is a thought, the poem, I have argued, represents ambivalence about making a thought unconscious. Ambivalence is epitomized by the mourners, who could be understood to lament the burial of the thought, although, ultimately, in sitting for the ceremony, they also come to consent to it. Ambivalence is definitely underscored by the second of the variants and the variant grammar it gives the poem's final line (fig. 10, second manuscript page of "I felt a Funeral, in my Brain"). For that variant, written below and to the right of the word on the line, makes it unclear whether knowing is finished (there being no longer any knowing, but only unconsciousness), or whether what is "Got through—" is the experience of unconsciousness, which leaves "knowing" in its wake. In the second way of reading the poem's last line, according not only to its variant but also to its variant grammar, knowing is what *begins* at the poem's end, rather than what concludes. Finally, a third way of reading the variants is to see them in relation: that is, they precisely dramatize the conflict registered throughout the poem, and, as I have tried to illustrate, throughout the earlier poems in the fascicle. As noted, this conflict is registered in miniature by the alternative words—and the alternative punctuation of the same words, as exemplified by the possibly implicit but absent comma of "Finished[,] knowing—then—" and the absent comma of "Finished knowing—then—." Thus the implicit double grammar, raised both by the variant and by a closer scrutiny of the line itself, equivocates whether knowing is *finished,* or whether it *survives* when the experience recorded by the poem is finished.

A related ambiguity is reiterated in the poem's fourth line, where "Sense . . . breaking through—" connotes that sense is either "breaking down" or, idiomatically, "emerging." In the first understanding, sense's breaking through consciousness means the speaker's breaking down because sense falls out or away once it breaks through (not because the verb "breaking" itself necessarily means "collapsing"). And a similar ambiguity is reiterated in the peculiar formulation of the second to last stanza: "I, and Silence, some strange Race." The line raises the question of whether the status of personhood is being conferred upon silence or of whether the speaker, by allying herself with something non-human, inanimate, not even palpable, is herself ceding that status. For the speaker seems to personify silence and identify herself with it. If the conjunction is so construed, she and silence might have equal status, might even be considered to form a "Race." Alternatively, since silence doesn't have the status of a person, the speaker's identification could be regarded as working to cancel the speaker's *own* personhood. In the second way of reading the line, despite the attempt to personify silence, the speaker rather depersonalizes the self to the point of obliteration. Or, finally, like the other two lines that must be read in contradictory ways, this one invites not a double reading but, more specifically, two readings that contend with each other, enacting at the level of the individual line the conflict registered in the poem and, more generally, in the fascicle as a whole.

A refusal to see begins the fascicle; ambivalence about seeing intervenes in "I felt a Funeral, in my Brain"; and, as I shall argue, a refusal to see is repeated in the first part of the fascicle's final poem. But before examining the poems that complete the fascicle, consider the poem that follows "I felt a Funeral, in my Brain," P 281:

> 'Tis so appalling—it exhilirates—
> So over Horror, it half Captivates—
> The Soul stares after it, secure—
> To know the worst, leaves no dread more—
>
> To scan a Ghost, is faint—
> But grappling, conquers it—
> How easy, Torment, now—
> Suspense kept sawing so—
>
> The Truth, is Bald, and Cold—
> But that will hold—
> If any are not sure—
> We show them—prayer—
> But we, who know,
> Stop hoping, now—
>
> Looking at Death, is Dying—
> Just let go the Breath—
> And not the pillow at your Cheek
> So Slumbereth—

Others, Can wrestle—
Your's, is done—
And so of Wo, bleak dreaded—come,
It sets the Fright at liberty—
And Terror's free—
Gay, Ghastly, Holiday!

2. it half Captivates] it   4] A Sepulchre,
   dumb fascinates—   fears frost, no more—

The antecedent for the "it" is not specified at the beginning of the
poem. It is multiply specified within the poem—as "a Ghost," "Torment," "Truth," "Death," and "Wo"—each of these being a metaphor for
states in which extremity is embraced, rather than tentatively courted.
What is distinguished, then, is the relationship between process and its
termination, between dread and the definitive actuality of the dreaded
object, as in "To scan a Ghost, is faint——/ But grappling, conquers it—."
Emphasized throughout is not the *content* of the superlative (which is left
blank), but rather the mastery of the experience through "grappling"
with the superlative; hence the experience's conclusion. For to have
reached the ultimate of an experience is logically to achieve liberation
from further, and more severe, aspects of it. In this context, death epitomizes, metaphorizes, and most precisely *instantiates* the ultimate without (however peculiar this may sound) *particularizing* the ultimate. But if
literal death only epitomizes the state of finality, literal death is not the
subject which the poem represents. It is thus metaphorically that we
must understand "Looking at Death, is Dying—." For if the utmost is
represented as different from anticipation of the utmost, also represented
is the outrageous understanding—outrageous because of the prior discriminations that would seem precisely to have militated against this
conclusion—that to see rather than to anticipate is to be fully enveloped
by the utmost implications of that which is seen. In this poem, then,
death is a vehicle for a statement about vision—about the degrees of
vision, as "scan[ning]," "star[ing]," "Looking" imply. It is also a vehicle
for a statement about the gripping implications of vision, once it is inescapably present. Or it is, to my mind, decidedly such a poem outside of
the fascicle context.

In the fascicle context, the topics of death, vision, choice seem in fact
inseparable, as are, therefore, the poems that connect them. For though

the three topics do not converge in all of the poems, they do so in a sufficient number that they inevitably implicate those other poems that represent one of the three topics in isolation. Thus the inseparability of the topics, and of the questions raised by their entanglement, is contagious. The questions of whether the speaker chooses vision (as "'Tis so appalling—it exhilirates—" and "I like a look of Agony" imply) or refuses vision (as "Before I got my eye put out—" implies); of whether the choice of vision is synonymous with the choice of death (as "Of nearness to her sundered Things" and "I like a look of Agony" imply); of whether vision and death are antithetical (as "How noteless Men, and Pleiads, stand," the poem which follows "'Tis so appalling" in the fascicle, implies); or, finally, of whether death is chosen, but chosen only as a metaphor for the most definitive vision possible (as in "'Tis so appalling—it exhilirates—"), remain ambiguous—an ambiguity itself dramatized by "I felt a Funeral, in my Brain." That ambiguity remains inhospitable to resolution because different poems have different answers to these questions, as well as to the single question—of whether death is chosen—that they collectively propose. But it also remains inhospitable to resolution because in some poems (for example, "'Tis so appalling") vision and death are treated as synonymous whereas in other poems—for example, the next poem in the fascicle, quoted below—they are treated as antagonistic because death is what incapacitates vision. Thus poems are mutually implicated in ways that are at once redundant and contradictory.

In "'Tis so appalling," the act of "Looking at Death, is Dying," but in the following poem death is precisely what looking can't ascertain:

How noteless Men, and Pleiads, stand,
Until a sudden sky
Reveals the fact that One is rapt
Forever from the Eye—

Members of the Invisible,
Existing, while we stare,
In Leagueless Opportunity,
O'ertakeless, as the Air—

Why did'nt we detain Them?
The Heavens with a smile,
Sweep by our disappointed Heads
Without a syllable—

9. detain Them] retain   12] But deign no syllable
them—/ [detain] it

Amid the vertigo created by the back-and-forth claims made by the poems in Fascicle 16, it is unclear how to account for the wild vacillations which the quoted poems represent. Why should vision so acute as to *cause* death, as to be *epitomized* by death, as to *illuminate* the dead, be, in "How noteless Men, and Pleiads, stand," vision alternatively described as presenting an opacity to death, as inadequate to penetrate to the dead? Why should a condition of inevitability turn to a condition of impossibility—a condition stressed, it should be pointed out, by the poem's variants, which emphasize the degrees according to which access is deemed impossible? (Thus "detain Them" is made to negotiate with "retain them—/ it," as the idea of *delaying* their going is converted into the idea of *preventing* their going, an aspiration "disappointed" from the margins as it is "disappointed" in the last stanza. Thus "Without a syllable" is made to contend with "But deign no syllable," so that the efforts at "detaining" the dead are more actively thwarted; the dead, understood as those who do not talk, are converted into the dead understood as those *unwilling* to talk.)

Why should the previous poems in the fascicle seem to ally themselves with either the inevitability or the impossibility of seeing or choosing death? For it seems that the poems examined thus far have either asserted allegiance to the idea that seeing death is inevitable, or to the idea that seeing death is impossible. "I felt a Funeral" would be an exception to such a characterization, since, in the ways described above, it manifests the conflict between "inevitable" and "impossible"—dramatizing, in effect, the inability to choose. The poem that follows in the fascicle (P 242, alluded to earlier) obliquely addresses these questions:

When we stand on the tops of Things—
And like the Trees, look down—
The smoke all cleared away from it—
And Mirrorrs on the scene—

Just laying light—no soul will wink
Except it have the flaw—
The Sound ones, like the Hills—shall stand—
No Lightning, scares away—

The Perfect, nowhere be afraid—
They bear their dauntless Heads,
Where others, dare not go at Noon,
Protected by their deeds—

The Stars dare shine occasionally
Upon a spotted World—
And Suns, go surer, for their Proof,
As if an Axle, held—

7. shall stand] stand up—   11. go at Noon] walk at noon—
8. scares] drives—   16. an Axle, held] A Muscle—
10. dauntless] fearless—   held
     / tranquil—

The poem represents a moment of illumination. But it also represents
the vantage of illumination and, in some respect, the speaker's absorp-
tion of illumination. As the sun reflects the stars, so the speaker seems
to reflect both. To assume such a vantage, the vantage from "the tops of
Things," is to be able to stand light, as "Before I got my eye put out—"
suggests the inability to stand it. (In the poem's second stanza, I suspect
one hears an echo of "allaying" in "laying," which helps to mediate the
difference between the two relations to light.) Moreover, in this poem to
tolerate light and to produce light are connected, first, because "laying
light" seems to come from the self as well as from the mirrors, in that
self and world are, in the concluding stanza, made effectively inseparable. "Suns" (which go surer) are implicitly compared to the speaker
because both "stand on the tops of Things" and differently "look down."
Sun and speaker are more emphatically connected as the variant to the
poem's last line suggests. They are at once held together by the integrity
of the world (as the word "Axle," implying part of a revolving mechanism, indicates) *and* by the integrity of self (as the word "Muscle," implying part of the human anatomy, suggests). There is no more distinction
between self and world in this poem than there is between any other two
incomplete perspectives advanced throughout the poem.

Thus the poem represents the experience of seeing from a totality. Its
first line even comes to seem a metatextual self-naming and perspective
upon the other elements of the fascicle. In fact one way of reading the
poem is as *resolving* the ambiguity of whether death, the lover (in the
fascicle's concluding poem, which I shall cite in a moment), or vision is
being chosen or declined. Vision on the tops of things is vision of a total-

ity which dismisses questions of choice because it implicitly rejects the partiality that would necessitate such a choice. Since choice, by definition, implies separations, if only of perspective, with reference to those separations it could always only occasion ambivalence. On the one hand, then, the poem resolves the conflicts of allegiance in the other poems in the fascicle—and does so because it offers an alternative to the way they partialize the world. On the other hand, as I have observed, it is only a middle poem, asserting its principle of wholeness of perspective not from an end point, not even from a point signalized as central, but only from in between. Yet if the poem is not a real alternative to the divisions represented in and among the fascicle's other poems, nevertheless, because the poem shares certain terms with these poems, and because it also *changes* the common terms, "When we stand on the tops of Things—" could be seen as governing other poems, even from a middle perspective which cannot technically be called central.

Three poems conclude the fascicle: "'Twas just this time, last year, I died" (P 445), in which the speaker imagines how death will affect the living in order to imagine the living from the vantage of her own death; "Afraid! Of whom am I afraid?" (P 608), in which the speaker asserts a superiority over death, life, resurrection successively; and the poem which concludes the fascicle, P 446, quoted again below:

> He showed me Hights I never saw—
> "Would'st Climb"—He said?
> I said, "Not so."
> "With me"—He said—"With me?"
>
> He showed me secrets—Morning's nest—
> The Rope the Nights were put across—
> "And now, Would'st have me for a Guest?"
> I could not find my "Yes"—
>
> And then—He brake His Life—and lo,
> A light for me, did solemn glow—
> The steadier, as my face withdrew
> And could I further "No"?

11. steadier] larger—

In the fascicle's last poem its three topics—death ("And then—He brake His Life"), vision ("and lo,/ A light for me, did solemn glow"), and choice ("I could not find my 'Yes'")—come together. The poem is fascinating for its potential refusal and—in the question with which the poem concludes—its potential negation of the refusal to choose. It is also fascinating because, as indicated earlier, there is another version of the poem, though not within the fascicles. As noted, Dickinson sent the following to her sister-in-law, Susan Dickinson, roughly, it is speculated, at the same time that she copied and bound the previously quoted poem as the last in Fascicle 16:

> I showed her Hights she never saw—
> "Would'st Climb," I said?
> She said—"Not so"—
> "With *me*—" I said—With *me*?
> I showed her Secrets—Morning's Nest—
> The Rope the Nights were put across—
> And *now*—"Would'st have me for a Guest?"
> She could not find her Yes—
> And then, I brake my life—And Lo,
> A Light, for her, did solemn glow,
> The larger, as her face withdrew—
> And *could* she, further, "No"?

The two versions of the poem replicate the stances toward vision adopted in the fascicle as a whole: in the fascicle version and context, the unwillingness to choose vision or light and, in the version sent to Susan Dickinson, the imperative to choose—in this case, to get the *other* to choose. As indicated earlier, in the copy sent to Susan Dickinson the gender is changed, and, as much to the point, so are the positions of lover and speaker, hence of the one who supplicates and of the one who refuses to acquiesce to the supplication. Since the "public" version—the one sent to Susan Dickinson—contains the feminine pronoun, we might suspect that the masculine pronoun, emerging only in the fascicle context, is kept covert. In both versions, to acquiesce to the light represented in the last four lines is to acquiesce to the seduction warded off throughout. Thus what might be concealed in the version sent to Susan Dickinson is that this is a love poem, in which a male lover is refused by the speaker even as he continues to be regarded.

Even outside of the comparative context, "He showed me Hights I never saw—" raises the question of whether seeing (often seeing light in the earlier poems) is connected, by displacement, to the subject of accepting a lover. Since the two topics are inseparable in this poem, they may also, retrospectively, appear connected in previous poems. For here the withdrawal from the light and the withdrawal from the "He" are all but indistinguishable. Since the fascicle's first and last poems represent refusals to see, "He showed me Hights I never saw—" also raises the question of whether the *ultimacy* of refusal structures the fascicle's intermediate ambivalence. Or should we rather emphasize not the ultimacy of negative choice, but the ambivalence that lingers even at the end of the fascicle's last poem? Specifically, the final question, considered rhetorically, suggests the lover might be seen as chosen. Or, as the stress on the question left *unanswered* differently suggests, he might be seen as declined. In these disparate ways the concluding poem in the fascicle reiterates the questions raised by poems throughout the fascicle: about choice differently determined, hence unstably determined, or, to put this in other terms, about choice *multiply* determined. For much like variants to individual lines, as well as variant allegiances within Fascicle 16, the two versions of the poem, and the variant ways of reading its ending, leave us uncertain about how to construe a choice that either cannot be made or that, once made, is made again and made differently.

I want in concluding the discussion of the fascicles read as discrete entities to consider a series of related questions. How is the problem of choice at the level of variants related to the choices left unmade by the poems in Fascicle 16 and related as well, if oppositely, to choices explicitly made in Fascicle 20? To choose—whether in the case of variant words or of variant positions—is to submit to substitution. It is to consent to "this" in lieu of "that." And such a concession produces wholeness, whether with respect to lines or poems construed as non-problematic entities. For the integrity of an entity depends on its single identity, which, once established, resists reversal, complication and change.

In Fascicle 20 we see how thoroughly wholeness is contingent on substitution: of the speaker's choice for God's choice, of the speaker's body for the lover's, of the strains of music for the strains of memory, of the logic of dispossession for the logic of claim ("Mine—[long as/while] Ages steal!"), of the many sacrificed for the one who is chosen ("I've known her—from an ample nation—/ Choose One—/ Then—close the [Valves/lids—] of her attention—/ Like Stone—"). Conversely, in Fascicle 16, because the poems produce non-definitive positions, alternative claims are made to supplant each other. Poems are *variants* that revise, but not consequentially so, what has preceded them. And the effect of the equivocation—of all, even opposites, being entertained—is that we do not know whether something is chosen, or whether it is declined. We do not know the relation of one of the fascicle's topics to another, each visibly yet unclearly implicated in the other. Finally we do not know whether choice itself, as thematized in the poem that concludes Fascicle 16, is declined or ultimately made. For the absence of substitution—in effect the *refusal* of substitution—appears to lead to a commensurate evasion, even withholding, of completion. That is, while the possible refusal to choose between the variant endings does not necessarily imply a critique of wholeness (since the refusal to choose could be seen to make the variant part of the poem), from one vantage it would appear that the pressure to choose and the inability to choose between the variant endings does constitute such a critique—at least a critique of wholeness as contained. Similarly, the poems in Fascicle 16, alternately endorsing disparate, often antithetical positions with respect to the same topic, declare a critique of wholeness and of the integrity of a single perspective. For in Fascicle 16 no perspective is made hierarchically definite, none allowed either to govern or to be discrete.

As a consequence of Dickinson's refusal, in Fascicle 16 the problem of reading becomes the problem of choosing. Since choice is declined in the concluding poem, and differently declined in earlier poems, *made* inconclusive because of their variant reconstructions of subjects, how we construe wholeness is contingent on how we privilege parts as governing wholes. For instance, by light of "When we stand on the tops of Things—," nothing is chosen. But—this is crucial—nothing is chosen because from the vantage of totality, nothing *needs* to be. Perspective is whole, even though that wholeness is manifested through the fragmentation of the poem's variants—the integrity of a world, as figured by the "Suns," complemented by the integrity of the self, as figured by the "Muscle." From the vantage of "He showed me Hights I never saw—," nothing is chosen, despite the fact that the imperative to choose is three times deliberated in the poem's progressive qualifications of ambivalence: "I said, 'Not so.' . . . I could not find my 'Yes'—. . . And could I further 'No'?" The imperative to choose is reiterated even as choice is negated. According to "When we stand on the tops of Things—," choice is unnecessary because nothing requires sacrifice. According to "He showed me Hights I never saw,—" choice is required even as it is also eschewed.

It will have become apparent that I have throughout these pages considered the same examples, but not the same questions with respect to
those examples, the point being to investigate the various levels of
averted choice made apparent by the so-called same poems. At the beginning of the preceding chapter I raised the following question: Did Dickinson not publish because she couldn't do so; because she chose not to; or
because she couldn't choose? That question is pertinent to the ones already considered here. For choosing not to publish (or not being able to
choose *how* to publish); not choosing among variants to words; not choosing among variant, even antithetical, relations established by poems in a
single entity (an entity, like Fascicle 16 or 20, *made* single by the recurrence of certain topics as well as by the physical manifestations of copying
and binding); and, finally, the thematics of choice (choice made in "The
Soul selects her own Society—" and choice refused to be made in "He
showed me Hights") are related issues.

In confronting this array of different choices refused, it seems important to consider what is at issue in choosing and not choosing. Does "not
choosing" cancel power or confer it? It might be said that choosing and
not choosing afford different kinds of power. For instance, as a consequence of choosing, entities become discrete. They are so, I have argued,
by virtue of substitution—whether the substitution manifests itself at
the level of the individual word or at the entirely different level of the
speaker's body for the lover's body. Substitution empowers because, by
means of it, identity is made absolute—although, in the case of the
partialization of body and soul, where the substitution seems initially to
fragment, completion is presumptive, even if only anticipatory. Yet if
wholeness is speculative, if waiting is required to make the speculative
concrete, waiting is also compensatory, since deferring completion aug-
ments the idea of what completion might be. For the wholeness guaranteed rests not simply upon the return of the ceded bodily part (to be
exact, upon the return to the speaker of her body), but also upon the
return of the ceded part of the identity—the lover reconceived as integral
to the speaker. The wholeness guaranteed depends upon construing the
other and the self as one entity. Choosing, then, empowers by establishing or demarcating identity—and, not incidentally, by supplementing
the sense of what such an identity might be. But *not* choosing empowers
in an entirely different way. For if everything is inconclusive, if nothing
is absolute, then, also, nothing is excluded. Thus choosing and not
choosing suppose different understandings of totality: one predicated on

substitution and discrete identity, the other predicated on identity that is inclusive, even illusorily infinite—a conclusion pertinent to a possible way of understanding the advantages implicit in Dickinson's not publishing.

Choosing and not choosing, with respect to the lover ("I've known her—from an ample nation—/ Choose One—"; "And could I further 'No'?")—as well as the different forms of power attendant on choosing and not choosing—are properly understood in the context of related problems of equivocation raised by Dickinson's poetry. First, in this poetry it is often unclear whether a subject—specifically, death—is to be understood metaphorically or literally. Thus, for instance, in "I like a look of Agony" and in "'Tis so appalling," death's finality is a metaphor for the definitive and for the absolute, respectively. But as one poem elaborates on the details of physical death ("The Eyes glaze once—and that is Death—"), and as the other, it seems gratuitously, investigates the consequences of death ("Looking at Death, is Dying—/ Just let go the Breath—/ And not the pillow at your Cheek/ So Slumbereth—"), we are left with an indisputable double sense. Death is being made metaphoric in these poems, and as any such vehicle, it is subordinate to some other primary topic which it is enlisted to express. But death itself is *also* represented. Thus we remain in no doubt that in each of these poems *other* topics—"Truth," the utmost, making something unconscious (in "I felt a Funeral, in my Brain")—are, respectively, *primarily* rendered. But that primacy is not consonant with the vitality of the vehicle, depicted so "literally" in its own right that at some second level it remains unclear why the tenor of the metaphor is nevertheless strongly invested with an autonomous palpability. For in these poems death is employed as a metaphor, *chosen* as one, without maintaining the subordination that a metaphor would have. In this respect, the question of whether the poetic discourse is "literal" or "metaphoric" is comparable to that raised by the variants. For something is chosen, and like the word set resolutely on the line in the poem—set on the line, but supplemented by the word(s) in the margins or at the poem's end—the "choice" isn't a choice (in the case of the variants) or the choice hasn't the implications of one (in the case of literal or metaphorical status).

An analogous equivocation is whether the death written of—inscribed and reinscribed in many of Dickinson's poems—is that of the speaker or of a lover. In certain poems an answer is decisive: "Because that you are going" (P 1260) clearly represents the speaker's response to the death of another, as "Going to Heaven!" (P 79) clearly represents a speaker's imagined response to her own death. In other poems, whose death is being represented is less easy to determine, as exemplified by "Because I could not stop for Death—" (P 712). Almost every analysis of this poem assumes what it must account for is the speech of a person presumed to be dead. When the poem is read in the fascicle context, it seems as likely that the speaker is accompanied by consciousness of a death that is not in fact her own. Yet as with the metaphoric or literal status of death, whether a lover's death or a speaker's own death is being represented by these poems is chosen between without consequence— and so is not really or fully chosen. Whose death is depicted cannot easily be settled, because the speaker and the lover—like the lover's body and the speaker's soul—have repeatedly been represented as inseparable.

If words are chosen that are not ultimately chosen (as in the case of the variants); if the question "Is death literal or metaphoric?" is a question that is answered without consequence; if the attempt to determine whether the death represented is the speaker's or the lover's cannot in fact succeed because the *initial* answer to the question is always, by definition, implicated in the *ultimate* answer to that question, indeed, is implicated because the literal death of the lover's body requires the speaker to relinquish *her* body in the temporary exchange discussed earlier—then these multiple refusals of choice explain the prevalence of paradox and antithesis at a deeper level in Dickinson's poetry. They explain that the kind of paradox or antithesis which initially seems to define the poetry is superficial, since more fundamentally at issue are questions of choice. Finally the multiple refusals of choice indicate why readings that cast the conjunctions and divisions we have seen throughout the fascicle in the narrative terms of a love affair or a marriage seem explanatorily deficient, as do readings that oppositely make conjunctions and divisions wholly identic, psychological or self-referential. For identity as deployed in these poems, and in the fascicles that organize them, is neither wholly relational nor wholly self-referential—thereby precluding the exclusivity of either of these interpretations. Thus if subjects, conventionally understood, are redefined in Dickinson's poetry, so too—in the last of these evaded choices—is subjectivity.

4

THE INTERIOR REVISION

I WANT, IN CONCLUDING, to consider the implications of the characteristics of Dickinson's fascicles—specifically to consider the implications of "not choosing" as they emerge through the continuously renegotiated connections of part to whole. I have examined this problem as it is differently raised by the relation between variant and poem, between one poem and another, and among poems in a single fascicle. I shall conclude by explaining how the relations between part and whole are also economized in Dickinson's poems read as individual lyrics. For, as one would expect, the fascicles teach us the comprehensive terms by which to read Dickinson's poems taken singly. Before proceeding, however, I reiterate the argument of the examination in the previous pages, as well as the questions raised by that argument.

In chapter 1, I claimed that with respect to the variants, and to poems in the fascicles, Dickinson economizes meaning. She regulates the relation between part and whole so that the question What is a subject? becomes What are its parameters? including What are its textual parameters? This is really a question of the in(ter)determinacy of meaning, whether with respect to the relation *among* poems in a fascicle or with respect to variants *in* poems. Meaning in Dickinson's poems is thus understood as relational. Moreover, it is produced by relations that evolve and shift. Given this interdeterminacy, Dickinson's texts reveal a poetry of excess rather than a poetry of leanness.

In chapter 2, I examined the specific ways in which the variants raise the question, What is the relation between part and whole? It will be remembered that, with respect to the variants in "I gave myself to Him—," the part *reiterates* the whole. With respect to the variants in "If I may have it, when it's dead," the part *contests* the whole. With respect to the specific variant considered in "One need not be a Chamber—to be Haunted—" and "Dare you see a soul at the 'White Heat'?" part and whole are made *commensurate*, because if the variant to one poem returns as the submerged line of another, "part" and "whole" are inadequate designations, since these terms suggest inequality. Yet inequality is belied by a conjunction which implicitly *equates* the variant from one poem and the line from another, for, as in this example, the position occupied by the part makes it into a whole. Oppositely, in the separate poems that represent variant visions, "Of Bronze—and Blaze—" and "There's a certain Slant of light," wholes are made into parts between which, it appears, we must choose.

In fact, to recapitulate my argument, the variants reiterate the question, What is a subject, and how is it bounded? Each reiterates the question in slightly different terms. For instance, if there are parts, what is their relation? The relation may be conjunctive and continuous and even, we could say, additive, as in the "'White Heat'" and "Haunted Chamber" poems. It may be reiterative, as in the case of the conflict in the margins that repeats a conflict in the center of a poem—in effect, bringing together margin and center. It may be contestatory in that the variants make questionable what the poem "proper" attested to as certain. Or it may be genuinely substitutive, as the two versions of "I showed her Hights"/"He showed me Hights" would imply if they were in the same fascicle. In other words, as these differences suggest, it is unclear in what cases, and in what ways, we are meant to read ostensible substitutions as genuinely substitutive. The variants raise the question of how a subject is bounded. But they do so by predicating problems of boundary as specifically problems of choice. Thus we find ourselves asking whether the variants *to* poems and the poems which work like variants of each other suggest that something is being chosen or that choice is being declined.

A similar question was raised with respect to the proximities considered earlier, for example, between the poems "I read my sentence—steadily—" and "If I may have it, when it's dead," which precedes it on the fascicle page. Such proximity, in which *his* death becomes *her* sentence, can be seen to explain the multiple pronouns in "I read my sentence—steadily—"; oppositely, it can be seen to reiterate questions about the multiple pronouns. Proximities also exist between the poem "I had been hungry, all the Years—," which ends one fascicle, and the poem "Before I got my eye put out—," which begins the fascicle that presumably follows. For these two poems predicate alternative economies, as never having had is an alternative economy to having had too much. Proximities exist between (again, presumably) successive Fascicles 13 and 14, the first of which suggests that loss can be naturalized and the second of which suggests that it cannot be. Proximities, then, raise the question of how disparate entities are to be read—as *continuous* (the death in one poem explaining the multiple pronouns in the other); as *corrective* (the vision of surfeit subsuming that of deficit); or as not at all substitutive but rather *simultaneous,* since loss seen as naturalized and loss seen as personalized complement each other. So with respect to these progressively larger forms of proximity the question raised, as with the variants, is: Is something being chosen, or is choice being declined?

In chapter 3, I examined poems which are not proximate on the manuscript page but which in their respective fascicles are best comprehended as variants of each other. Thus in Fascicle 15 an experience thought to be over—to be proximate, rather than present—is not in fact over. In Fascicle 14, conversely, what ties poems together are their variant understandings of how to coerce the alien back into proximity. In this respect, a specific variant discussed earlier, "maddest/nearest," is a governing variant since in terms of linguistic and other forms of displacement it is the site of transition where (often through substitution) the alien is turned back into the proximate. Thus in Fascicle 14 proximity is adjusted, manipulated, transferred, arranged. In fact, the respective fascicles economize or regulate relations in opposite ways. There is the economy of repetition in Fascicle 15, and the economy of exchange in Fascicle 14, in which what is far is made near. The problem of choice is also implicated in these representations, since in Fascicle 15 repetition involves the absence of choice, indeed, in these poems, the impossibility of choice. The terrible experience cannot be escaped; whereas, when the experience *itself* escapes—as it does in the poems that make up Fascicle 14—retrieving it requires regulating the relation between the proximate and the alien. It requires choosing the alien as if it were the proximate, as the poems in this fascicle do.

In the latter part of chapter 3 I examined two fascicles as totalities— read as differently addressing the problem of choice as well as differently thematizing it. In Fascicle 20 the problem of choice is represented as specifically a problem of substitution: the speaker is characteristically construed in terms of soul, so that the dead lover can be construed in terms of a still palpable body. Such an economy of partialization is understood, however ultimately, to make for completion. What is rethought in Fascicle 20, then, is the status of personhood. Choice (of his body for her soul) initially involves radical substitution. But ultimately it involves radical recompense. Conversely, in Fascicle 16 no choice is made; no relations are advanced with substitutive stability, even as expectations of choosing continue, poem by poem, to be perpetuated. Moreover, "not choosing" in this fascicle is understood in different ways. From the vantage of a middle poem, "When we stand on the tops of Things—," choice is unnecessary, but from the vantage of the final poem in the fascicle, choice is, rather, impossible: "And could I further 'No'?"

I have enumerated some of the questions raised by the poems when read in the fascicles: the kinds of power that inhere, differently, in choosing and not choosing; the way in which not choosing involves a redefinition of subjectivity, as well as a redefinition of the boundaries of the poetic subject; the terms in which reading Dickinson becomes a question of choosing how Dickinson should be read. I have also considered the way in which choice is implicated in the related questions of whether death is literal or metaphoric, of *whose* death is being represented, and of whether division and conjunction can best be explained by the formal properties of narrative or of variant. To these considerations I would again add that there are two kinds of totality presumed by choosing and by not choosing. In the case of *choosing,* as in Fascicle 20, the part anticipates the whole: the integrity of body and soul and of two selves which will become one. In the case of *not choosing,* the part *is* the whole, or is made inseparable from the whole, or comes to subsume the whole. For in Fascicle 16 there is no clear way of isolating parts from wholes.

Dickinson's lyrics—poems read individually, to which I now turn—illustrate the way in which not choosing governs the relation between part and whole in terms criticism has not yet, without benefit of the fascicles, fully considered. For if lyrics are parts of wholes (the fascicles), the latter teach us that the relation between part and whole is mobile. Having read the whole, we are in a position to read even the part as a whole, since no boundedness guarantees that closure which would seal in or out—or in any other way make inevitable—the identity of a given utterance. Moreover, by reading the poems in the fascicles we are able to recognize the real issue of the poems read as lyrics. In individual lyrics as in fascicle texts, choices appear to be made that are not being made—a phenomenon that could be understood as a theme. Yet it is more than this. For positional complexity—in which "this" seems to exclude "that," but is in fact integral to it—is enacted in these poems, as it is enacted in the fascicles, although, as noted above, not necessarily recognized as such before a reading of the latter.

In the three poems I shall discuss below, boundaries are suggested in relation to positions that are not real boundaries. What is visible "in" the three poems that is also visible "in" the fascicles is an identity of positions initially thought both discrete and opposed. If what is re-delimited in the fascicles are the boundaries of a text, as this issue is inseparable from a question about the boundaries of a subject, in the poems discussed below boundaries around subjects are similarly made questionable. For while the fascicles raise questions about boundaries with respect to the deliberated limits of subjects and texts, the texts of lyrics no less than those of fascicles call into question whether a reader is confronted with a part or a whole and, as much to the point, with how a whole is defined. The three poems examined below begin, it should be noted, with three parallel negations, "I cannot"/"I would not"/"I cannot," which they continue to reiterate. These poems participate in negative choices that result in the apparent negation of choice. For in all three poems what is emphasized is the inability to choose what the speaker presumably desires to choose. Notwithstanding the proclaimed inability to choose, we shall see what such declarations of disablement have it in their power to accomplish:

> The Tint I cannot take—is best—
> The Color too remote
> That I could show it in Bazaar—
> A Guinea at a sight—
>
> The fine—impalpable Array—
> That swaggers on the eye
> Like Cleopatra's Company—
> Repeated—in the sky—
>
> The Moments of Dominion
> That happen on the Soul
> And leave it with a Discontent
> Too exquisite—to tell—
>
> The eager look—on Landscapes—
> As if they just repressed
> Some Secret—that was pushing
> Like Chariots—in the Vest—
>
> The Pleading of the Summer—
> That other Prank—of Snow—
> That Cushions Mystery with Tulle,
> For fear the Squirrels—know.

Their Graspless manners—mock us—
Until the Cheated Eye
Shuts arrogantly—in the Grave—
Another way—to see—

16] [Like] Columns—in the   19] [That] covers mystery with
Breast—   Blonde—

In "The Tint I cannot take" (P 627) (cannot take in or absorb, as in "am not permitted to," but also, secondarily, cannot tolerate, as in "am not able to"), something said not to be had is in fact had. In the disparate tropes of the four middle stanzas it is extravagantly enumerated as had, and is moreover implicitly explained in terms of the phenomenology that facilitates possession. In effect, *moments* have dominion. Even moments that disappear do. For the thing that cannot be had is not so much a vision—which is adequately recorded in five stanzas of the poem—as the duration and consequent palpability of vision. So this thing that cannot be had because it is superficial (happening *on* the soul rather than *in* it), fleeting, mysterious, concealed, and, in the word of the last stanza, asserted therefore to be "Graspless," has, with reference to the plenitude displayed ostentatiously in each stanza, nevertheless been grasped. The variant to line 16 reiterates the question of where the secret is located (at what level of internality), and the variants read in relation to each other raise the question of whether the pressure of the secret's revelation is fixed, as "Columns" implies, or mobile, as "Chariots—in the Vest—" implies. In fact, the variants of line 16, read in relation, inaugurate a movement from the fixed to the mobile as well as from the internal to the external. For a "Secret . . . pushing/ Like Chariots—in the Vest—" is one that moves outward, emerging triumphantly. Thus the variants repeat the dialectic between depth and surface articulated in the poem as a whole. And, more to the point, they also privilege the surface to the extent that the variant associated with force as well as with exteriority is made central rather than marginal. It could further be said that "Chariots—in the Vest—" are associated with power *because* they are associated with the mobility and externality ostensibly contested.

The eye is said to be "Cheated," then, but seen *not* to be. It is seen not to be because "Another way—to see," alluded to in the last stanza, is not only prospective (something that will ultimately, after death, be possible), but also belongs to the present tense. So, if two states are claimed, those of seeing and not seeing, *not* seeing, as recorded in the poem, has the *status* of seeing. Indeed, it has the status of seeing *better*. For not seeing, or seeing otherwise, seeing fleetingly or partially, has the apparent range and adequacy that a totality would have. Given the dominance of *what* is seen ("The fine—impalpable Array—/ That swaggers on the eye"), the distinction between the seeing in the poem and the seeing anticipated in the last stanza becomes immaterial. For the putative inadequacy of the speaker's vision is canceled by the imperialism of its effects. As the word "swaggers" (which characterizes the way of seeing as well as the transit and style of the object seen) inevitably implies, the vision in the poem has an "arrogan[ce]" of its own.

The way of seeing exemplified by the poem (claimed to be inadequate, predictive rather than present, indistinct and ineffable) is, then, in five distinct instances comprehensively enumerated. Vision may be in moments, rather than in, say, periods of time. It may be of surfaces rather than of depths. But surfaces become depths as they are internalized in the vision of this poem. They are not remote at all but rather perfectly absorbed or "grasped." In effect, those moments—partialities and piecemeal visions—take dominion everywhere. They show where dominion is, and even *what* dominion is, so that the way of seeing said to be coveted, the way deemed inaccessible, is also, implicitly, the way demonstrated to be unnecessary. For the very superficiality of the sights (on the eye, on the soul), lamented as inadequate, rather sharpens vision, makes it even excessive. It spills out of the eye, into the splendors represented by the vision said not to be seen, known, told, kept. Thus the "Tint I cannot take" *is* "best" because dominion is redefined as residing only in the momentary—in the particular piecemeal moments reiterated in this poem as both comprehensive and unforgettable. Other poems in Fascicle 32, in which "The Tint I cannot take" is copied, not incidentally also represent vision, specifically also represent *double* visions. See, for example, "Like Eyes that looked on Wastes—" (P 458); "A Wife—at Daybreak—I shall be—" (P 461); "I live with Him—I see His face—" (P 463). And it should be noted about these double visions that the one claimed to be insufficient—even non-existent in the sense of only projected, recollected or imagined—is, in these other poems as well, shown to be superior. Consider, for example, the conclusion of "A Wife—at Daybreak—I shall be—," where the speaker encountering God discredits what she sees, or demotes it to the secondary: "Master—I've seen the Face—before—." (In another manuscript the first word of this final line is, more pointedly, "Savior" rather than "Master.") Thus double visions, or other ways to see, are repeatedly *better* ways to see. In "The Tint I cannot take—is best—," "Moments of Dominion . . . happen on the Soul" because dominion happens in moments—in moments and on surfaces and not in duration and depth.

Consider, now, P 505, the justly celebrated poem that follows:

I would not paint—a picture—
I'd rather be the One
It's bright impossibility
To dwell—delicious—on—
And wonder how the fingers feel
Whose rare—celestial—stir—
Evokes so sweet a Torment—
Such sumptuous—Despair—

I would not talk, like Cornets—
I'd rather be the One
Raised softly to the Ceilings—
And out, and easy on—
Through Villages of Ether—
Myself endued Balloon
By but a lip of Metal—
The pier to my Pontoon—

Nor would I be a Poet—
It's finer—own the Ear—
Enamored—impotent—content—
The License to revere,
A privilege so awful
What would the Dower be,
Had I the Art to stun myself
With Bolts of Melody!

3. bright] fair
7. Evokes] provokes
11. the Ceilings] Horizons
12. out] by—

14. endued] upheld/upborne
    /sustained
21. privilege] luxury

Again, something said not to be desired—actively to paint, play, write—said even to be declined, is not declined. It is rather possessed. For the speaker experiences the feelings that accompany creation, ostensibly refused, because she is the source of the power she says she desires to be affected by. Thus in the first stanza to "wonder how the fingers feel" is not to be at a loss for words. It is rather to know that "rare—celestial—stir" and to recollect, as well, the affect that accompanies the labor of creation. Thus the experience wondered about has the textural detail and extravagance of an experience that does not need to be wondered about; albeit disclaimed, it has nonetheless been had.

In the second stanza, the speaker does not play, but rather listens to the music. But she is a listener who is moved, as if she *were* the music, to a place where the music is. And in describing herself as being where the music is, becoming in effect indistinguishable from the music, she produces an impression of her own relation to the music that is essentially equivalent to producing the music (hence, her intimate knowledge of the instrument, the "lip of Metal," from which it issues). In the third stanza, the speaker is ostensibly the ear, rather than a writer of the words received by the ear. But she is an ear that reflects the power of the words which are produced, as if the ear at once received and "revere[d]" the words the self simultaneously produces. Thus the claimed incapacity reveals capacity. It reveals the capacity it in fact produces. Most relevantly, in all these instances, what is being occupied is not one position rather than another. And what is being made is not the "choice" that the poem's overt logic of dichotomy advances. Instead, a single position, assumed here to be partial, in fact generates a newly defined totality. "Despair" can be said to be "sumptuous," then, because it is precisely not experienced but rather created. Or it is experienced only after and as a consequence of its creation. Hence its sweetness arises from viewing it, not from feeling it. Specifically, its sweetness arises from viewing it with the detachment of the one who has created it rather than merely observed it. Or, say, despair is being surreptitiously experienced from the vantage of the one who produces it, but who claims not to produce it, and who is hence surprised by the production—you could even say stunned.

Again, something is said to be declined—the power to create—which is not declined. Something is said to be dichotomized and chosen between which is not chosen between. The part or position said to be chosen—of witnessing (of looking, listening, hearing) rather than creating—subsumes the whole or is shown to be equivalent to it. The suppositional is shown to be actual. "Had I the Art" becomes *having* the art.

And this explains the relations within the series "Enamored—impotent—content." For the passive or "impotent" infatuation turns into "content," as it turns into power. The consequences, not warded off at all, are rather experienced as explosive as the speaker becomes, ostensibly unwittingly, the experiencer of the "Bolts" which she has herself created. Or, rather, power occurs at the precise moment the speaker is struck by the inseparability of the two roles. Thus, although the experience is repeatedly defined as partial (the one who witnesses versus the one who creates), and although the speaker claims to ally herself with the part or position of impotence, this position so completely imagines the creation it eschews that it encroaches upon that creation. For the possible relations to the experience, as understood throughout the poem (of the one who creates and the one who attends), are redefined by the poem's conclusion. Retrospectively, it becomes clear they have also been redefined throughout. Thus the one who attends or responds *becomes* the one who *has* created; the sum, in this case, is produced by one of the parts, which remains "more" than it. In this case, too, then, "choosing not" to be the "one who" means the ability to redefine how position itself is chosen, and how it is in effect expanded so that attending *is* creating, which is then attended to.

In fact, since the speaker is consistently seen to occupy the positions of the one who creates *and* of the one who attends, "choosing not" to create is in this poem the precise strategy for not choosing at all. Like "I would not paint—a picture—," the other poems copied in Fascicle 17 similarly represent experiences in excess of the speaker's avowed ability to designate *what* is experienced. The poems in the fascicle represent positions which they do not acknowledge, or which they acknowledge only at the poem's end, usually inadvertently or negatively. "It was not Death, for I stood up" (P 510) is another poem which works its way into positional complexity specifically by negation (see *LT,* pp. 48–53). In "The Soul has Bandaged moments—" (P 512), a dichotomy, analogous to that of witnessing and creating—in this case a dichotomy between "Bandaged moments" and "moments of Escape"—is similarly represented. For such moments are not seen as associated until the poem's end, when, having spoken of what is "Bandaged" or restrained and of what is "Escape[d]" or liberated as implicitly opposite, the speaker acknowledges the two experiences as related in a summary claim: "These, are not brayed of Tongue—." In "I felt my life with both my hands" (P 351), "Being" is said to require being "turned . . . round" in order for the speaker to recognize where she is. Thus the poems in the fascicle are poems that redefine position. They do so even while claiming—in fact specifically *by* claiming—to be disabled from knowing or saying what that position is. In "I would not paint—," not knowing a position is related to disavowing it. But not knowing and disavowing are the specific conditions that facilitate a position's being enlarged so that it can then be occupied.

Consider now another poem, P 640, that begins "I cannot":

I cannot live with You—
It would be Life—
And Life is over there—
Behind the Shelf

The Sexton keeps the Key to—
Putting up
Our Life—His Porcelain—
Like a Cup—

Discarded of the Housewife—
Quaint—or Broke—
A newer Sevres pleases—
Old Ones crack—

I could not die—with You—
For One must wait
To shut the Other's Gaze down—
You—could not—

And I—Could I stand by
And see You—freeze—
Without my Right of Frost—
Death's privilege?

Nor could I rise—with You—
Because Your Face
Would put out Jesus'—
That New Grace

Glow plain—and foreign
On my homesick Eye—
Except that You than He
Shone closer by—

They'd judge Us—How—
For You—served Heaven—You know,
Or sought to—
I could not—

Because You saturated Sight—
And I had no more Eyes
For sordid excellence
As Paradise

And were You lost, I would be—
Though My Name
Rang loudest
On the Heavenly fame—

And were You—saved—
And I—condemned to be
Where You were not—
That self—were Hell to Me—

So We must meet apart—
You there—I—here—
With just the Door ajar
That Oceans are—and Prayer—
And that White Sustenance—
Despair—

35. excellence] consequence   49. Sustenance] exercise—
                                          /privilege—

The poem overwhelms with its multiple manifestations of distance:
"Life is over there—/Behind the Shelf . . . One must wait/ To shut the
Other's Gaze down—/ You—could not—." Even in supposition what is
predicated is distance. The only subjunctive apparently susceptible of
being imagined is a condition of (more) distance: "And were You—
saved—/ And I—condemned to be/ Where You were not—/ That self—
were Hell to Me—." Yet if distance, everywhere present, makes it
imperative to "choose" to renounce the lover, it is repeatedly shown as
possible to regulate. In fact, regulating the distance also regulates the
choice; renunciation as represented here demonstrates why the lover that
must be given up cannot be given up, and why, though his renunciation
is asserted, he is not in fact given up. For "meet[ing] apart" is nonethe-

less meeting. It could even be argued that meeting apart—"You there—
I—here"—is a condition which enables the renegotiation of distance and
effectively does away with it.

The last stanza illustrates. For it shows *what* distance is, by clarifying
how much distance there is. Specifically, it does this by indicating how
distance is variously measured, and, hence, how it is discrepantly understood. For instance, as signified by "the Door ajar": distance is not very
much. As signified by "Oceans": it is much, an immensity. As signified
by "Prayer": it is not very much. As signified by "that White Sustenance"
(which—in its proximity to "Prayer," in its connotation of something
partaken, in its slant echo of "That Whiter Host," finally in its demon-
stratively symbolic and hence synecdochic status—I take as the communion wafer in which Christ's body is literally incorporated): it is nothing at all. As signified by "that White Sustenance" understood as despair:
distance is everything. But the choices "nothing/everything" which occupy structurally opposite positions are demonstrated to be equivalent,
and the vacillations between one trope, which designates the *absence* of
distance, and another, which demonstrates the *enormousness* of distance,
are advanced with such rapidity that the distinctions in meaning disappear. Thus the emphasis does not fall on nothing. Or it falls on how
nothing becomes everything, even as part becomes the totality—the
communion wafer being the part that both represents and *is* the bodily
whole. So, again, something said to be declined or not chosen—proximity to the lover—is shown not to be declined. For the "White Sustenance," the very trope that designates despair over the loss of the lover's
body, is also the trope that asserts the *incorporation* of the body said to be
given up. And this would be the case even if one did not read "that
White Sustenance" as the communion wafer (as the variants might dis-
courage us from doing), since throughout the poem in general, as well as
in the vacillations of the last stanza in particular, renunciation is consistently the strategy for retaining the one who is renounced.

Consider the ninth stanza with its barely concealed sexual metaphor.
What happens to the eyes in that stanza is inevitably comprehensible in
terms of what happens to the body in its entirety: "Because You saturated
Sight—/ And I had no more Eyes/ For sordid excellence/ As Paradise. . . ." "Saturated," in this context, is a word which does double
service, precisely because it reiterates that the eyes can be filled and sa-
tiated, even as the scopic image only half displaces a second bodily context for penetration and surfeit. In these lines, then, the sexual means of

incorporation complement the religious means of incorporation (transubstantiation), almost, it would seem, rendering the latter gratuitous. Except one could say that it is the heresy of the poem, or perhaps its point, to equate an image for transubstantiation with an image for sexual intercourse, redefining, as it were, how the speaker's encounter with the lover is conceived. Thus although a negative choice is ostensibly made (the speaker appears to choose not the lover but God in the lover's stead), choosing not to be with the lover turns into not choosing at all. Choosing not to be with the lover (choosing to leave him) turns into choosing the terms on which to meet him. And the terms on which to meet him depend on equating him with the God for whom he has ostensibly been renounced. They depend on *not* making the very choice between the lover and God that the poem presumably laments. For if, as the poem's middle stanza suggests, God is less than the lover, according to the last stanza the lover gains proximity, even access, to the speaker, specifically as God does.

It may seem, then, that the three poems considered—"I would not paint—a picture—," "The Tint I cannot take—is best—," and "I cannot live with You—"—exemplify negative choices. In fact, in all three instances no choice is being made. Although one poem calls for "Another way—to see," it also dismisses the idea of "Another way" as necessary. Vision, as represented in the poem, is not only adequate but superfluously acute. The lover is not being declined. Rather choice is being declined. And "I would not paint—a picture—" is a poem that specifically redefines choosing negatively as not having to choose at all, since it is by choosing negatively that the speaker sees that no choice is required. Thus positions said to be rejected are not rejected. Parts are juxtaposed to wholes as if they were equivalent to wholes; moments of dominion are juxtaposed to presumptive moments of duration, witnessing to creating, the white sustenance of the communion wafer to the immanence it signifies. And these parts are then made not alternative to, but rather subsumptive of, the wholes. At the beginning of the discussion of Dickinson's fascicles I suggested that, with respect to the particular situation of publishing—a situation whose conditions or explanatory possibilities are, as we have seen, applicable to other aspects of the poetry—"she wasn't able to or couldn't," "she chose not to," "she couldn't choose," were different descriptive options. But with respect to these three poems, "couldn't" (as in "The Tint I cannot take—is best—"), "chose not to" (as in "I would not paint—a picture—"), and "couldn't choose" (as in "I cannot live with You—") are in fact the same option. For they are all strategies for arriving at the single position that dismisses choosing as necessary.

This, in effect, is what looking at the three lyrics teaches us, although, as I have argued, without the prior lesson of the fascicles we would not necessarily see the lyrics as governed by "not choosing" as a specific form of enablement. It may in fact no longer be possible to read the lyrics as distinct from questions about choice in which the fascicles embroil them. Such a statement returns us to a somewhat different question about the relation between lyric and fascicle texts, a relation that we are now in a position fully to comprehend. Finally, to see the necessity for choice in these lyrics as a necessity that is thematically subverted enables us to ask about "not choosing" in the broadest terms supplied by alternative ways of reading lyric and fascicle texts. In the broadest context of the textual issues, then, when Dickinson chooses not to choose, what does she choose not to choose between?

She is not problematizing identity with respect to reading one of her poems next to a poem of Whitman's or Yeats's. The point of my argument has not been to make the trivially true but irrelevant claim that the meaning of poems alters when they are placed next to poems by other poets. Nor has it been to suggest indiscriminate boundarilessness, where everything belongs to everything else, or where relations between poetic entities are limitless.

And Dickinson is also not problematizing identity with respect to reading one of her own poems next to any other of her own poems, although there might be reason to embark on such an intertextual reading.[1] What Dickinson *does* problematize are the following two things:

---

1. There are certainly reasons—biographical, thematic, structural—why one might wish to read Dickinson's poems intertextually. For instance, to read "I showed her Hights she never saw—" in relation to "He showed me Hights I never saw—," raises questions, as indicated earlier, about whether the "he" is a cover for the "she" in the poem sent to Susan Dickinson, or whether the "she" in the poem sent to Susan Dickinson is rather a cover for the fact that this is a love poem. Such juxtapositions of related poems raise biographical questions from one perspective, and questions about gender from another. For instance, to juxtapose "There's a certain Slant of light" to "A Light exists in Spring" (P 812) is to ask how Dickinson differently represents the evasiveness of a natural phenomenon when it cannot be apprehended. This is a thematic question. To read "An altered look about the hills—" (P 140), written in 1859, against "Further in Summer than the Birds" (P 1068), written in

first, within the fascicles, what it means to determine the identity of a poem, given the impossibility of choosing between its variants, whether variants are alternative words or alternative poems. What is not chosen here, as I have demonstrated, is x as opposed to y or y as opposed to x, rather than y or x as opposed to anything else. Second, Dickinson problematizes what it means to read a poem in a fascicle—in its place within a fascicle—as opposed to what it means to read the same poem unfascicled. In other words, what Dickinson chooses not to choose between is whether to read a given poem in a fascicle or outside: whether to read "I cannot live with You—" as preceded by "I am ashamed—I hide—" (P 473) and followed by "Size circumscribes—it has no room" (P 641), or to read "I cannot live with You—" as preceded by nothing and followed by nothing.

Yet the analysis of the poems just discussed demonstrates that once one has worked through the different ways of reading between which Dickinson refuses to choose, one inevitably sees an individual poem as

---

1866, is to raise questions about chronology in relation to a poet's syntactic development. Finally, to read "There came a Day—at Summer's full—" (P 322) against "I cannot live with You—" (P 640) is to raise questions about the relation between the sacred and the secular, since in both poems communion epitomizes the sexuality that is also said to oppose it. But even in the last of these cases (where the relation between the secular and the sacred in "There came a Day" has clear analogies with that same relation as presented in "I cannot live with You—," read either as a single lyric or in its fascicle context), what we are reading when we read intertextually are analogues or relations. Thus to read Dickinson's poems intertextually is to raise questions about the relation of poems rather than about how poetic identity is constructed.

Therefore, once one has read through Dickinson's poems both individually and in the fascicles, the question may arise: How about any poem next to any other poem? Having worked through the argument of my book, however, the reader should not be able to say, "Now I must read through all the fascicles and see how this obtains, and having done that, I can take account of any relation—it won't matter whether the relations noticed are in the same fascicle." For while it is useful to widen the set of possibilities for reading, it must be clearly determined whether one is reading relations or identities. It must be determined whether one is reading within the presumed intention, or outside of and despite it. Thus while seeing the ways in which the boundaries of poems are destabilized by the fascicle context gives one license to see different ways of reading proximities and *relations* independent of the fascicles, it does not invite one to see different ways of reading *identities* independent of them.

something different from what an individual poem was before one read the fascicles. For the individual poem now is interpenetrated or saturated with the kind of connections revealed by reading Dickinson in the fascicles. The individual poem is overdetermined by such connections, but the poem is also fragmented, so that, rather than being subjectless, it has too many subjects. These subjects, one might argue, can only fully be explored by looking back to the fascicle context.

Nor, without the fascicles, would we necessarily understand the dominant relation of part to totality, in apparently different contexts. For instance, in speaking of parts and totalities I have thus far been calling attention to the relation of formal entities (variants and lines; one poem and a putative other; lyric and fascicle) or of thematized relations (moments of dominion versus presumptive temporal wholes). But what of the bodily parts that dominate—even as they are fragmented in—Dickinson's poetry? It is true that the reduction of the self to an alternative body or soul is explained by the economic distribution of body and soul in the poems that represent recompense for a lover's death. But this economy does not explain the reduction of the self to a *part* of the body. It does not explain the isolated ear, eye, feet, heart, brain. For it is bodily *parts* that dominate Dickinson's poetry: specifically, the eye in "The Tint I cannot take—is best—," the ear in "I would not paint—a picture—," and the eye in "I cannot live with You—." What explains this dominance?

One of the effects of the synecdoche by which the body is reduced to a part—for example, the other's gaze in "I cannot live with You—" is not simply that the part is made representative, but also that, because it has been reduced to manageable size, it can in this case be palpably possessed. Indeed, the implications are that it already has been. The gaze—not exactly part of the body, but rather a phenomenon generated from a part of the body—has even been exchanged and reciprocally taken in. One relevant comment on the double incorporation is that it yet again presents not choosing the lover as here not *needing* to choose him because, as the reciprocity in the implied past tense demonstrates, the speaker has already done so. Another observation to make about the double incorporation is that, by its very displacement, the gaze redefines internality. For if the self and the other are represented by mutual exchange of the gaze, there are no boundaries to the self being represented, as in the poem's repeated hyperbolic formulations there are no prohibitions of access. Thus the representation of the self, when it has been forsaken by the lover, is here epitomized as "my homesick Eye—." By this I understand that her eye, at his prospective death, has been estranged from its object, that is, from its habitation. Yet in relation to the line "Because You saturated Sight—," the terms in which the estrangement and loss are expressed ("no more Eyes") insist on an earlier plenitude. Their respective eyes, together, have been made "more," in the sense of "made indistinguishable."

Thus what is being represented is not simply the self as a bodily part. Also represented is his self as that part of *her* body which, once absorbed, in effect continues to occupy her. She has, then, "no more Eyes" than the ones to contain him, no more than his eyes, no more eyes of her own at all, since she has lost his, or since, even having lost his eyes, she nonetheless retains the vision of him—retains the gaze that *isn't* lost. Even once he is dead, she will have, as the poem repeatedly makes clear, no extra, vacant vision. In the simultaneity of these disparate but not cross-canceling connotations, selfhood is variously economized, exchanged, used up, forfeited, and declined to be forfeited. For the gaze is repeatedly reassessed. It is differently located and quantified, even as the part of the body—the eyes—from which it issues is similarly made, first implicitly, more and then less, is first made abundant and then diminished. In the poem's last stanza, previously considered, we see, in another register, analogous additions and subtractions to those earlier illustrated corporeally. We see negotiations of distance which are construed as at once absolute and non-existent.

In Dickinson's poetry, then, the point of partializing the body, like the point of partializing the owned position, is to arrive at wholeness. Differently understood, the enterprise makes parts so indistinguishable from wholes that the difference is immaterial. Moreover, if one thus confuses parts with wholes, it is unclear whether something is lost or gained. This ambiguity is the case in "I cannot live with You—," where the eye, the gaze, in addition to connecting the speaker and the lover, is also, by being partialized, made potent: "Your Face/ Would put out Jesus'—/ That New Grace/ Glow plain—and foreign/ On my homesick Eye—." It is the case in "As the Starved Maelstrom laps the Navies," in which desire laments the absence of its object only to epitomize it: "I, of a finer Famine/ Deem my Supper dry/ For but a Berry of Domingo/ And a Torrid Eye" (P 872). And it is even the case in "Because I could not stop for Death—," where the speaker is simultaneously blocked by the vision of the "Horses Heads . . . toward Eternity" and rests upon that vision—as nowhere else in the poem—as upon a destination.

It has become apparent that it is difficult to establish a hierarchy among the questions raised by the fascicle texts, questions that could be summarized as: How is substitution consequentially subverted with respect to the variants and to variant poems? What constitutes a poem's textual identity and its demarcated subject? Given the shifting borders that frame the subject or the text, what is the poem's interior? The inability to construct a hierarchy among such questions is, it should by now be clear, connected to the shifting relation of part and whole. Because this relation shifts, whole poems are made into parts, as when "There's a certain Slant of light" is read in relation to "Of Bronze—and Blaze—"; parts become wholes, as when the variant to the line of one poem is read against the line proper of another poem; the unit thought to *be* a redefined whole (Fascicle 14, for instance) loses such definition when it is read against the fascicle that follows it. It is difficult to establish a hierarchy among the questions raised by the fascicles because the material that seems to dictate these questions also appears to shift. Specifically, if relations are economized, and the boundaries of subjects continuously renegotiated, it is unclear how we should consider them. Moreover, there are shifting ways to understand the relation between part and whole. Part *anticipates* whole—as in Fascicle 16, where the body and soul are partialized, but only temporarily so. Or part *is* the whole already effectively redefined in the course of the poem—as illustrated by "The Moments of Dominion," as well as by the position of witnessing endorsed in "I would not paint—." No less illustrative are the eyes which allow the gaze to epitomize all in the final poem this discussion considers. Further, the choices of part over whole, which seem to be made in the last of these instances ("I would not paint—a picture—/ I'd rather be the One") are not being made. And this radical reassessment of the relation of part to whole, as well as these repeated instances of choosing negatively ("I cannot," "I would not," "I cannot")—in which choosing negatively has enabling consequences because it is made precisely equivalent to not choosing at all, and of not needing to do so—makes the reading of this poetry (or the understanding of that experience) uniquely vertiginous.

That the fascicles extend such an issue as the relation between part and whole—rather than, say, clarifying it—and that they bring to light another issue ("not being able to" choose as "not needing to" choose) may indeed be one of the disappointments of a certain way of reading them, or of a nostalgia for a certain kind of coherence. It may explain why most assessments of the fascicles have declared them arbitrary. The longing for coherence assumes that the whole explains the part. It likewise assumes that what the whole "is" can be recognized. In distinction to these conceptions, it is the genius of this poetry, or you could say its perversity, to decline—and in complex terms—precisely such assumptions.

In fact, one of the reasons Dickinson's fascicles might not be understood to explain Dickinson's poetry is that the fascicles, no less than individual lyrics (and, since they are ostensible "wholes," perhaps more ostentatiously), problematize the relation between part and whole. No less relevantly, to the extent that the fascicles privilege one of these terms, it would be, as I have demonstrated in a number of contexts, the part rather than the whole that is insisted upon as dominant. This privileging of the part—whether the part is understood as a poetic variant; as a corporeal entity (the "no more Eyes" or the "Horses Heads"); as one position rather than another, putatively endorsed and then occupied (as in "I would not paint—a picture—/ I'd rather be the One"); or as the lover's body gained for the speaker's soul that "selects" it—has radical consequences. For if the fascicles are construed as a systematized entity, they constitute a failed, or rather, as I have argued, a subverted enterprise. It is therefore no wonder that, misassessed in these terms, the fascicles might never be understood as coherent in their own terms, or as anything but marginal to the achievement of Dickinson's poetry. Yet to understand the fascicles properly—that is, in the terms they predicate— is to understand the deep structure of Dickinson's poetry. For the fascicles illustrate structure conceived not as a demarcated entity but rather as a federation whereby power, initially thought to be centralized, is ultimately distributed to constituent parts, which are then deemed representative. In this way, the fascicles redefine how Dickinson understood totality.[2]

***

2. Given such a claim, it might be asked how my position differs from Hartman's, disputed in the first chapter. In saying that the "hyphen-hymen" that "both joins and divides . . . persephonates Emily," Hartman is essentially discussing the divisions in Dickinson's poetry and their consequence, in his understanding of them as disjunction and blankness. For Hartman the dash both connects and disconnects, but the result is paradox stripped of representational content. Since I have claimed that Dickinson's poems read in the fascicle context characteristically partialize—

"'Tis Units—make the Swarm—" (P 565), Dickinson had written, a line of poetry that could also characterize the distinguishing features of her own poetry. For it is units—as well as questions raised by what constitutes units with respect to words separated (or joined) by dashes, to poems copied proximately, to poems linked by non-contiguous associations, or to juxtaposed fascicles—that are repeatedly offered as indeterminate in the poetry. In each of these cases what something "is," whether a part or a whole, and how parts fit together—questions raised with respect to disparate and even incomparable entities—are just what the poetry brings into view and then problematizes.

If the fascicles frustrate conventional understandings of connection and totality, they concomitantly frustrate the desire to know why so many of the poems begin in the middle, at an unexplained crisis. While reading Dickinson's lyrics deprives us of the answer to this question, so does reading Dickinson's fascicles. Such fascicles, for instance, as 15 or 23 (beginning with "The first Day's Night had come—" and "Because I could not stop for Death—" respectively), merely punctuate the intermediate ground of this poetry. Yet if speech in the fascicles often erupts, it seems, from an unexplained center or middle—it is nevertheless not speech that is ungrounded. One of the effects of detaching utterance from recognizable situational anchors is that it paradoxically allows speech to *be* centered in new terms—terms that depend upon the very strategies of disorientation that disable predictable explanation. Thus "When we stand on the tops of Things—" is a poem that clarifies, even resolves, certain conflicts of the fascicle it appears to govern. But, as I have argued, it clarifies these conflicts from a moment shown as passing. Thus "When we stand on the tops of Things—" redefines clarification itself as something transient.

Moreover, the fascicles illustrate, as in "When we stand on the tops of Things—," that the self's partializations, whether of (his) body from

---

privilege the part and the partial—I obviously agree that the poems legislate against completion conventionally understood. Yet I would argue that the consequence of the dash is to amplify the sense of the multiple phenomena that *can* be connected. Thus what the dash emphasizes is not in fact singularity, "stasis," or "impasse," as Hartman claims, but rather that unboundedness which admits of making radical connections. For as I have repeatedly demonstrated, the point of Dickinson's partializing is to redefine totality, not to be dispossessed of it. The extreme benefit of such a redefinition, I shall argue, is to get rid of exteriority.

(her) soul, or of thought from sequential thought in "I felt a Cleaving in my Mind—" (P 937), are directly contingent on the double sites of these poems. It is in relation to a place of origin that the self is often partialized. In other words, the poem's locations are plural. They are plural because, in "I cannot live with You—," for instance, two sites are inhabited simultaneously—the one occupied by the speaker and the one occupied by the lover. But since it is the poem's intense objective to dissolve the distinction between two distinct "persons" in ways discussed previously, the "two" locations have an autonomous status *and* interpenetrate. In other poems, location, hence groundedness, is plural because the same person is demonstrably situated in two distinct landscapes. Thus "Of Bronze—and Blaze—" represents a speaker looking up at the night sky, and past the death scrutinized, whereas "There's a certain Slant of light" locates that speaker looking down and *at* death, which can't be seen past. In the intersection of these disparate visions or disparate voices—or in the intersection of this single voice at disparate moments of its utterance—location is charted. The consequence is not the scenelessness that the criticism ascribes to Dickinson's poems. It is rather, in this case, the representation of two scenes initially observed as proximate but ultimately superimposed. Thus the fascicles reiterate, italicize, and, I shall argue, finally *explain* at another level the concerns raised by Dickinson's poems read singly.

Although the subjects I have touched on—the intermediate, the partialized, the superimposed, the non-chosen—seem diverse, not, as I have noted, hierarchically organized, they are in fact related by the problem of variants. For "variants" are a logistical as well as a formal issue in the poetry. The issue emerges in the broadest context, as I observed initially, because reading Dickinson's fascicles is not in fact an alternative to reading Dickinson's lyrics, since Dickinson never chose whether she wished her poems to be read as single entities or as single entities subordinate to the larger structure of the "books" the fascicles construct of them. Variants are also a substantive matter in the poetry because the power of "choosing," as it privileges substitution and wholeness, is itself only an alternative to the power of "not choosing," which in its turn reveals "not choosing" as "not needing to do so." Thus choosing and not choosing, apparently crucial alternatives in the poetry, are, from another vantage, made complementary. We have observed this equivocation in individual fascicles, which variantly endorse the option of "choosing" and that of "not choosing," options between which the fascicles only vacillate. Thus choosing and not choosing are marked in the poetry as variant possibilities which, much like words in the margin that seem initially alternative to each other, turn out to be non-exclusive options. They have an additive or transformative, rather than a substitutive, relation to each other.

Similarly, positions or places that are first demarcated as separate and then superimposed also operate as variants. For the *natural* perspective in "Of Bronze—and Blaze—" could be seen as yielding to the *person's* perspective in "There's a certain Slant of light," even as that way of formulating the relation of the two poems belies a double perspective. The perspective is held as double because the commerce between the two views that would legitimate a word like "yield" is never acknowledged, does not in fact exist. Thus there cannot be a transition from one view to another. Instead, both (contradictory) visions are held in suspension or, as I have noted, superimposed. Variants also govern the intermediacy of speech. For since there is no stance from which to identify what is initial or definitive, there is also no place from which to mark a beginning or an end to utterance. Rather, the variant positions, and the variant ways of regarding the relation of positions, maintain the sense—indeed create the fact—of speech that can always only be surmised as speech from a "middle," from a position that is by definition shifting and partial. Here it should be reiterated that since nothing is "outside" the poem, the inclusion of the variants, or giving them equal status with the words on the line, has this particular consequence: It invalidates the distinction between interiors and exteriors on which a poem's integrity is thought to depend.

Finally, in relation to the double stances that "Of Bronze—and Blaze—" and "There's a certain Slant of light" both adopt and epitomize, one can ask: What is the motive for choosing not choosing, for being indifferent to choosing? And, second: What is the relationship between the indifference frequently thematized *in* the poetry and the indifference to choice which is the stance Dickinson takes *with respect to* the poetry? Is the position which Dickinson has reached as a consequence of choosing not choosing someplace where choice has been transcended or gone beyond? What is such a place? In a sense, this question is rhetorical, or it implies its own answer, for the position of not choosing could only be one of sublimity. From such a position there could be only indifference to questions of distinction and questions of the human—for from such a position the speaker is self-described as "Disdaining Men, and Oxygen,/ For Arrogance of them" (P 290). What is enacted in not choosing is indifference to difference. Thus "indifference" to difference characterizes "Of Bronze—and Blaze—." It characterizes Dickinson's refusal to choose between the antithetical visions—the person's perspective and the natural perspective—represented by the two poems. And it characterizes the repeated stance of choosing not to choose that these two poems only epitomize. Maybe this refusal and the place from which it originates help to explain why so many of Dickinson's poems appear inaccessible. What cannot be identified or reached is the sphere in which they take place, for that sphere does not formally admit of *her* mortality. In that sphere Dickinson's speakers simulate a stance—here simulate utterance—that she once attributed to the dead as "Sublimer thing—than Speech—" (P 310). The position of the speakers, like the position of the dead ("Untouched by Morning/ And untouched by Noon—") in "Safe in their Alabaster Chambers—" (P 216), is beyond, inhuman, indifferent, sublime. Their speech issues from a place beyond "internal difference,/ Where the Meanings, are." Only from such a vantage "on the tops of Things" can those differences—on which the coherence of the human world presumably rests—be seen and seen beyond.

Say the characteristics I have described are uniquely Dickinsonian. Then what, linguistically and philosophically, do they epitomize? If there is a philosophical problem that emerges from these characteristics, what is it and how could it be described? I ask these questions because they insist on the importance of identifying what specifically is revealed in distinguishing the features of a given body of poetry. I take it that the task of "identifying" the characteristics of a poetic oeuvre is in some sense only preliminary—that which helps us to see what set of problems is being worked out; the terms in which these problems are understood and negotiated; and the grounds of their appeal to us. To say less is to mistake why linguistic questions interest us.

Dickinson's poetry dramatizes the impossibility of wholeness understood as boundedness. It does so in its almost incomprehensible adherence to piecemeal utterance, in the refusal of the syntax to endorse resolutions marked by conventional grammatical pauses, connections, or punctuated units of sense. This allegiance and resistance, in ways that have now been adequately remarked upon, demonstrate defiance of totality at fundamental levels. Dickinson's language is language that is broken. Thus, if language marks rupture, it does so for the sake of italicizing the arbitrariness of units of sense understood as conclusive. Just as radically, the poetry dramatizes the impossibility of wholeness in its preference for synecdoche—whether with respect to the body, with respect to a position said to be chosen (even as the chosen position is then transgressed), with respect to "whole" poems made into parts by association with the other poems that call their discrete status into question, or with respect to parts made into wholes when variants to lines are treated as commensurate with lines that are *not* variants. Most stunningly, Dickinson dramatizes the impossibility of wholeness by privileging variants as the essence of her poetry. Variants, we could say, are the single unit "predictably" constitutive of an utterance's instability. For variants undermine "wholes" as discrete entities. They do so by pointing specifically to the economies that constitute structures that are not—and could never be—made stable and totalized. Another way to say this is that when totality is negated, what is called into question is the status of an exterior that stays codified as such.

If Hart Crane's poetry, in Allen Grossman's formulation of it, is "difficult" in its attempt to coerce relations that persons cannot have and in its insistence on producing utterances that persons cannot "say,"[3] it could be argued that Dickinson's poetry is "difficult" in its attempt to contest the presumption of boundaries, hence the presumption of adequacy, which lies at the heart of our understanding of the satisfactions of poetic utterance. For the adequacy of words—or, to be more precise, the adequacy of certain words—to represent a stance in a definitive way is precisely what Dickinson's poetry disputes. Even the topic of pain is a less central feature of this poetry than the partializing phenomenon to which we are continually returned.

It may be that Dickinson's poetry promises, by problematizing, the very coherence which her poetry also withholds. It promises totality even as it represents speech that survives outside of the conditions that ostensibly make discrete "sense." Then the promise of Dickinson's poetry is continually broken. What Dickinson's poetry epitomizes is the fracture of sense. In fact, to comprehend Dickinson's speech is also often to sever

---

3. See Grossman's extraordinary discussion of the suppositions behind the difficulty of Crane's poetry in "Hart Crane and Poetry: A Consideration of Crane's Intense Poetics with Reference to 'The Return'" in *Critical Essays on Hart Crane,* ed. David R. Clark (Boston: G. K. Hall, 1982), pp. 224, 226, 238, and inclusively 221–54.

speech from its proximities—of variants, of other poems—which the fascicles make integral to it. Thus there is the violence *of* the poetry, and the violence we do *to* the poetry when we read violence out of it by instituting boundaries around a structure that in fact eschews them. If the description seems to exaggerate the situation of reading Dickinson, we have only to consider an uncharacteristic poem of hers, "The last Night that She lived" (P 1100), in which narrative creates a consecutive and discrete utterance that is framed and that itself frames as unified the event (of another's death) which is represented. That this poem should be atypical reminds us of the normative situation for reading Dickinson's poems. It reminds us of the extremes on which the poetry seems to insist: either Dickinson's utterance is partialized and variant, or it is doggerel. "The last Night that She lived" is a rare instance of speech that negotiates the range of these extreme possibilities: no completion in conventional terms or completion achieved at the cost of sense, which is trivialized.

In fact, as I have noted, to see the characteristics of Dickinson's poetry is to see its deviance from those characteristics we customarily identify with poetic utterances.[4] Thus, to return to Grossman's *Summa Lyrica,* which specifies the identifying, generic features of poetry, we see the degree of Dickinson's violation of conventions of poetic speech as represented by the fascicles. Thus, for instance, Grossman: "In closure, the poem is characterized as an interior, the relationship of which to the rest of being, or other being, is as an interior to an exterior" (39.1).[5] But what we have seen in the context of Dickinson's fascicles is precisely the

---

4. I am not retracting the claims I made for Dickinson's poetry in *Lyric Time,* but I would reformulate them as follows: Dickinson's poetry exaggerates the temporal features of the lyric as a genre. This phenomenon still seems to me true of individual lyrics. But the degree of the ensuing dislocation, and what I now understand to be its source—the inability to settle on a phenomenon as a single entity or to represent it except variantly—changes what I first understood as a question of degree into a question of kind. Thus, while the temporality in Dickinson's lyrics taken singly is an emblematic, if extreme, manifestation of a generic feature, once read in the fascicle context the poems no longer look representative because they no longer look like lyrics. Only as a consequence of reading the lyrics in the context of the reconstructed fascicles is it possible to see this.

5. Grossman writes about Dickinson explicitly here and elsewhere in *Summa Lyrica.* But he sees her poems as preserving the very distinction between the interior and the exterior that I have argued her poems contest. For a discussion of Dickinson's poetry as one of closure rather than aperture, see 39.1–40.8.

inability to demarcate "interior" and "exterior," either with respect to the margins of a poem when it is marked by variants, or with respect to the boundaries of an utterance which is often "continued" in lyrics that no longer look discrete but rather look related, even "integral." Thus, for instance, Grossman: "Neither of the terms [I or you] can be conceived of without the other; they are complementary, although according to an 'interior/exterior' opposition" (24.1). But, as we have seen, the "you" in Dickinson's poems is precisely not exterior, hence not opposed, to the "I" who is speaking—as instantiated, for example, in "I cannot live with You—" or "The Soul selects her own Society—." Nor in these poems, as we have also seen, is the "you" outside of the poem. Or if, as in "The Soul selects her own Society—," the other, here called "One," is initially situated "outside," that other is ultimately invited within—the intent of this specific poem being to dramatize as well as to represent the consequence of that internalization. In poems like this one, the polarity Grossman assumes as an identifying feature of poetry frequently does not identify Dickinson's poetry.

Thus, further, Grossman: "The minimal function of closure is to fence the poem from all other statements, and most strenuously from alternative statements of the same kind" (4.5). But in the fascicles alternative statements, as constituted by the variants, are precisely integral to a *single* poem of Dickinson's as we have deliberated it. In the same vein, Grossman writes, "If the text is lost, the poem is lost" (22.6). And further, in the same section, he presumes an identity between text and poem. "All poems have a fixed text, for the poem is a manifestation and manifestation cannot be this way *or* that. All alternate versions of poems (drafts, revisions, alternative singings, miscopyings) are alternative poems." But Dickinson's poems dispute these assertions, for alternative words do not indicate discrete poems but are rather integral to one poem, presumed to be a single structure. Again, Grossman: "In constructing poetic utterance we contrive singular and unexchangeable routes through global, linguistic and, perhaps also, experiential resources" (25.1). But such determinacy is not a principle of Dickinson's fascicles, in which language, experience, and representation itself are emphatically not singular. The principle of Dickinson's poetry is, as I have noted, economic and depends on exchange. Finally, Grossman: "The form of the poem is principally a phenomenon of centering" (28.3). Dickinson's poems defy such a notion. They do so not simply because the poems lack a center but, more emphatically, because they contest the stability that a center would confer (as, for instance, the fascicle's treatment of "When we stand on the tops of Things—" does).

In reiterating the ways in which Dickinson's poems contest propositions about poetry, I intend to ask again about the way we are implicated in this speech. For Dickinson's poetic speech—not whole, not bounded, not centered, not unique, not discriminating between the I and the you, not, in some sense, social—teases us with the promise of the characteristics exemplified by other poems, even as it frustrates the discovery of those properties we associate with poetic communicability. Why then, to repeat a question asked earlier, do we read Dickinson?

Say we are implicated in this speech not as its object or as the person addressed but as a consequence of its invitation to us to stand alongside of, although not in place of, the speaking subject. For the presumption of speech is not that it is *to* us, but that it is *ours*. Hence poems that seem propositional may issue not from a speaker who says "I" but from a speaker who says "One" ("One need not be a Chamber—to be Haunted—") or whose declarative assertions arise so loosely from a source that we *become* the source when we assent to claims which strictly speaking are not "owned," as in "The Soul selects her own Society—," "Pain—has an Element of Blank—" (P 650), "A Route of Evanescence" (P 1463), and "Further in Summer than the Birds" (P 1068). Even when there is an articulated "I," as in "I got so I could [hear/think—/ *take*—] his name—/ Without—Tremendous gain—" (P 293), it is the function of the poetry to unravel the coherence of that "I" so that speech is dislocated, has no discrete origin (see *LT,* pp. 58–61).

In Dickinson's poems we see unboundedness with respect to whom these words may be said to belong. One important aspect of the fallout from a poetic utterance in which subjectivity is so split and conflicted, oscillating and polymorphous that the poems end up seeming to speak *for* rather than to us, is a certain sense in which the variants could precisely be reimagined as alternatives which no single voice, neither author's nor reader's, could utter simultaneously with any coherence. In this way the impinging presence of the variants would further testify— within the poem taken as *utterance*—to a suspension of normal either/or disjunctions between self and other, origin and destination, address and attention within the extruded interiority of these lyrics.

Consequently, to read Dickinson's poems, and specifically the fascicles, is to be lodged within a spaciousness so unfamiliar that it is experienced as disorienting. Put in different terms, what these poems make available is interiority itself—interiority without either origin or outside. To read Dickinson in the fascicles is to encounter an interiority found there as if it were our own. Thus the claims made by this poetry are fundamentally presumptive. To the extent that its stress is on unboundedness itself, whatever the manifestations of it, we may even question whether the properties of this discourse are less poetic than religious.

I raise this question because I suppose religious language to be concerned not with the world of persons but rather with the world of spaces. Consider again "I saw no Way—The Heavens were stitched—/ I felt the Columns close—," in which space that conceals, and that also excludes, yields to space that reveals and inexplicably opens up: "The Earth reversed her Hemispheres—/ I touched the Universe—/ And back it slid—and I alone—/ A Speck upon a Ball—/ Went out upon Circumference—/ Beyond the Dip of Bell—" (P 378). Such a concern with spaces and, more specifically, with the *opening* up of spaces permeates the poetry, as in "A Pit—but Heaven over it . . . It was a Pit—with fathoms under it" (P 1712). As in: "The Only News I know/ Is Bulletins all Day/ From Immortality" (P 827). As in: "There is a solitude of space/ A solitude of sea/ A solitude of death, but these/ Society shall be/ Compared with that profounder site/ That polar privacy/ A soul admitted to itself—/ Finite Infinity" (P 1695). As in "The Brain—is wider than the Sky—/ For— put them side by side—/ The one the other will [contain/ include]/ With ease—and You—beside—" (P 632). The last example is a good one on which to pause. For it insists that although Dickinson's poetry charts the opening of outer spaces ("And back it slid—and I alone—/ A Speck upon a Ball—/ Went out upon Circumference—/ Beyond the Dip of Bell—" [P 378]), the latter is only symptomatic of the opening of inner spaces. Such an opening is daring precisely to the extent that it equates *all* space with *inner* space, refuses to recognize a difference between inner and outer, so equivalent has the poetry discovered the two to be, as in the last stanza of the poem already quoted: "The Brain is just the weight of God—/ For—Heft them—Pound for Pound—/ And they will differ— if they do—/ As Syllable from Sound—" (P 632).

All the poems that produce imaginary geographies, as, for instance, "Our journey had advanced—" (P 615) does, are predicated on the equivalence of the space opened up within and the space traversed without. This equivalence is what keeps discoveries from becoming abstractions:

"Eternity's White Flag—Before—/ And God—at every Gate—" is not an observation about an exterior landscape. It is an observation about a landscape that can be attested to because there is no ascertainable difference between the space that reveals itself from within and that which reveals itself from without. Indeed, one could argue that one of the reasons the question of whether something is literal or metaphoric in Dickinson's poetry is only superficially sensible (and frequently unanswerable) is that "sense" would depend on a distinction between outside and inside that the poetry disputes.

The single most prominent feature of Dickinson's poetry, then, is the opening up of spaces. It is the opening up of spaces allowed to remain open. This is why reading the poems in the fascicle context is not only an alternative to reading the poems as single lyrics but also explains something about the properties of these poems read singly. For the spaces *between* the poems, more drastically than the spaces *in* the poems, though not essentially different in kind from the latter, illustrate the uncontainability of what is being represented. What is represented is the determination of Dickinson's utterance to penetrate divisions, to explicitly connect one entity with another that might be understood as severed from it—though the point of such a connection is, as I have noted, neither completion nor equation. Nor does this interpenetration result in the scenelessness of chapter 1, for the openness of Dickinson's poems is not evacuated of scene. Indeed, as I have observed, the poems supply a plenitude of scene, even a superimposition of multiple scenes, as there is a plenitude of coordinate points by which these scenes may be demarcated.

Moreover, what is open and unbounded is not blank, though it penetrates blankness ("The Forest of the Dead—," for instance). For the speaker in these poems, travelling through blankness, always arrives somewhere: whether at the "precarious Gait/ Some call Experience" (P 875) or at "God—at every Gate" (P 615) or at the vision of the "Horses Heads" (P 712). In this poetry God, the gait, and the horses' heads are equivalent destinations. What is "open," moreover, is not indeterminate, though it may be multiply determined, as the variants, for example, illustrate multiple determinacy. And what is revealed in the openness is, as I have noted, not division. For what is repeatedly insisted upon is radical connection—as poems are not divided, as the dead and the living are not divided, as the "I" and the "you" are not divided, as speech from the center and speech from the margin are not divided, as the presumptive speech of the speaker and the presumptive speech of the reader are—can be said—not to be divided. To read Dickinson's poetry is to be thrust into territory where words issue from her consciousness as if it were our own. From the vantage of these observations we see why the lyrics are not only untitled but never could be titled. For with regard to the poems as single utterances it is unclear what would designate the "topics" they explore, since they are in the process of redefining conventional understandings of such topics. From the vantage of the fascicles there would be no way to posit titles since there is no (single) way to posit boundaries *to* subjects. Finally, from the vantage of ascribed and ascribable utterance, if the poems speak our thoughts as well as hers, then no one is left with the authority to title them as issued utterances.

Why do we read Dickinson's poetry? To answer that question I must have recourse to another poet, writing in another language and in another century. In *Duino Elegies,* and differently in *Sonnets to Orpheus,* Rilke discovers—or is given—a similar unboundedness, what he names "the Open,"[6] which the *Elegies,* especially, explore. I say "is given" because the compositional history of these poems, as reported by Rilke, seems to me crucial to our understanding: Rilke describes himself as essentially taking dictation of them. The compositional history is crucial because the discovery which Rilke transcribes in the poems is at once interior in origin, expressing something within, and no less exterior, given from without. In effect, what Rilke transcribes is the dissolution of the boundary between these locations. In the *Elegies,* evoked and represented is first the yearning for what the Eighth Elegy calls "the Open," ultimately discovered in the Ninth Elegy as not elsewhere but here: "Perhaps we are *here* in order to say: house,/ bridge, fountain, gate, pitcher, fruit-tree, window—/ at most: column, tower. . . . But to *say* them, you must understand/ oh to say them *more* intensely than the Things themselves/ ever dreamed of existing." In *The Sonnets to Orpheus,* saying "the Things themselves" involves viewing them—viewing being—as an essence that will not be partialized. This is what the conclusion to Sonnet II, 23, informs us when its speaker predicates distinctions no longer understood as distinctions, or still understood as distinctions but subsumed by

6. The translations from Rilke's *Elegies* and *Sonnets to Orpheus* are Stephen Mitchell's from *The Selected Poetry of Rainer Maria Rilke* (New York: Vintage, 1984).

praise: "because we are the branch, the iron blade,/ and sweet danger, ripening from within." Thus openness for Rilke requires surrender to unboundedness taken up as a subject; to the implications of unboundedness the self, in the *Elegies,* is progressively made susceptible. "The Open" is a space in which our vision is not obscured with recognizable objects and which cannot be arranged.[7]

Openness for Heidegger—what he calls "unconcealedness" (in "The Origin of the Work of Art") and "the Open" (in "What Are Poets For?" which takes up Rilke's Eighth Elegy)—is theorized specifically as the "ground" of poetry. Thus, from the first essay: "Poetry is the saying of the unconcealedness of what is."[8] "Such saying is a projecting of the clearing, in which announcement is made of what it is that beings come into the Open *as*" (p. 73). And from "What Are Poets For?" which is more difficult to excerpt: The "Open . . . happens in the world's inner space. That space touches man when, in the inner recalling of conversion, he turns toward the space of the heart" (p. 138). Thus for Heidegger, explicating Rilke, the "unconcealed" is the Open understood to tra-

---

7. In passing so quickly over this sense of "the Open" I am necessarily eliding stages of Rilke's discovery as recorded by the progression of the *Elegies.* For it could be argued that, in the Eighth Elegy, "the Open" is the place where only angels and animals live. But if the Eighth Elegy makes this distinction between "the Open," which is accessible to the angels, and some other, inner space accessible to us, the two concluding elegies place the speaker in a habitation similarly unbounded by objects and similarly transcending dualism. The angels are, of course, those in whom a transformation is unnecessary, for they are what presence consists of when it is not already split. As a consequence they are in the Open, as arguably we could never be. Yet in the Ninth and Tenth Elegies, an analogous space is available to us. For to "say these things"—to apprehend without appropriating—is to be in a space similarly cleared. As a consequence of leaving things as they are, as a consequence of pure perception, there is access to the Open, for to let things be is not to differentiate, to be and to see simultaneously. Thus although the Open is thought to be unavailable, a space initially yearned for and ultimately relinquished as first conceived, it is not, if we perceive purely, quite unavailable. If we apprehend purely, we see, as Rilke writes in a letter to Witold von Hulewicz: "We of the here and now are not for a moment hedged in the time-world, nor confined within it; we are incessantly flowing over and over to those who preceded us. In that greatest *'open'* world all *are,* one cannot say 'simultaneous,' for the very falling away of time determines that they all *are*" (*Letters of Rainer Maria Rilke 1910–1926,* trans. Jane Bannard Greene and M. D. Herter Norton [New York: Norton, 1969], p. 373; subsequently cited, parenthetically, as Greene and Norton).

8. In *Poetry, Language, Thought,* trans. Albert Hofstadter (New York: Harper & Row, 1971), p. 74. Subsequent page references are supplied in parentheses.

verse boundaries between the interior and the exterior, that is, between "the world's inner space" and "the space of the heart."[9] For Heidegger, as for Rilke, "the Open" is that objectless place where innerness is discovered, is "found" in and for itself. Hence its designation as "pure existence." It is objectless because it has no goal except simply to be: "the hard thing consists . . . in the . . . going over from the still covetous . . . work of the eyes, to the 'work of the heart.'" The "hard" thing being described is the exchange of one way of discerning completion or perfection (in and through discrete entities, which are seen and coveted) for the perfection of mere being, in which nothing can be owned because nothing is bounded, hence nothing is discrete. Thus the innerness that is discovered is said to belong both to the world and to the self, with no distinction between the two: the "inner space" of consciousness is unified with "the world's inner space." In more fundamental terms, the inspiration of Rilke's poems, which is also the dictation of them, had compositionally elided the difference between these dichotomized terms of inner and outer. Thus Rilke describes the "single breathless act of obedience" (Greene and Norton, p. 327) to the presence to which he is attending: "Transiency everywhere plunges into a deep being" (p. 373). But he also describes the origin of vision as interior: "It is our task to imprint this provisional, perishable earth so deeply, so patiently and passionately in ourselves that its reality shall arise in us again 'invisibly'" (p. 374). In this way the understanding revealed *in* the writing about the relation of interior and exterior is mirrored—or is itself dictated—by the understanding of the origin *of* the writing.

But what Rilke thematizes and what Heidegger theorizes as essential to being and as the only real work of poetry, Dickinson's fascicles more simply exemplify. In Dickinson's fascicles inwardness has no goal or no point except that of manifestation.

9. Heidegger elaborates: "The hard thing is to accomplish existence. The hard thing consists not only in the difficulty of forming the work of language, but in the difficulty of going over from the saying work of the still covetous vision of things, from the work of the eyes, to the 'work of the heart.' The song is hard because the singing may no longer be a solicitation, but must be existence" (pp. 138–39). In other words, in song—or poetry—what must be exchanged is *bounded* objects for vision unimpeded by objects. Space without objects is space in which nothing is there to be "solicited" or procured. In a world not bounded by objects, the self rests in being, but in being that cannot be "located." This is just to say that interior and exterior no longer make categorical sense, because the experience of being is no longer the experience of separation.

Then to answer the questions: What claim does Dickinson have on us? Why do we read this poetry? What in the fascicles is exemplified and extended to us? Call it multiple manifestations of inwardness—so that there is no aspect of the poems which is closed to these manifestations, and no place to which inwardness does not penetrate. Given this, how could the poems be "titled," conventionally ordered, or understood to manifest order? For it is in violation of these categorical limits that the poetry speaks, spreading "innerness" in Heidegger's vocabulary, or "the Open" in Rilke's words, or, in Dickinson's terms, flaunting the transgressive indifference to all those distinctions on which speech that has limits manifestly depends. Precisely because in Dickinson's poetry objects and subjects are not in fact discrete—are not, that is, bounded—the relation between them and, significantly, the ways of measuring relation dispute conventional designation. Objects and subjects, like variant poems, or like words and variants to words, are not greater than, not less than, not even equal to each other—these being terms of measurement to which Dickinson's speech initially seems confined, but from which it is ultimately released. I conclude by particularizing the claim with reference to P 632, which proposes categories of measurement like "greater than" and "equal to," which are then repudiated.

> The Brain—is wider than the Sky—
> For—put them side by side—
> The one the other will contain
> With ease—and You—beside—
>
> The Brain is deeper than the sea—
> For—hold them—Blue to Blue—
> The one the other will absorb—
> As Sponges—Buckets—do—
>
> The Brain is just the weight of God—
> For—Heft them—Pound for Pound—
> And they will differ—if they do—
> As Syllable from Sound—
>
> 3. contain] include

The brain and sky, brain and sea, brain and God are juxtaposed so that we may see that the brain apparently *contains/includes* the sky, as it contains the self to which it is therefore implicitly not equal. (Here one could say that in centralizing "contain," or in putting it on the line, Dickinson avoids the semanticity of the rhyme between "include" and "God" which, however separated by intervening lines, she would nonetheless have heard; as she also avoids the assonance of the uncharacteristic triplet. Moreover, to the extent that equivalence is still preliminarily contemplated, she is marginalizing or interlineating "include" and centralizing "contain," for "include" is permeable. Hence "contain" is preferable, for both comparison and equivalence require non-identity.) So too the brain *absorbs* the sea, having apparently more amplitude. (Apparently more amplitude. Even ultimately more amplitude, although "Sponges" absorbing "Buckets" disturbs the equilibrium of the brain's greater spaciousness, understood in any facile way. For if sponges absorb buckets, they only do so gradually. And this fact would suggest that the brain *can* contain the sea, but not all at once or simultaneously. If so, the exact relation between brain and sea that is in one sense specified is in another equivocated.) And these specifications of relation, with their diminished second terms of "Sky" and "sea," are themselves transformed in the third of the stanzas. "Just the weight of God" would suggest a rectification of the comparative terms by the making of an equivalence. But it is not equivalence on which the last stanza closes. For "Syllable" is what manifests "Sound." Syllable is the articulation of sound, the voicing or uttering of it.

Here *within* a poem, as in the fascicles we have seen *between* poems, entities are connected—even as the nature of their connection cannot categorically be stabilized. Here *within* a poem, as in the fascicles between poems, the "You" in the first stanza is only another name for the speaking "I," so that there is no otherness to which the poem admits. And, since this poem is propositional, there is for us, as for the speaker, also no otherness that is *ours*—the "You" referring to the speaker no less than it refers to us. Here *within* the poem, as in the fascicles between poems, there is no outside to the experience, for the poem precisely narrates the way in which the outside is first *contained,* then *absorbed,* and finally *sounded* by the inside which it gives forth, gives back—one could say: makes available.

Like the relations between variant and word, poems in the fascicles and single lyrics, one poem and the "other" poems that sustain that poem's interiority from "outside" its apparent boundaries, the I and the you, and the chosen and the not chosen, so the "Brain" is also measured comparatively, as "just the weight of God"—though it is unclear what this would ultimately mean, since God could only be conceived as fundamentally weightless. This economizing of their relation indicates neither a difference between, nor a sameness of, the two. The brain compared to a syllable, and God, its manifestation, here compared to sound, instead exemplify how interiority is voiced, given in all its substantiality, but no less in its infinity. For if the infinite and the exterior are absorbed by the finite and the interior, they are then returned. To ask what is returned is to see how the poem incapacitates any distinction that could be made with respect to the two entities, no longer discrete but also not identical. For the last stanza conceives "Brain" and "God"—those most monumental synecdoches of the inner and the outer respectively—as variants of each other that require each other to reveal the inner, on the one hand, and to extend it, on the other. But what "reveals" and what "extends" are finally not assignable to "Brain" or "God" respectively. This is just to say that neither entity after all has priority and neither can be weighed. Or the entities cannot be weighed separately—for it has been precisely the point of the poem, or the sign of its task's having been carried out successfully, to make the two permeable.

In all three stanzas Dickinson wants to specify what the difference between entities would be while at the same time insisting on the possibility that the entities do not differ. What she here chooses not to choose between are the two claims that the entities differ and that they do not. The refusal to choose is insisted upon and made clearest in the poem's last stanza, which separates the claim that God and the brain are the same ("The Brain is just the weight . . .") from the claim that they are different ("And they will differ . . . As Syllable from Sound") by an interpolated question about whether they are really different ("And they will differ—if they do—/ As Syllable from Sound—"). The dashes around "if they do"—like the dashes in Dickinson's poems generally—are the marks Dickinson uses to open spaces for alternative words, alternative arrangements of words, alternative ideas, which no amount of pausing will allow her to choose among.

Appendix A

Transcripts from Fascicles
13, 15, 16, 20

For a description of the contents of Appendix A, see Textual Note, pp. xiii–xiv above.

FASCICLE 13

290

Of Bronze—and Blaze—
The North—Tonight—
So adequate—it forms—
So preconcerted with itself
So distant—to alarms—
An Unconcern so sovreign
To Universe, or me—
Infects my simple spirit
With Taints of Majesty—
Till I take vaster attitudes—
And strut upon my stem—
Disdaining Men, and Oxygen,
For Arrogance of them—

My Splendors, are Menagerie—
But their Competeless Show
Will entertain the Centuries
When I, am long ago,
An Island in dishonored Grass—
Whom none but Daisies, know.

10. attitudes} manners   19. Daisies} Beetles—
18. An} Some—

258

There's a certain Slant of light,
Winter Afternoons—
That oppresses, like the Heft
Of Cathedral Tunes—

Heavenly Hurt, it gives us—
We can find no scar,
But internal difference,
Where the Meanings, are—

None may teach it—Any—
'Tis the Seal Despair—
An imperial affliction
Sent us of the Air—

When it comes, the Landscape listens—
Shadows—hold their breath—
When it goes, 'tis like the Distance
On the look of Death—

FASCICLE 15

410

The first Day's Night had come—
And grateful that a thing
So terrible—had been endured—
I told my Soul to sing—

She said her Strings were snapt—
Her Bow—to Atoms blown—
And so to mend her—gave me work
Until another Morn—

And then—a Day as huge
As Yesterdays in pairs,
Unrolled it's horror in my face—
Until it blocked my eyes—

My Brain—begun to laugh—
I mumbled—like a fool—
And tho' 'tis Years ago—that Day—
My Brain keeps giggling—still.

And Something's odd—within—
That person that I was—
And this One—do not feel the same—
Could it be Madness—this?

411

The Color of the Grave is Green—
The Outer Grave—I mean—
You would not know it from the Field—
Except it own a Stone—

To help the fond—to find it—
Too infinite asleep
To stop and tell them where it is—
But just a Daisy—deep—

The Color of the Grave is white—
The outer Grave—I mean—
You would not know it from the Drifts—
In Winter—till the Sun—

Has furrowed out the Aisles—
Then—higher than the Land
The little Dwelling Houses rise
Where each—has left a friend—

The Color of the Grave within—
The Duplicate—I mean—
Not all the Snows c'd make it white—
Not all the Summers—Green—

You've seen the Color—maybe—
Upon a Bonnet bound—
When that you met it with before—
The Ferret—Cannot find—

414

'Twas like a Maelstrom, with a notch,
That nearer, every Day,
Kept narrowing it's boiling Wheel
Until the Agony

Toyed coolly with the final inch
Of your delirious Hem—
And you dropt, lost,
When something broke—
And let you from a Dream—

As if a Goblin with a Guage—
Kept measuring the Hours—
Until you felt your Second
Weigh, helpless, in his Paws—

And not a Sinew—stirred—could help,
And sense was setting numb—
When God—remembered—and the Fiend
Let go, then, Overcome—

As if your Sentence stood—pronounced—
And you were frozen led
From Dungeon's luxury of Doubt
To Gibbets, and the Dead—

And when the Film had stitched your eyes
A Creature gasped "Repreive"!
Which Anguish was the utterest—then—
To perish, or to live?

580

I gave myself to Him—
And took Himself, for Pay,
The solemn contract of a Life
Was ratified, this way—

The Wealth might disappoint—
Myself a poorer prove
Than this great Purchaser suspect,
The Daily Own—of Love

Depreciate the Vision—
But till the Merchant buy—
Still Fable—in the Isles of Spice—
The subtle Cargoes—lie—

At least—'tis Mutual—Risk—
Some—found it—Mutual Gain—
Sweet Debt of Life—Each Night to owe—
Insolvent—every Noon—

1. myself to Him] Him all   11. Still] How—/So—
    myself—

415

Sunset at Night—is natural—
But Sunset on the Dawn
Reverses Nature—Master—
So Midnight's—due—at Noon.

Eclipses be—predicted—
And Science bows them in—
But do one face us suddenly—
Jehovah's Watch—is wrong.

419

We grow accustomed to the Dark—
When Light is put away—
As when the Neighbor holds the Lamp
To witness her Goodbye—

A Moment—We uncertain step
For newness of the night—
Then—fit our Vision to the Dark—
And meet the Road—erect—

And so of larger—Darknesses—
Those Evenings of the Brain—
When not a Moon disclose a sign—
Or Star—come out—within—

The B[r]avest—grope a little—
And sometimes hit a Tree
Directly in the Forehead—
But as they learn to see—

Either the Darkness alters—
Or something in the sight
Adjusts itself to Midnight—
And Life steps almost straight.

420

You'll know it—as you know 'tis Noon—
By Glory—
As you do the Sun—
By Glory—
As you will in Heaven—
Know God the Father—and the Son.

By intuition, Mightiest Things
Assert themselves—and not by terms—
"I'm Midnight"—need the Midnight say—
"I'm Sunrise"—Need the Majesty?

Omnipotence—had not a Tongue—
His lisp—is Lightning—and the Sun—
His Conversation—with the Sea—
"How shall you know"?
Consult your Eye!

421

A Charm invests a face
Imperfectly beheld—
The Lady dare not lift her Vail
For fear it be dispelled—

But peers beyond her mesh—
And wishes—and denies—
Lest Interview—annul a want
That Image—satisfies—

577

If I may have it, when it's dead,
I'll be contented—so—
If just as soon as Breath is out
It shall belong to me—

Until they lock it in the Grave,
'Tis Bliss I cannot weigh—
For tho' they lock Thee in the Grave,
Myself—can own the key—

Think of it Lover! I and Thee
Permitted—face to face to be—
After a Life—a Death—We'll say—
For Death was That—
And This—is Thee—

I'll tell Thee All—how Bald it grew—
How Midnight felt, at first—to me—
How all the Clocks stopped in the World—
And Sunshine pinched me—'Twas so cold—

Then how the Grief got sleepy—some—
As if my Soul were deaf and dumb—
Just making signs—across—to Thee—
That this way—thou could'st notice me—

I'll tell you how I tried to keep
A smile, to show you, when this Deep
All Waded—We look back for Play,
At those Old Times—in Calvary.

Forgive me, if the Grave come slow—
For Coveting to look at Thee—
Forgive me, if to stroke thy frost
Outvisions Paradise!

2. so] now—
6. Bliss] Wealth I cannot
   weigh/Right
8. own] hold
14. Bald] Blank—
20. across] it seemed

21. notice] speak to—
25. come] seem
26. Coveting] eagerness—
27. stroke] touch/greet
28. Outvisions] [Out]
    fables—

412

I read my sentence—steadily—
Reviewed it with my eyes,
To see that I made no mistake
In it's extremest clause—
The Date, and manner, of the shame—
And then the Pious Form
That "God have mercy" on the Soul
The Jury voted Him—
I made my soul familiar—with her extremity—
That at the last, it should not be a novel Agony—
But she, and Death, acquainted—
Meet tranquilly, as friends—
Salute, and pass, without a Hint—
And there, the Matter ends—

416

A Murmur in the Trees—to note—
Not loud enough—for Wind—
A Star—not far enough to seek—
Nor near enough—to find—

A long—long Yellow—on the Lawn—
A Hubbub—as of feet—
Not audible—as Our's—to Us—
But dapperer—More Sweet—

A Hurrying Home of little Men
To Houses unperceived—
All this—and more—if I should tell—
Would never be believed—

Of Robins in the Trundle bed
How many I espy
Whose Nightgowns could not hide the Wings—
Although I heard them try—

But then I promised ne'er to tell—
How could I break My Word?
So go your Way—and I'll go Mine—
No fear you'll miss the Road.

417

It is dead—Find it—
Out of sound—Out of sight—
"Happy"? Which is wiser—
You, or the Wind?
"Conscious"? Wont you ask that—
Of the low Ground?

"Homesick"? Many met it—
Even through them—This
Cannot testify—
Themself—as dumb—

418

Not in this World to see his face—
Sounds long—until I read the place
Where this—is said to be
But just the Primer—to a life—
Unopened—rare—Upon the Shelf—
Clasped yet—to Him—and me—

And yet—My Primer suits me so
I would not choose—a Book to know
Than that—be sweeter wise—
Might some one else—so learned—be—
And leave me—just my A—B—C—
Himself—could have the Skies—

581

I found the words to every thought
I ever had—but One—
And that—defies me—
As a Hand did try to chalk the Sun

To Races—nurtured in the Dark—
How would your own—begin?
Can Blaze be shown in Cochineal—
Or Noon—in Mazarin?

1. words] phrase   7. shown] done

413

I never felt at Home—Below—
And in the Handsome Skies
I shall not feel at Home—I know—
I dont like Paradise—

Because it's Sunday—all the time—
And Recess—never comes—
And Eden'll be so lonesome
Bright Wednesday Afternoons—

If God could make a visit—
Or ever took a Nap—
So not to see us—but they say
Himself—a Telescope

Perennial beholds us—
Myself would run away
From Him—and Holy Ghost—and All—
But there's the "Judgment Day"!

578

The Body grows without—
The more convenient way—
That if the Spirit—like to hide
It's Temple stands, alway,

Ajar—secure—inviting—
It never did betray
The Soul that asked it's shelter
In solemn honesty

1. without] outside   8. solemn] timid—
4. Temple] Closet

579

I had been hungry, all the Years—
My Noon had Come—to dine—
I trembling drew the Table near—
And touched the Curious Wine—

'Twas this on Tables I had seen—
When turning, hungry, Home
I looked in Windows, for the Wealth
I could not hope—for Mine—

I did not know the ample Bread—
'Twas so unlike the Crumb
The Birds and I, had often shared
In Nature's—Dining Room—

The Plenty hurt me—'twas so new—
Myself felt ill—and odd—
As Berry—of a Mountain Bush—
Transplanted—to the Road—

Nor was I hungry—so I found
That Hunger—was a way
Of Persons outside Windows—
The Entering—takes away—

7. Wealth] Things   19. Persons] Creatures—
8. for Mine] to earn

FASCICLE 16

327

Before I got my eye put out—
I liked as well to see
As other creatures, that have eyes—
And know no other way—

But were it told to me, Today,
That I might have the Sky
For mine, I tell you that my Heart
Would split, for size of me—

The Meadows—mine—
The Mountains—mine—
All Forests—Stintless Stars—
As much of noon, as I could take—
Between my finite eyes—

The Motions of the Dipping Birds—
The Lightning's jointed Road—
For mine—to look at when I liked—
The news would strike me dead—

So safer—guess—with just my soul
Upon the window pane
Where other creatures put their eyes—
Incautious—of the Sun—

15. Lightning's jointed
    Road] Morning's Amber Road—

607

Of nearness to her sundered Things
The Soul has special times—
When Dimness—looks the Oddity—
Distinctness—easy—seems—

The Shapes we buried, dwell about,
Familiar, in the Rooms—
Untarnished by the Sepulchre,
The Mouldering Playmate comes—

In just the Jacket that he wore—
Long buttoned in the Mold
Since we—old mornings, Children—played—
Divided—by a world—

The Grave yields back her Robberies—
The Years, our pilfered Things—
Bright Knots of Apparitions
Salute us, with their wings—

As we—it were—that perished—
Themself—had just remained till we rejoin them—
And 'twas they, and not ourself
That mourned.

8. The] Our

279

Tie the Strings to my Life, My Lord,
Then, I am ready to go!
Just a look at the Horses—
Rapid! That will do!

Put me in on the firmest side—
So I shall never fall—
For we must ride to the Judgment—
And it's partly, down Hill—

But never I mind the steepest—
And never I mind the Sea—
Held fast in Everlasting Race—
By my own Choice, and Thee—

Goodbye to the Life I used to live—
And the World I used to know—
And kiss the Hills, for me, just once—
Then—I am ready to go!

5. firmest] tightest
/ highest—
8. And it's partly] And it's
many a mile—

9. steepest] Bridges
15] Here's a keepsake for
the Hills
16. Then] Now

241

I like a look of Agony,
Because I know it's true—
Men do not sham Convulsion,
Nor simulate, a Throe—

The Eyes glaze once—and that is Death—
Impossible to feign
The Beads upon the Forehead
By homely Anguish strung.

280

I felt a Funeral, in my Brain,
And Mourners to and fro
Kept treading—treading—till it seemed
That Sense was breaking through—

And when they all were seated,
A Service, like a Drum—
Kept beating—beating—till I thought
My Mind was going numb—

And then I heard them lift a Box
And creak across my Soul
With those same Boots of Lead, again,
Then Space—began to toll,

As all the Heavens were a Bell,
And Being, but an Ear,
And I, and Silence, some strange Race
Wrecked, solitary, here—

And then a Plank in Reason, broke,
And I dropped down, and down—
And hit a World, at every plunge,
And Finished knowing—then—

19. plunge] Crash—   20. Finished] Got through—

281

'Tis so appalling—it exhilirates—
So over Horror, it half Captivates—
The Soul stares after it, secure—
To know the worst, leaves no dread more—

To scan a Ghost, is faint—
But grappling, conquers it—
How easy, Torment, now—
Suspense kept sawing so—

The Truth, is Bald, and Cold—
But that will hold—
If any are not sure—
We show them—prayer—
But we, who know,
Stop hoping, now—

Looking at Death, is Dying—
Just let go the Breath—
And not the pillow at your Cheek
So Slumbereth—

Others, Can wrestle—
Your's, is done—
And so of Wo, bleak dreaded—come,
It sets the Fright at liberty—
And Terror's free—
Gay, Ghastly, Holiday!

2. it half Captivates] it   4] A Sepulchre, fears frost,
   dumb fascinates—   no more—

282

How noteless Men, and Pleiads, stand,
Until a sudden sky
Reveals the fact that One is rapt
Forever from the Eye—

Members of the Invisible,
Existing, while we stare,
In Leagueless Opportunity,
O'ertakeless, as the Air—

Why did'nt we detain Them?
The Heavens with a smile,
Sweep by our disappointed Heads
Without a syllable—

9. detain Them] retain   12] But deign no syllable
    them—/ [detain] it

242

When we stand on the tops of Things—
And like the Trees, look down—
The smoke all cleared away from it—
And Mirrorrs on the scene—

Just laying light—no soul will wink
Except it have the flaw—
The Sound ones, like the Hills—shall stand—
No Lightning, scares away—

The Perfect, nowhere be afraid—
They bear their dauntless Heads,
Where others, dare not go at Noon,
Protected by their deeds—

The Stars dare shine occasionally
Upon a spotted World—
And Suns, go surer, for their Proof,
As if an Axle, held—

7. shall stand] stand up—   11. go at Noon] walk
8. scares] drives—   at noon—
10. dauntless] fearless—   16. an Axle, held] A
    / tranquil—   Muscle—held

445

'Twas just this time, last year, I died.
I know I heard the Corn,
When I was carried by the Farms—
It had the Tassels on—

I thought how yellow it would look—
When Richard went to mill—
And then, I wanted to get out,
But something held my will.

I thought just how Red—Apples wedged
The Stubble's joints between—
And Carts went stooping round the fields
To take the Pumpkins in—

I wondered which would miss me, least,
And when Thanksgiving, came,
If Father'd multiply the plates—
To make an even Sum—

And would it blur the Christmas glee
My Stocking hang too high
For any Santa Claus to reach
The Altitude of me—

But this sort, grieved myself,
And so, I thought the other way,
How just this time, some perfect year—
Themself, should come to me—

608

Afraid! Of whom am I afraid?
Not Death—for who is He?
The Porter of my Father's Lodge
As much abasheth me!

Of Life? 'Twere odd I fear [a] thing
That comprehendeth me
In one or two existences—
Just as the case may be—

Of Resurrection? Is the East
Afraid to trust the Morn
With her fastidious forehead?
As soon impeach my Crown!

7. two] more—   8] As Deity decree—

446

He showed me Hights I never saw—
"Would'st Climb"—He said?
I said, "Not so."
"With me"—He said—"With me?"

He showed me secrets—Morning's nest—
The Rope the Nights were put across—
"And now, Would'st have me for a Guest?"
I could not find my "Yes"—

And then—He brake His Life—and lo,
A light for me, did solemn glow—
The steadier, as my face withdrew
And could I further "No"?

11. steadier] larger—

FASCICLE 20

1725

I took one Draught of Life—
I'll tell you what I paid—
Precisely an existence—
The market price, they said.

They weighed me, Dust by Dust—
They balanced Film with Film,
Then handed me my Being's worth—
A single Dram of Heaven!

1761

A train went through a burial gate,
A bird broke forth and sang,
And trilled, and quivered, and shook his throat
Till all the churchyard rang;

And then adjusted his little notes,
And bowed and sang again.
Doubtless, he thought it meet of him
To say good-by to men.

364

The Morning after Wo—
'Tis frequently the Way—
Surpasses all that rose before—
For utter Jubilee—

As Nature did not care—
And piled her Blossoms on—
And further to parade a Joy
Her Victim stared upon—

The Birds declaim their Tunes—
Pronouncing every word
Like Hammers—Did they know they fell
Like Litanies of Lead—

On here and there—a creature—
They'd modify the Glee
To fit some Crucifixal Clef—
Some Key of Calvary—

524

Departed—to the Judgment—
A Mighty Afternoon—
Great Clouds—like Ushers—leaning—
Creation—looking on—

The Flesh—Surrendered—Cancelled—
The Bodiless—begun—
Two Worlds—like Audiences—disperse—
And leave the Soul—alone—

3. leaning] placing   7. disperse] dissolve—
5. Cancelled] Shifted   / withdraw—/ retire—
7. Two] the—

525

I think the Hemlock likes to stand
Upon a Marge of Snow—
It suits his own Austerity—
And satisfies an awe

That men, must slake in Wilderness—
And in the Desert—cloy—
An instinct for the Hoar, the Bald—
Lapland's—nescessity—

The Hemlock's nature thrives—on cold—
The Gnash of Northern winds
Is sweetest nutriment—to him—
His best Norwegian Wines—

To satin Races—he is nought—
But Children on the Don,
Beneath his Tabernacles, play,
And Dnieper Wrestlers, run.

6. And] Or   7. Hoar] drear—
7. instinct] hunger   12. best] good

365

Dare you see a soul at the "White Heat"?
Then crouch within the door—
Red—is the Fire's common tint—
But when the quickened Ore

Has sated Flame's conditions—
She quivers from the Forge
Without a color, but the Light
Of unannointed Blaze—

Least Village, boasts it's Blacksmith—
Whose Anvil's even ring
Stands symbol for the finer Forge
That soundless tugs—within—

Refining these impatient Ores
With Hammer, and with Blaze
Until the designated Light
Repudiate the Forge—

4. quickened] vivid   6. She] It
5. sated] vanquished

526

To hear an Oriole sing
May be a common thing—
Or only a divine.

It is not of the Bird
Who sings the same, unheard,
As unto Crowd—

The Fashion of the Ear
Attireth that it hear
In Dun, or fair—

So whether it be Rune,
Or whether it be none
Is of within.

The "Tune is in the Tree—"
The Skeptic—showeth me—
"No Sir! In Thee!"

11. none] din—

301

I reason, Earth is short—
And Anguish—absolute—
And many hurt,
But, what of that?

I reason, we could die—
The best Vitality
Cannot excel Decay,
But, what of that?

I reason, that in Heaven—
Somehow, it will be even—
Some new Equation, given—
But, what of that?

527

To put this World down, like a Bundle—
And walk steady, away,
Requires Energy—possibly Agony—
'Tis the Scarlet way

Trodden with straight renunciation
By the Son of God—
Later, his faint Confederates
Justify the Road—

Flavors of that old Crucifixion—
Filaments of Bloom, Pontius Pilate sowed—
Strong Clusters, from Barabbas' Tomb—

Sacrament, Saints partook before us—
Patent, every drop,
With the Brand of the Gentile Drinker
Who indorsed the Cup—

12. partook] indorsed   15. indorsed] enforced
14. Brand] Stamp

366

Although I put away his life—
An Ornament too grand
For Forehead low as mine, to wear,
This might have been the Hand

That sowed the flower, he preferred—
Or smoothed a homely pain,
Or pushed the pebble from his path—
Or played his chosen tune—

On Lute the least—the latest—
But just his Ear could know
That whatsoe'er delighted it,
I never would let go—

The foot to bear his errand—
A little Boot I know—
Would leap abroad like Antelope—
With just the grant to do—

His weariest Commandment—
A sweeter to obey,
Than "Hide and Seek"—
Or skip to Flutes—
Or All Day, chase the Bee—

Your Servant, Sir, will weary—
The Surgeon, will not come—
The World, will have it's own—to do—
The Dust, will vex your Fame—

The Cold will force your tightest door
Some Febuary Day,
But say my apron bring the sticks
To make your Cottage gay—

That I may take that promise
To Paradise, with me—
To teach the Angels, avarice,
You, Sir, taught first—to me.

367

Over and over, like a Tune—
The Recollection plays—
Drums off the Phantom Battlements
Cornets of Paradise—

Snatches, from Baptized Generations—
Cadences too grand
But for the Justified Processions
At the Lord's Right hand.

670

One need not be a Chamber—to be Haunted—
One need not be a House—
The Brain—has Corridors surpassing
Material Place—

Far safer of a Midnight—meeting
External Ghost—
Than an Interior—Confronting—
That cooler—Host.

Far safer, through an Abbey—gallop—
The Stones a'chase—
Than Moonless—One's A'self encounter—
In lonesome place—

Ourself—behind Ourself—Concealed—
Should startle—most—
Assassin—hid in our Apartment—
Be Horror's least—

The Prudent—carries a Revolver—
He bolts the Door—
O'erlooking a Superior Spectre—
More near—

4. Material] Corporeal
8] That Whiter Host.
17. The Prudent] The Body
17. a] the

19–20] A Spectre—infinite—
accompanying—
He fails to fear—
19–20] Maintaining a
Superior Spectre—
None saw—

302

Like Some Old fashioned Miracle—
When Summertime is done—
Seems Summer's Recollection—
And the Affairs of June—

As infinite Tradition—as
Cinderella's Bays—
Or little John—of Lincoln-Green—
Or Blue Beard's Galleries—

Her Bees—have an illusive Hum—
Her Blossoms—like a Dream
Elate us—till we almost weep—
So plausible—they seem—

Her Memory—like Strains—enchant—
Tho' Orchestra—be dumb—
The Violin—in Baize—replaced—
And Ear, and Heaven—numb—

   5. infinite] Bagatelles—   13. enchant] Review—
  12. plausible] exquisite   14. be] is
  13. Memory] Memories

303

The Soul selects her own Society—
Then—shuts the Door—
To her divine Majority—
Present no more—

Unmoved—she notes the Chariots—pausing—
At her low Gate—
Unmoved—an Emperor be kneeling
Upon her Mat—

I've known her—from an ample nation—
Choose One—
Then—close the Valves of her attention—
Like Stone—

3. To] On   8] On [her] Rush mat
4. Present] Obtrude   11. Valves] lids—

368

How sick—to wait—in any place—but thine—
I knew last night—when someone tried to twine—
Thinking—perhaps—that I looked tired—or alone—
Or breaking—almost—with unspoken pain—

And I turned—ducal—
That right—was thine—
One port—suffices—for a Brig—like *mine*—

Our's be the tossing—wild though the sea—
Rather than a Mooring—unshared by thee.
Our's be the Cargo—*unladen—here*—
Rather than the *"spicy isles—"*
And thou—not there—

528

Mine—by the Right of the White Election!
Mine—by the Royal Seal!
Mine—by the Sign in the Scarlet prison—
Bars—cannot conceal!

Mine—here—in Vision—and in Veto!
Mine—by the Grave's Repeal—
Titled—Confirmed—
Delirious Charter!
Mine—long as Ages steal!

4. Bars] Bolts   9. long as] while
8] Good affidavit—

369

She lay as if at play
Her life had leaped away—
Intending to return—
But not so soon—

Her merry Arms, half dropt—
As if for lull of sport—
An instant had forgot
The Trick to start—

Her dancing Eyes—ajar—
As if their Owner were
Still sparkling through
For fun—at you—

Her Morning at the door—
Devising, I am sure—
To force her sleep—
So light—so deep—

370

Heaven is so far of the Mind
That were the Mind dissolved—
The Site—of it—by Architect
Could not again be proved—

'Tis vast—as our Capacity—
As fair—as our idea—
To Him of adequate desire
No further 'tis, than Here—

APPENDIX B

FACSIMILE OF FASCICLE 20

For a description, see Textual Note, pp. xiii–xiv above.

The Morning after Wo—
'Tis frequently the Way—
Surpasses all that rose before—
For utter Jubilee—

As Nature did not care—
And piled her Blossoms on—
And further to parade a Joy
Her Victim stared upon—

The Birds declaim their Tunes—
Pronouncing every word
Like Hammers—Did they know they fell
Like Litanies of Lead—

On here and there—a Creature—
They'd modify the Glee
To fit some Crucifixal Clef—
Some Key of Calvary—

FIG. 11.   Fascicle 20, bf1, 2nd recto

Departed - to the Judgment -
A mighty - Afternoon -
Great Clouds - like Ushers -
+ Leaning -
Creation - looking On.

The Flesh - Surrendered -
+ Cancelled -
The Bodiless - began -
+ Two Worlds - like Audiences -
+ disperse -
And leave the Soul - alone

+ placing + shifted + the -
+ dissolve . withdraw . retire -

FIG. 12. Fascicle 20, bf1, 2nd verso

I think the Hemlock
likes to stand
Opon a marge of Snow –
It suits his own Austerity
And satisfies an awe

That men, must slake in
‡ Wilderness ✝ Or
✝ And in the Desert – cloy –
An ✝ instinct for the ✝ Hoar, the
Bald – ✝ hunger ✝ drear –
Lapland's – necessity –

The Hemlock's nature thrives
on cold –
The Gnash of Northern winds
Is sweetest nutriment to him –
His ✝ best Norwegian Wines –
✝ good

To satin Races – he is nought –
But Children on the Don,

FIG. 13.   Fascicle 20, bf2, 1st recto

Beneath his Tabernacles, play,
And Whisper Wrestlers, run.

³ ———————————

Dare you see a Soul at the
"White Heat"?
Then Crouch within the Door.
Red - is the Fire's common tint
But when the +quickened Ore
                    +vivid

+vanquished
Has +called flames' Conditions
+She +it quivers from the Forge
Without a Color, but the Light
Of unanointed Blaze.

Least Village, boasts its Black-
smith
Whose Anvils' even ding
Stands symbol for the finer Forge
That soundless tugs - within

Refining these impatient Ores
With Hammer, and with Blaze
Until the designated Light
Repudiate the Forge -

To hear an Oriole sing
May be a Common thing -
Or only a divine.

It is not of the Bird
Who sings the same, unheard,
As unto Crowd -

The Fashion of the Ear
Attireth that it hear
In Dun, or fair -

So whether it be Rune,
Or whether it be + none
Is of within. + din

FIG. 15. Fascicle 20, bf2, 2nd recto

the "Tune is in the Tree." —
the Skeptic — showeth one —
"No Sir! In thee!"

I reason, Earth is short —
And Anguish — absolute —
And many hurt,
But, what of that?

I reason, we could die —
the best Vitality
Cannot excel Decay,
But, what of that?

I reason, that in Heaven —
Somehow, it will be even —
Some new Equation, given —
But, what of that?

(63)

FIG. 16. Fascicle 20, bf2, 2nd verso

To put this World down,
Like a Bundle -
And walk steady, away,
Requires Energy - possibly Agony -
'Tis the Scarlet way

Trodden with straight renunciation
By the Son of God -
Later, his faint Confederates
Justify the Road -

Cavers of that old Crucifixion -
Filaments of Bloom, Pontius Pilate
sowed -
Strong Clusters, from Barabbas'
Tomb -

                    + indorsed
Sacrament - Saints + partook before us -
Patent, every drop,
                   + stamp
With the + Brand of the Gentile Drinker
        + Entorced
Who + indorsed the Cup -

FIG. 17.   Fascicle 20, bf3, 1st recto

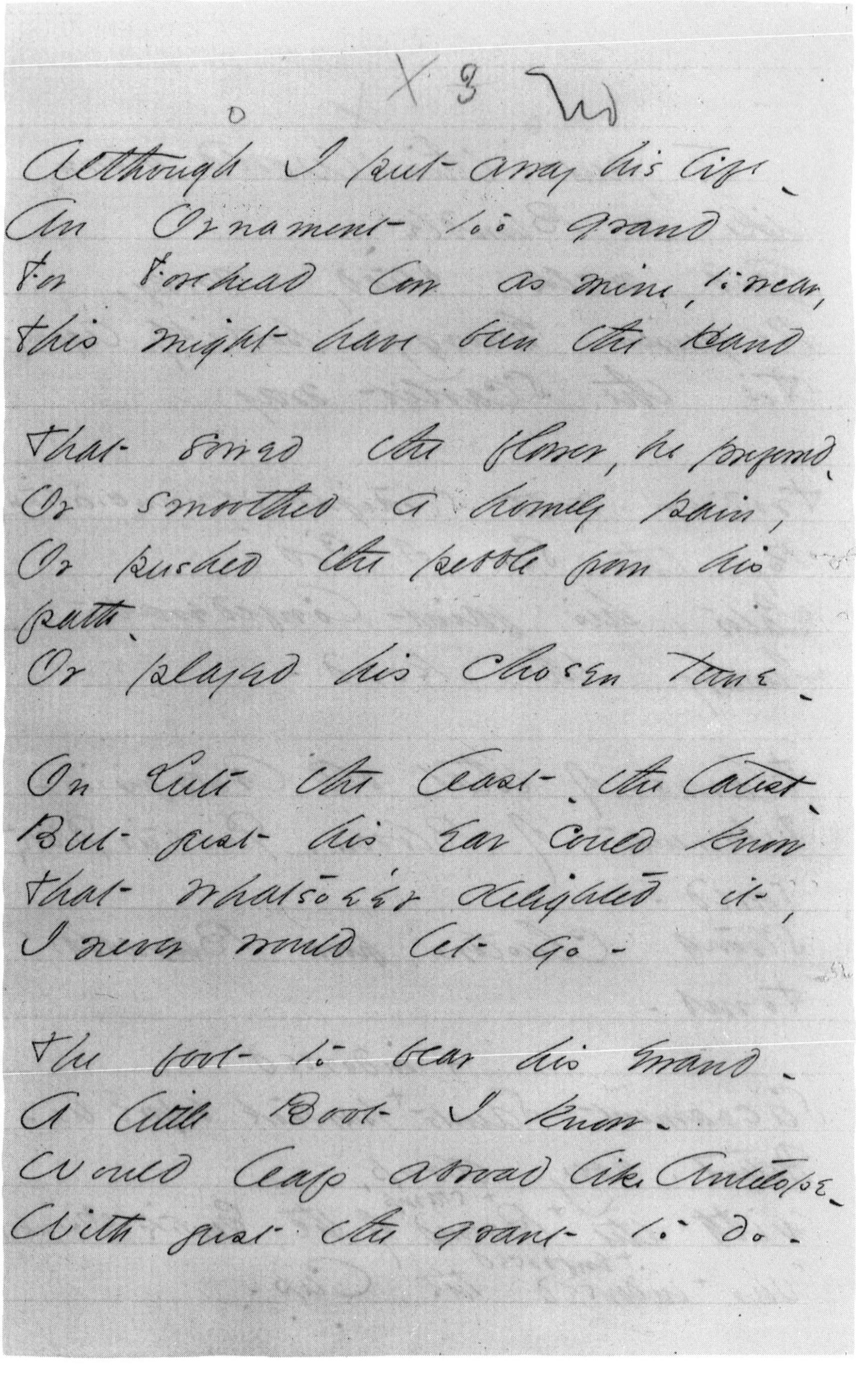

His meanest Commandment-
A smaller to "obey,"
than "hide and seek"-
Or skip to flutes-
Or all day chase the Bee-

Your Servant, Sir, will weary-
the Surgeon, will not come-
the World, will have its own to do-
the Dust, will vex your fame-

the Cold will force your tightest
Door
Some February day,
But say my Apron bring the
sticks
to make your Cottage gay.

that I may take that promise
to Paradise, with me-
to reach the Angels, avarice,

FIG. 19. Fascicle 20, bf3, 2nd recto

You, Sir, Taught first – to me.

Over and over, Like a Tune.
the Recollection plays.
Drums off the Phantom
Battlements
Cornets of Paradise –

Snatches, from Baptized
Generations –
Cadences too grand
But for the Justified
Processions
At the Lord's Right hand.

(64)

FIG. 20. Fascicle 20, bf3, 2nd verso

3 +

One need not be a Chamber
to be Haunted -
One need not be a House -
the Brain has Corridors
surpassing
+ Material Place -

+ Far safer of a Midnight -
meeting
External Ghost -
than an Interior - Confronting -
+ that Cooler - Host -

+ Far safer, through an Abbey -
gallop -
the Stones a'chase -
than Moonless - One's A'self
Encounter -
In Lonesome Place -

FIG. 2I. Fascicle 20, bf4, 1st recto

Ourself - behind Ourself -
Concealed -
Should startle most -
Assassin - hid in Our Apart-
ment -
Be Horror's least -

the +Prudent - Carries +a
Revolver -
He bolts the Door -
+O'er looking a Superior Spectre
More near -

+ Corporeal + that Whiter Host -
+ A Spectre .infinite .accom-
panying . he fails to fear -
+ the Body + the
+maintaining a superior spectre.
none can -

FIG. 22.   Fascicle 20, bf4, 1st verso

Like some old fashioned
Miracle -
When Summer time is done -
Seems Summer's Recollection
And the Affairs of June

As + infinite tradition. as
Cinderella's Bays -
Or Little John - of Lincoln-
Green -
Or Blue Beard's Galleries

Her Bees - have an illusive Hum -
Her Blossoms. Like a dream
Elate us. till in almost weep -
So beautiful. they seem -
+ Memories   + Review -
Her memory - like Strains. Enchant-
tho' Orchestra + is + a dumb -
the violin - in Baize - replaced -
And Ear. and Heaven. numb -

(right margin: + Bagatelles. + exquisite +)

FIG. 23.   Fascicle 20, bf4, 2nd recto

the Soul selects her own Society -
then - shuts the Door -
To her Divine Majority -
Present no more -

Unmoved - she notes the Chariots - pausing -
At her low Gate -
Unmoved - an Emperor be kneeling
Upon her Mat -

I've known her - from an ample
nation -
Choose One -
then - Close the Valves of
her attention -
Like Stone -
+ On +obtrude + On + Rush mat - + lids -

FIG. 24. Fascicle 20, bf4, 2nd verso

How sick - to wait - in any
place - but thine -
I knew last night - when
some one tried to trim -
+ thinking - perhaps - that
I looked tired - or alone -
Or breaking - almost - with
unspoken pain -

And . I turned - ducal -
that - night - was thine -
One port - suffices - for a
Brig - like mine -

Our's be the tossing - wild
though the sea -
Rather than a mooring -
unshared by thee.
Our's be the Cargo - unladen - here -
Rather than the "skies" 1865 "
And thou - not there -

FIG. 25.   Fascicle 20, bf5, 1st recto

Mine - by the Right of
the White Election!
Mine - by the Royal Seal!
Mine - by the Sign in
the Scarlet prison -
+ Bars - cannot Conceal!

Mine - here - in Vision - and
in Veto!
Mine - by the Grave's Repeal -
+ titled - Confirmed -
+ Delirious Charter!
Mine - + long as Ages steal!

_____

+ Good affidavit -   + While
+ Bolts

FIG. 26.   Fascicle 20, bf5, 1st verso

She Ca, as if at play
Her life had Leaped away.
Intending to return.
But not so soon.

Her merry Arms, half dropt.
As if for Cues of short.
An instant had forgot.
the trick to start.

Her Dancing Eyes. ajar.
As if their Owner were
Still sparkling through
For fun. at fun.

Her Morning at the Door.
Venising, I am sure.
To force her sleep.
So light. So deep.

FIG. 27. Fascicle 20, bf5, 2nd recto

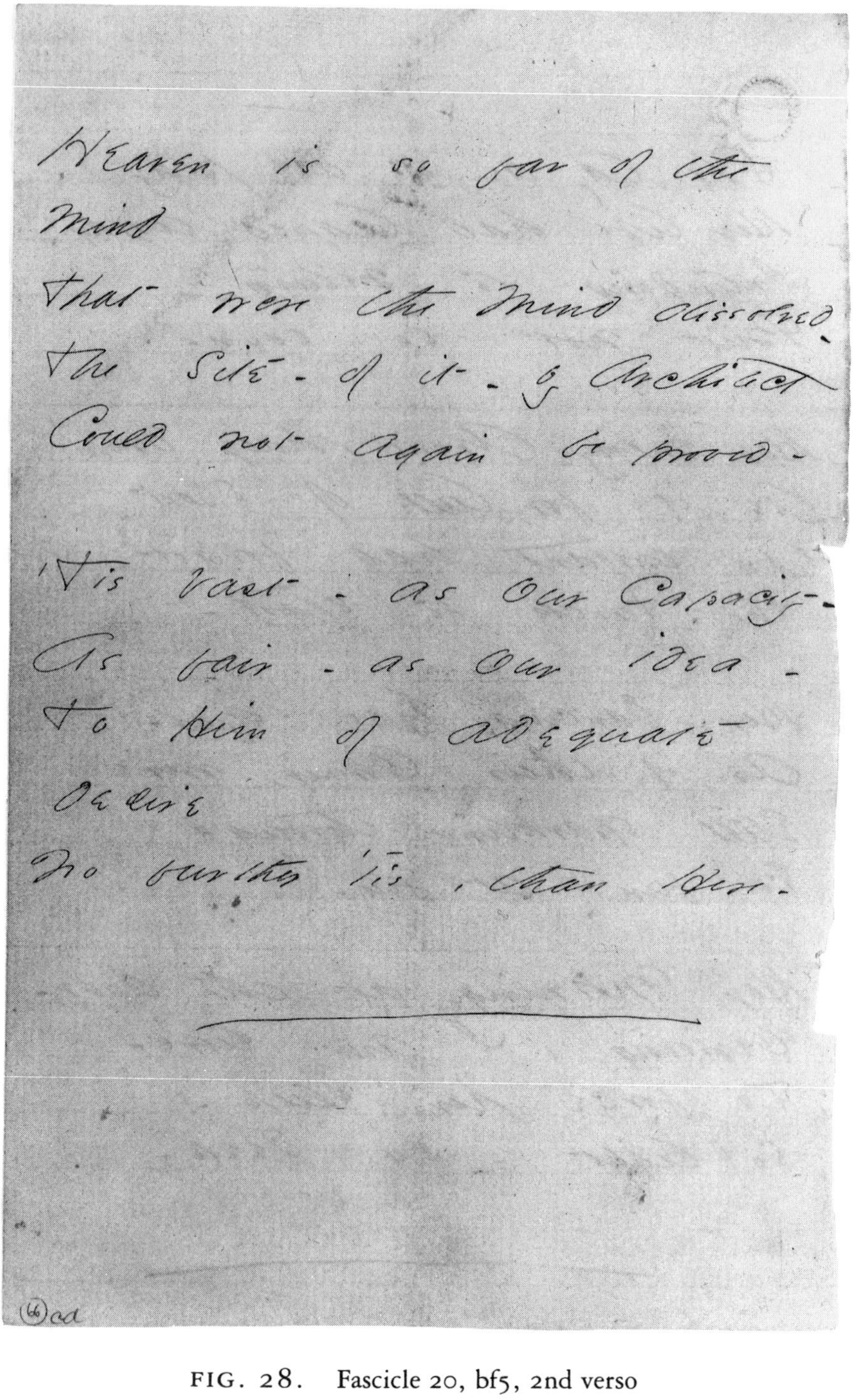

FIG. 28. Fascicle 20, bf5, 2nd verso

Index of Names

INDEX OF FIRST LINES

Figures reproducing manuscript pages are indicated by an "f" following the page number.